# COSMIC SUGAR

# COSMIC SUGAR

✦

## The Amorous Adventures of a Modern Mystic

*LEELA JONES*

2/1/13

to Patty –

enjoy!

Leela
(aka Joan)

iUniverse, Inc.
New York  Bloomington  Shanghai

# COSMIC SUGAR
## The Amorous Adventures of a Modern Mystic

iUniverse books may be ordered through booksellers or by contacting:

iUniverse
1663 Liberty Drive
Bloomington, IN 47403
www.iuniverse.com
1-800-Authors (1-800-288-4677)

Because of the dynamic nature of the Internet, any Web addresses or links contained in this book may have changed since publication and may no longer be valid.

ISBN: 978-0-595-49228-2 (pbk)
ISBN: 978-0-595-61016-7 (ebk)

Printed in the United States of America

I have changed all the names and identifying characteristics of anyone in this book who might be embarrassed or otherwise hurt. I have done this in the hope of not incurring any bad karma or lawsuits.

I have told my version of the truth of my life with as much clarity and 20/20 hindsight as it is possible for a psychic, with a blind spot in the romantic area. Of course, it is only *my* version. There is always *their* version and the version that is *the* objective truth.

My primary intentions in writing this memoir are to entertain, enlighten and do no harm. If I have succeeded in the first two but not the last, I am truly sorry.

*To the*

*B E L O V E D*

*in all of his guises*


*"Out of eternity*

*I turn my face to you*

*and into eternity ...*

*we have been in*

*love that long."*

*RUMI*

# *Contents*

# *Prelude*

I knew one day I would write about my sexual adventures. In my imagination, it would be when I was in my eighties. By that time, I presumed I could write my history with the amused detachment of one long past things sexual. In addition, it would not affect my reputation professionally and, even though I have changed all the names to protect the "innocent," time would also serve as a safeguard.

Close friends who have heard me recount tales of my exploits encouraged me repeatedly to write these stories down before, in the haze of memory, they lost their piquant freshness. I always resisted the temptation.

Now, in my forty-fifth year, at a time in my life where I am slowly approaching my peak, sexually as well as psychically, I have developed a near obsession with getting all of this down on paper. This is not a rational act. However, writer friends assure me that I should follow my muse and worry about the consequences later.

I am in the middle of writing my second nonfiction book in my field, have a steady private practice as a psychic and spiritual counselor, and yet recording this now is consuming almost all of my waking thoughts. *So be it.*

*Leela Jones*
*December 1998*
*New York City*

# Introduction

Everyone comes into their life with a mission, an assignment, a soul purpose. Sometimes I like to joke about it, especially when I look around me. I see lots of people scurrying around without a clue as to what their sojourn on earth is really all about. I call this condition "deep cover." It's very common. It means they're on assignment—they've just forgotten what it is.

One of my functions is helping people remember why they're here. Not every life is lived with the same intentions from the soul's perspective. But most incarnations are for healing and learning on many different levels, usually with a specific karmic focus that permeates the life.

My desire in writing this book arose out of specific karmic themes that I am here to heal and bring into balance. My hope is that I will undergo a deeper healing of the split in my being by transmitting this information to you. Then I can move to the next level of my growth with more integration and wholeness.

My primary karmic split is between two series of lives. The first cycle in my reincarnational development is one in which I developed psychically and spiritually as a priestess, oracle, sage, seer, and prophet—to name a few. My primary bond was with the Higher Forces. I was either committed to a path of celibacy, or more commonly, utilized my sexual energies for healing or ritual as a vehicle for communion with the Divine. I had no personal relationships. All were trans-personal in their emotional nature as channels for spiritual union.

The other series of lives that created this split has to do with a cycle in which I have become overly fond of and attached to. You guessed it! This was a series of lives in which I developed along the second chakra. That is, lives primarily focused and lived through the expression of sensual, sexual and creative energies. I had such a good time in many of those lives—as a concubine, temple dancer, harem girl, hetaera and, my absolute favorite, a Brahmin courtesan—I developed what I have come to call a "karmic rut."

My definition of a karmic rut is: any series of lives focused on a specific theme that has become so overly developed, no more growth potential is available there. This creates an imbalance. My experience with thousands of clients is that the majority of us have karmic ruts which we have become attached to for our identity.

We actually have to choose to come into an incarnation to specifically bottom out on our karmic ruts. The way it works is: first we need to fully activate our rut, which usually takes at least thirty to forty years, and *then* we need to consciously choose to move out of this way of being. It doesn't matter how good we are at it or how enjoyable it is. Our attachment to any specific type of development for identity is a losing proposition once it has become stagnate. That is because the name of the game in the earth plane is growth. We are all actors on the great stage of life and learning to play new roles is the only way we can continuously expand.

Obviously, there are as many types of karmic ruts as there are types of soul development. We won't even go into development in other dimensions in this book. Unfortunately, not everyone's karmic rut is as pleasant as mine has been. In fact, most of the karmic ruts of clients I have worked with over the last thirty years have been decidedly less pleasurable than mine.

I have observed monk ruts, nun ruts, ascetic ruts, control freak ruts, pain in love ruts, overly mental ruts, warrior ruts, long-suffering martyr ruts (very popular). Shall I go on? I have seen power ruts, lack of power ruts, money ruts, poverty ruts, external focus ruts, lack of focus ruts. The list goes on and on, with an almost infinite variety of sub-ruts one can fall into.

One of my hopes in writing this memoir about my desire rut is to inspire others to get over their ruts, no matter how safe and cozy they've become. Many of us go to great lengths to rationalize our ruts. We decorate them, hang curtains, look around and exclaim, "It's not so bad!"

I can promise you that there is no place like home, but, in the end, it can never be found in a rut. Most of us don't even realize we're in one until we fully activate it and *then* remember when we have that old déjà vu feeling of, *"Haven't I done this all before?"* Still, we usually need to repeat the pattern at least one more time to fully bottom out with conscious awareness. For those of us who are especially resistant to change (all bottoms have infinite trap-doors), we may have to keep repeating our karmic patterns until aversion fully sets in. But, sooner or later, in this life or the next, we will choose to go for the growth.

Then, we can, hopefully, get on with why we are *really* here and move to the next level of the game.

I'll show you mine—if you show yourself yours.

# PART I
## *PRECOCITY*

# 1

## *Setting the Tone*

Energy is the currency that fuels this world. While I didn't access my psychic energy until I was nineteen, and I didn't access my sexual energy until I was a preteen, my earliest conscious memories, at age three, remind me of my first lessons in managing this currency.

My parents separated when I was three and my brother Phillip was seven. My mother, brother and I moved into a residence hotel. I spent my days with my mother who tried to keep me entertained on the toddler swings at a local park while my brother was at school. My mother was very emotionally distraught during this period. When she was pushing me on the swing, I felt as if she was trying to push me away from her because I was too much for her to handle.

Like most three-year-olds, I was a bundle of energy demanding constant attention. Nonetheless, I formed a very strong belief on that swing. If I was too much for my mother to handle, then I probably would always be too much for most people to handle if I let my full light shine. I decided right then that it would be better for me to spread my light around and not focus it too brightly on any one being for too long.

Not only did that decision inspire me to become extremely extroverted and very much of a social being as a coping mechanism, it also later influenced my impression that I am not monogamous by nature. If my energy was so forceful, so powerful, so yang (male) as a little girl, then I needed to take care of my resources skillfully so as not to alienate people. I also realized that I would have to take care of myself from then on, since I was more than my mother could handle. I became my own parent, as well as assuming a caretaking role with others. Over time, this became such a strong part of my identity, it was natural for me to be drawn to a helping profession.

That's a lot to learn from a swing ride—especially since I still hold most of those beliefs to this day, although in a slightly more balanced and mature way. Now, I am more comfortable being introverted as well as outgoing, and I have magnetized many friends and lovers into my life over the years who can handle (more or less) my intensity.

Looking back with hindsight, which is always 20/20, I believe I was born to be intense and outgoing. I just used that experience as a "swing-board" to activate and reinforce the basic karmic nature I came with—to help stabilize it as the foundation for my self-image early in life.

My next memory during this period was continually asking where daddy was and being informed that he was home fixing the plumbing. This seemed to make sense at the time as he was in the construction business.

One night, several months into my parent's separation, I accidentally locked myself into the hotel bathroom and couldn't get out. The lock seemed stuck. I cried and screamed until I wore myself out, sobbing on the white tile floor. My mother called my father, in addition to the hotel maintenance man, and after what seemed like an eternity, I was released from my prison.

The good news was that my father was there when I got out and, better yet, when I woke up in the morning, he had slept over in the same bed as my mother. Best of all, the next day we all moved back home and stayed together as a family unit for nine more years.

Wow! Talk about power. I could get what I wanted—in this case, Daddy. All I had to do was put a "door" up between me and any male energy I wanted to draw to me—and pouf! Like magic, it has been working, most of the time, ever since. This was my first lesson in the feminine yin power of magnetic attraction.

# 2

## *Braces and Boners*

I grew up in a silent household in Chicago. My parents led predominately and increasingly separate lives. We all dined at different times. My father, who owned his own company, rarely arrived home until several hours past a normal dinner hour for kids. He ate in the dining room with my mother in attendance. My brother and I ate in the kitchen at separate times because we bickered. Coming from an upper-middle-class Jewish background, we had a succession of black live-in maids, and I usually ate with one of them.

There was no casual nudity that I can remember in our home, which was a large, rather formal eleven-room pre-war apartment. There were no private or public displays of affection. I knew that I was loved, even if it was never expressed. I never remember being hugged or even touched. As an infant, I was bottle-fed in a stand, instead of being held.

When I was four years old, on one of my pre-school outings with an outfit called Busy Beaver Day Camp (believe it or not), I was instructed to strip down to my underpants to frolic in the kiddie pool/sprinkler at a local park. It was a very hot summer day. All of the other kids had bathing suits, but someone had neglected to pack one for me. The counselor, a good-looking young man in his twenties, tried to encourage me to strip and go play. But my sense of propriety was already well established. I informed him, "That just wasn't done."

Being a pretty tightly wound little kid was an excellent set-up for quite an uninhibited explosion when I finally did discover sex. But, even after I was completely unwound, when "anything goes" became my motto in the bedroom, my four-year-old self still monitored any latent tendencies for exhibitionism by prohibiting any PDAs (public displays of affection) as something that "wasn't done."

In the meantime, I was a very cute, precocious little girl. I was petite for my age and almost looked like a china doll, from my coloring to my manner. While I was a tomboy until about the age of twelve, especially around my peers at play time, I seemed to like older men's attention whenever possible.

From the ages of eight to fifteen, I was sent to overnight camp for eight weeks every summer. I remember enjoying sitting on male counselor's laps, usually college boys, whenever I could and flirting with them. The rest of the time, I was off riding horses, doing gymnastics, or canoeing; I seemed to prefer non-team sports.

My father had taught me to say, "Thank you," when I received a compliment, and I did seem to get more than my fair share of attention and praise wherever I went. Therefore, by the time I was twelve and discovered boys my own age, I had developed a relatively strong and healthy ego structure and self-image.

Unfortunately, I also had a couple of things that were not in my favor in the "attracting boys department:" I wore braces and eyeglasses. Worst of all, I was the smartest kid in my class, even smarter than all the boys. I had gotten off to a slow start academically, but picked up speed by age seven and then rapidly outstripped all my peers on standardized IQ tests with a reading level of twelfth grade. This made the teachers single me out for special educational opportunities.

While the other kids got to square-dance, I was sequestered with kids a couple of grades ahead of me doing advanced math and reading. I became a teacher's pet, which I enjoyed, but I was also in danger of becoming a geek or even worse in those days, a bookworm.

I became very skillful at getting my needs met outside of the home, as nothing much was happening there in terms of emotional nourishment. By the age of ten, I had become best friends with the cutest, most popular girl in school, Marcie. When it came time for boy/girl parties and having a special boyfriend, I was in the perfect position to be invited to all the best parties and have my pick of boys, even if they were Marcie's cast-offs or second choices.

We used to play spin the bottle at parties and other variations of games I used to invent. I seemed to be very creative at escalating the "dirty" component of these games so they weren't so innocent. At school, the day after these parties, all the boys would look at each other and point and laugh if their lips were cut, because it meant they had been kissing me at the party. My braces were a serious weapon—but I didn't let that slow me down.

By the age of twelve I was still pre-pubescent and had no breasts at all. One of my boyfriends, while riding me on his handlebars, looked down my loose tank-top and yelled to the rest of the gang, "There's nothing there!" I was really embarrassed, especially since one of the girls in my circle, Carol, already had her period and was a 36D. My mother bought me a training bra to hide my shame. To make up for what I lacked in certain areas, I compensated in others—I didn't let it slow me down.

One time, just after my parents separated again and my mother started work-ing as a secretary, I invited my boyfriend and two other "couples" over to my house after school for an impromptu party. It quickly turned into a make-out ses-sion, with each couple occupying a different bedroom. Fully clothed, mind you, it was 1965, but pretty steamy nonetheless.

My mother arrived home early (or I lost track of the time), and she discovered my boyfriend lying on top of me in the master bedroom. She screamed. Couples flew out of other bedrooms. "What are you running here, a bordello?!" She shrieked. Little did she know I was just getting warmed up—my hormones hadn't even kicked in yet.

One of my girlfriends confided that my boyfriend Alan was bragging that whenever we kissed he got a "boner." I was so innocent and naive about male anatomy, I hadn't a clue what she was talking about or even whether it was a compliment or not. I was too embarrassed to ask and reveal my ignorance; I didn't find out what a boner was until I was fifteen. At least, by then, it was first-hand experience.

# 3

## *Lil' Oscar Saves the Day*

My pre-pubescence went on for another three and a half years, until I was almost sixteen. All my girlfriends had their periods by thirteen. I felt like a freak of nature. When I looked puberty up in the dictionary, it was defined as a purely physiological event. Adolescence, it said, had physical as well as psychological components. By that definition, I had a prolonged and crazy-making psychological adolescence, with minimal physical effects. This produced an interesting latency period for me.

My parents finally divorced. By the age of thirteen I was living alone with my mother in a smaller apartment in the same neighborhood I grew up in. My brother was away at college, and my father had quickly remarried. Emotionally, I was devastated by the divorce. I was mortally afraid it would disrupt my known and safe little universe—and it did. More importantly, I felt as if I had no say in this event; I was just informed of it and had absolutely no control over it.

My reaction to this experience of powerlessness was to make a decision. I decided to never let anyone get close to me again and, thereby, not risk getting hurt again. I shut the door to my heart and threw away the key. I didn't even remember I had made this decision until I was in my late twenties. In the interim, I became consumed with allowing in only good feelings and especially pleasurable sensations. This initiated my budding identity as a hedonist, as well as my attempt to separate sensual pleasure from matters of the heart.

Around this time, I discovered that if I allowed a strong jet of water in the shower to hit my clit, at just the right angle with enough force for about ten or fifteen minutes, something amazing happened. I had an orgasm. Of course, being a complete sexual innocent, I didn't know what I was having or what it was called. I only knew it was the best thing I had ever felt. I proceeded to do this whenever possible.

Within a very short period of time, I was getting completely waterlogged and my skin was looking decidedly prunish. Whenever my mother came looking for me, nine times out of ten, I was in the shower. I don't know if my mother ever figured out what I was up to, but she did offer me the most amazing gift and shower substitute.

She gave me a vibrator and told me, "If you hold it on your 'thing,' [my clitoris, I figured out] it will make you feel good and keep you out of trouble with boys until you're ready." That's how my lifelong relationship with Lil' Oscar, my beloved vibrator got started. My mother was right. Not only did it keep me out of trouble with boys until I was almost seventeen, Lil' Oscar (or his descendants) has been my devoted friend ever since.

I developed orgasmic capabilities with Oscar that were absolutely mind-blowing. I could come up to twenty times in an evening—and I counted. With the addition of smoking grass, which I discovered at sixteen, I created an expanded perceptual and sensual personal universe for myself. When I had the munchies, I ate bananas studded with M&Ms while listening to Santana and the Beatles. I was living a teenager's dream life—and this was only my private world.

In the outer world, I was transitioning in high school from being a very straight, sorority girl/cheerleader during my first two years of high school to a closet hedonist/hippie by my senior year. I was still hanging out with the smart popular crowd, but none of them smoked grass, so that became my secret vice. I smoked all day, every day, sneaking out between classes and at home in my room. Because my grades didn't suffer, and I had a lot of friends, my mother chose not to notice.

I had visions on grass of a computerized universe, alternately and at times simultaneously, with visions of a cartoon or farcical universe. It all made perfect sense to me at the time. Stoned, my inner world was equally as real as the outer world.

During this latency period, I had a few minor boyfriends, periodic dates and one semi-major boyfriend my senior year. One incidence I remember, when I was fifteen, occurred after a homecoming dance with a new date. We went to my girlfriend Marcie's house after the dance and proceeded to make-out in the den. I let him fondle my breasts under my training bra and immediately burst into hysterical sobs. "What did I do? What did I do?" He cried out frantically. I couldn't tell him exactly in any way that would have made sense to him. I only knew that letting him touch my breast was the beginning of the end for me, in terms of sexual innocence with boys. I could see and feel it coming. This was a very accurate premonition.

# 4

# *Infatuation*

In addition to my private world with Oscar and grass and my school and social life, my absolutely favorite part of every year was spent at Camp Judea, a kosher camp for boys and girls in Northern Wisconsin. My father went to this camp in the 1930s, as did his four sisters. In my generation, to maintain the family tradition, not only did my brother and I go, but so did two of my first cousins.

For eight weeks every summer, I was in heaven. I could make mischief, get into trouble with my cohorts and let go of the "good girl" persona I had at home. I wasn't really a good girl at heart; it was just the only way I could get attention in my family. My brother had already co-opted my preferred identity as the bad one. He got attention by being anti-social and not actualizing his mental brilliance with good grades.

I cherished the freedom of being away from my parents, living in a cabin in the woods on a beautiful lake and playing at different activities all day. I could flower at camp. I loved being in nature, especially on the water, and I was naturally athletic in just about every sport. But, what I loved most of all, by the age of twelve, was hanging out in the evenings with Frankie.

Frankie was a twenty-year-old counselor who was in charge of the boys' waterfront and a pre-med junior at Stanford. He looked like Frank Sinatra, with a tanned, perfectly lithe, muscular body which he always showed off in very tight, skimpy Speedo briefs. Best of all, he seemed to like hanging out with me as much as I did with him.

Every evening, we had free time after supper. I would go out on a little fishing boat with Frankie—just the two of us. This went on for three summers. We flirted up a storm. He told me he was going to wait until I grew up to marry me while I wondered what was making that big bulge in his bathing suit.

Finally, the last summer season of Camp Judea was upon us. After more than forty years it was going to be sold. I was fifteen, and it was the last year I could be a camper there anyway. My favorite pine tree, which I meditated under for seven years, was dying. But my romance with Frankie was just heating up.

In the middle of the night, I sneaked out of my cabin, flashlight in hand, and ran on a trail through the woods for a scary ten minutes until I hit the boys' side of camp. I would tiptoe into Frankie's cabin, past all his sleeping boys and crawl into bed with him in his small cubbyhole of a room.

The first few times, all we did was kiss. Then, I let him fondle me a little, above and below the waist, which was all very exciting and pleasurable in a dangerous sort of way. Being twenty-four by this time and having waited patiently for me to grow up, Frankie finally made his move. He relocated my hand under the covers and placed it on his erect member. This scared the shit out of me, so much that I jumped out of bed and ran like I was being chased, all the way back through the woods to my bunk on the other side of camp.

I couldn't sleep all night. I had to figure out what to do with that huge thing he'd placed in my hand. I knew for sure it would never be possible for it to fit inside me. I sought instruction.

Ronnie Sue was the girl in my cabin with the worst reputation with boys. We all knew she snuck out at night to "do it" with her boyfriend on the mattresses at the rifle range. I told her my dilemma, and she gave me detailed instructions for how to give a hand-job. I practiced on a large flashlight until I gained confidence.

I went back to Frankie's the very next night, being extremely nervous, but a good trooper, and proceeded to demonstrate my newfound expertise. We ended the season at a solid third-base, with mutual promises to pick up where we left off the following summer.

By late the next summer, just before I turned seventeen, Frankie and I arranged to sneak off for a weekend. We ended up at Ma and Pa Otis's, in Pelican Lake, Wisconsin, with the sole purpose of consummating our romance. In the meantime, I had had some more experience with manual third base, both ways, with a cute Steve McQueen look-alike who was vacationing near my mother and step-father's summer home.

I was more than ready to lose the burden of my virginity, especially with someone like Frankie. He had waited so long for me, was older and experienced, and I felt safe and comfortable.

What happened was an embarrassing fiasco. Try as he might, Frankie couldn't ram himself inside me. I was so nervous my vaginal muscles froze tight. We tried all weekend until we were so sore that Frankie had to ice his prick to bring down the swelling and numb his pain. We finally gave up and promised each other we would try again over Christmas vacation. We consoled each other. It was very sad and disappointing, but we parted as loving friends.

When Frankie came to visit at Christmas, we tried again. I got very stoned on grass. I think he sort of got in, but I didn't really feel much because I had so anesthetized myself. If this was sex, I wasn't too impressed. I bid a fond farewell to Frankie who was finishing medical school in California. Being ever hopeful by nature, I got myself on the pill and prayed for better days.

Frankie showed up one more time in my life, four years later, when I was twenty-one and living in New York City. I felt as if a lifetime had passed since our camp days together. He wanted to pick up where we left off. I tried, for old-time's sake, but I felt no love, no desire, only nostalgia. He still thought we would get married someday, but I had changed too much. This was my first lesson with the concept that one can't step in the same relationship river twice, to paraphrase Heraclites.

# PART II

*LOOKING
FOR
ADVENTURE*

# 5

## *Chapel in the Pines*

By the time I graduated from high school in 1971, I was pretty much out of control. When the high school yearbook asked me what I wanted to be when I grew up, I impulsively told them I wanted to be a hedonist, even though I wasn't quite sure of all the ramifications of that intention. I *was* sure that I wanted to find out. When they said that was an unacceptable ambition considering I was salutatorian, I told them to leave it blank, as I had no other goal.

In my graduation speech, I quoted Thoreau's different drummer, of course. Instead of a formal speech, I put on a one-act play, in which I depicted all of us selling out to middle-class values by the time we were forty and giving up our idealistic dreams (as if I had any). Not only did this totally embarrass my family (like I cared), but, being totally stoned out of my gourd, I also squirted a water pistol at all my friends when they came up to get their diplomas from my prime seat on the stage.

Going on the pill in the middle of senior year gave me a zaftig hippie look. I think the extra hormones, plus my excitement/fear of leaving home and going to Barnard College in New York City in the fall, plus being stoned all the time, conspired to turn me into quite the little butterball, considering I was only 5'1" and had the continual munchies. I didn't let it slow me down, although it might have, if I wasn't so stoned. I weighed 130 and zoomed from a size 4 to a size 12. At least I finally had breasts—36D, no less!

That summer, I was a junior counselor at a girls' camp in Wisconsin. I was supposed to be specializing in teaching canoeing, but what I really focused on was looking for adventure on my days and nights off. At this time, I had straight dark hair half-way down my back, rose-colored glasses, a T-shirt that said, "LOVE," skin-tight, hip-hugger, bell-bottom jeans and a hot pink belt.

On my first day off, I canoed solo across the lake to a Baptist nature retreat camp. In the snack shop, I met a little brown-skinned man from Northern India, named Mo, for short. He plied me with ice cream and chocolate bars as he told me his story. He was on a Fulbright scholarship at Yale, writing a dissertation on Wittgenstein. At home, he used to spend his days knee-deep in rice paddies with his family. I had never met anyone so exotic.

We seduced each other, on the altar of a religious shrine in an outdoor chapel in the middle of a pine forest. There were Christian religious slogans carved on signs along the path leading up to this "chapel in the pines." I had my first orgasm with a man looking up at pine trees reaching toward God. Since I was an atheist at the time, as well as a budding hedonist/pothead hippie, it was all deliciously sacrilegious.

I soon tired of Mo when I realized indoors he smelled of some funky hair tonic as well as himself. I have always been sensitive to pheromones and other odors. So much so that it has become quite a warning sign and deal breaker for me in choosing lovers. I decided to seek new adventures.

On my next day off, I decided to hitchhike as far as I could get from camp by mid-day and then turn around and hitchhike back. My first ride was a gorgeous twenty-something Robert Mitchum twin in western wear named Johnny. I suggested we go to the Baptist camp to get high and hang out.

We started making out in a fire watchtower. It was so intense I got weak in the knees. I never have been able to stand up well, once I get excited. We rushed behind the watchtower and proceeded to strip in an open meadow. Just as Johnny was getting ready to enter me, I stopped him. "Why are you stopping me?" he gasped.

"I just want to see you entering me," I said. I am very visual and the sight of his very long, curved cock, nosing by my barely on shocking-pink lace bikini panties was a sight that has stayed with me. In the middle of our heated congress, we were interrupted by a Baptist family hiking by. One of the boys yelled, "What are they doing, Ma?" But we couldn't stop ourselves. We had to leave it to the good parents to steer their children away, while covering their innocent eyes.

Johnny and I continued to meet whenever we could for the rest of the summer. He was married, but his wife was eight months pregnant, so he was reasonably horny. I think he was lonelier than anything. He really just wanted to sit and talk. All I wanted to do was get it on with him, since I was so excited to have discovered that my multi-orgasmic capabilities were not limited to Lil' Oscar. We compromised. I would pretend to listen patiently to him, if he plied me with ice cream, and then we would do it. This was one of my first lessons in the art of relationship compromise.

# *Karmic Activation*

I didn't know it at the time, but my first sexually orgasmic experience with a man struck a number of karmic chords that have been reverberating ever since. The fact that my lover was from India activated memories of my life as a Brahmin courtesan, as well as the full cycle of my karmic development along sensual lines. I didn't remember it consciously yet, but my body did. It remembered how to open up its yin capacities completely and have full-bodied orgasmic capabilities developed through many lives of sexual play as an art form.

Then, the fact that we had sex on an altar in the middle of an outdoor chapel opened up my karmic memory of all the lives in which sex was utilized as a spiritual ritual for communion with the Divine. Talk about a one-two activation punch!

All these activations weren't consciously integrated mentally or emotionally until later—but the karmic clock had definitely started ticking. At the time, I didn't believe in karma or reincarnation. I had never even really thought about it. Moreover, I was a self-proclaimed atheist in rebellion against my Jewish upbringing, which seemed hypocritical because it felt more for show than anything else. Now, whenever anyone asks me about my childhood religion, I just say, "I'm Jewish on my parents side," to paraphrase Ram Dass.

Since that time, I have met dozens of men whom I have known as lovers from the cycle of lives along sexual themes. Much rarer, but more powerful, are those lovers whom I have known from lives in which we used our sexual energies for spiritual purposes.

Rarer still, I have occasionally met men with whom I had been happily married with children in past lives. These men usually became very good platonic friends, with minimal sexual charge, at least from my side. Because I am not in this life to activate karmic cycles of marital bliss, connections with most of my former spouses feel minor rather than major in terms of my purposes here. As such, they don't strike the right chords for sexual activation.

# 6

## New York, New York

### The Concord Hotel

My love affair with New York City, which hasn't ended to this day, began with a fateful visit to the Concord Hotel in the Catskills for the Christmas holidays when I was fifteen. My family, that is, my father, step-mother and two step-brothers, drove from Chicago in a caravan of two Lincoln Continentals to hold all our baggage.

At the time, I was a budding cheerleader. Two days before the trip, I did a round-off into splits and pulled a muscle in my inner thigh. I was in a lot of pain, and skiing was out of the question. This meant more time for mischief.

Not only did I find a cute boy my own age from Fairfield, Connecticut, to make out with, I also made friends with a girl my age from Bensonhurst, Brooklyn, named Celia Bernstein, who was as interested in boys as I was. The importance of this friendship, which I now call "connecting the dots," was that we kept in touch. A year and a half later, when I was sixteen, Celia invited me to spend part of the summer in New York with her.

Just to finish up the Concord, there is one more story to tell. On New Year's Eve, there was a big party with bottles of liquor on all the tables. I proceeded to fill up a glass with five or six assorted varieties of hard liquor and chug-a-lugged it down. No wonder I lost a contact, puked all over my first evening dress and sat on the lap of one of the middle-aged waiters I had been flirting with all week and made out with him in the middle of the ballroom. I was dragged out of the party by my father and one of my step-brothers and carried, by my arms and legs, back to my hotel room.

I remember briefly coming out of a blackout in the elevator and wondering how I got this way before passing out again. I had never had any experience with alcohol before, except Passover wine, and had not a clue that I shouldn't have mixed all the different types of liquor in one glass and gulped it down. This was to become, over time, my relationship with alcohol. I was highly allergic physically, with a very low tolerance in general. When I did drink in quantity, it led to a complete loss of inhibition and control, ending in grayouts or blackouts.

This lack of control with booze scared me so much that I became a very controlled drinker. That is, until I was twenty-seven, when I lost control and hit bottom. Since that time, I have remained sober. During the years when I controlled my alcohol consumption, I used grass daily and men regularly—as I seemed to have more of an illusion of control with them. I gave up the grass and other drugs a year after the booze. As for men—well, I'm still working on that—a day at a time.

## Sweet Sixteen in Bensonhurst

Celia lived in a big house in Bensonhurst with her soon-to-be divorced mother and younger brother. She worked during the week at a summer job with an advertising agency in the city. I took the train in with her every day and spent my days wandering around the city, especially Greenwich Village. I knew that I had to make New York City my home. The energy, the sights and sounds and especially the diversity of human nature enraptured me. I have felt that way ever since, although my need for time away from human nature and more in nature seems to increase every year.

My romantic life that summer took an unexpectedly clandestine turn. On the surface, I was hanging out nights and weekends with Celia and her boyfriend and some guy they fixed me up with who was the boyfriend's friend. There were picnics on the beach, Nathan's and Coney Island, make-out sessions with some pot smoking—nothing too exciting.

On the side, I was developing a very hot scene with the husband of Celia's mother's best friend. His name was Eduardo and he was Sicilian, twenty years older than me and very darkly handsome. He kept trying to seduce me. We made it to mutual oral sex, but I kept backing away because I was still a virgin—and something about him scared me a little.

After several secret rendezvous, Celia found out about Eduardo and me and told her parents. Because they were responsible for my safekeeping, they naturally freaked out. They literally tied me up with rope and got me on a plane back to Chicago. I swore undying lust for Eduardo, which only fueled my desire to get back to New York as soon as possible.

In the meantime, I managed to get through my senior year, lose my virginity with Frankie and deliberately screw up all my interviews with colleges like Stanford and Radcliffe so I could go to college in New York. I got accepted by New York University with a scholarship, though I didn't need aid. My father insisted I go to Barnard anyway, even though he had to pay. I resisted because it was on the Upper West Side, and I wanted to live in the Village where NYU was. He won out, in the short term. But I won out in the long run because, while I'm still on extended leave from Barnard, I have lived in the Village since 1974.

## College Days

By the time I arrived at college for orientation week in September 1972, I was a nervous wreck. I had gone to see a psychic card reader the week before I left home, and he was ethical enough to turn me away because he said my energy was too confused.

I guess I had a lot of fear about finally leaving home, even though I believed there was nothing left for me in Chicago. I had burned all my bridges and lost touch with all my friends, as we were growing in different directions. There was nothing left for me but to go. I felt like a human piranha who has eaten what food there was for me—whether people, places, or adventures—and it was time for me to move on.

I had put on 25 pounds in the year since Eduardo had last seen me, so, of course, when we met again, he wailed, "Oh, shit, you let yourself go to fat!" My worst fear—rejection. He gave me an obligatory fuck, for old time's sake, with no passion or feeling on either side. He was living in an empty apartment, except for a bed, as his wife had cleaned him out. He was spending his time with a topless dancer from Lake George. Our affair was over before it even began.

I did meet someone new at a party at Columbia during orientation week. His name was William, but I called him Woody, because he reminded me of a cross between Groucho Marx and Woody Allen. Woody was a Jewish third-year law student at Columbia. To save on rent, he was the resident manager of a freshmen boys' dorm floor. Even though he was very Jewish in looks and manner, I didn't hold it against him because he was six years older and sexually rapacious. I needed someone to find me sexually desirable after my disappointment with Eduardo.

Woody and I became an item for the fall term, with a lot of accommodating to each other's idiosyncrasies. To begin with, I was still pretty sexually naive. When he invited me to stay over in his room after I met him at the party, I told him I would have to go back to my dorm first and get some stuff. He probably assumed I was going to get birth control or something, but when I emerged from his bathroom, he got quite a shock. I came out dressed in pink flannel bunny-rabbit feetsy pajamas. I thought this is how one dressed for a "sleepover party," like I used to have with my girlfriends where we stayed up all night and ate and talked.

Fortunately, Woody had a good sense of humor and thought my innocence was adorable. Also, it made him hotter to break in such a little schoolgirl. I discovered rapidly that Woody had some of his own issues. Just as soon as he ejaculated, he would disengage and hop out of bed into the shower. Let's just say it was probably a combination of fear of intimacy issues mixed with some overly-developed cleanliness neurosis. He was also remarkably tight with money, figuring out our Chinese restaurant bills down to the penny. Oh, well.

I was learning rapidly what my priorities were. I was more than willing to make allowances for good sex if the chemistry was right. The "X-factor," as I call it. The relationship could be worked on—*not* the other way around.

The good news is that when we were fucking and sucking he was totally uninhibited; this allowed me to loosen up quite a bit. He had an old girlfriend named Carol who used to hang out with us sometimes. I learned a lot from her too. I went to a party at her business school dorm and, by accident, walked in on her sitting on this guy's face in her bedroom. I was shocked and mesmerized at the same time. Carol was a very big, buxom girl and every part of her was bouncing violently as she rode him while holding on to the bedposts for balance. I had never seen a woman be this sexually aggressive. Not just by her position, but also because she was moaning loudly and uninhibitedly and giving him commands, as she smothered his face in her juices.

That image stayed with me, even though it took until I was in my thirties to be comfortable enough with myself to be that assertive. I preferred playing a more passive role when I was getting head. I did sixty-nine in my teens and twenties, on top at times. However, I still feared being perceived as too much too handle, especially if I was on top and calling the shots.

My first and only menage-a-tois with another woman was with Carol and Woody. Carol got so absorbed in eating me out and fucking me with her hand that Woody ended up leaving the bed and taking his usual shower. After Carol brought me to orgasm, I was too afraid and inhibited to do anything much with her except cuddle, even though I found her very attractive.

At the age of twelve, I became convinced that I was a lesbian after reading a hidden paperback about them that I found in my mother's lingerie drawer. I now believe I'm bisexual by nature, although I've never acted on it overtly. However, I'm sure I would naturally switch to being with women if no men were available—although I do prefer the male equipment package. Many of my fantasies are about being a hugely large-breasted woman. I experience inhabiting that body and the man's simultaneously—now that's the best of both worlds.

## *Karmic Interlude—The Male Perspective*

Whenever I have sexual fantasies (which is always with Lil' Oscar, as I never choose to fantasize when I'm with a lover), I simultaneously feel myself as the woman (usually with humungous breasts, much larger than my 36Ds) as well as the man—or men. I experience my orgasm equally from the male perspective and the female at the same time—sort of like stereo. It's as if I can identify with a man's sexuality as much or more than being a woman.

It wasn't until I was in my thirties that I fully accessed memories of all my major male incarnations. But I was getting glimmers in my teens and twenties. The ones that have affected my sexuality the strongest have been a series of lives in which I was a male homosexual, which was a transitional cycle in my soul development. Though not in any chronological order, I have been evolving along a bell curve from male to female, with androgyny at the top—which is true for most souls involved over time in the reincarnational process.

Two of these lives have had an especially strong influence on me. In both, I was in positions of power which I abused, subjugating others to my desires. Most prominent was a life in ancient Persia in which I held the position of court astrologer. I was into young boys and had no scruples about having them made into eunuchs for my pleasure, as it enhanced their feminine natures.

The next most memorable life in this cycle, and perhaps even darker, was a life as a Spanish Inquisitor. Not only was I a religious hypocrite in that life, I was also a pederast who enjoyed torture as foreplay—and just for its own sake.

One of my therapy clients, a very beautiful woman, with whom I was doing a series of past life sessions, kept regressing to lives that were similar to my karmic patterns. This was happening with no mention of any of my past lives. It was eerie. I could handle that she was a Chinese concubine, a Balinese temple dancer and a Brahmin courtesan, like me—but when she got to the Spanish Inquisitor, my astonishment knew no bounds.

As I listened to her describe herself in trance as a pederast, a sadist, a religious hypocrite *and* a glutton (she choked to death on a ham bone in that life), I couldn't resist blowing my karmic cover with her after the session. I did this also because she was feeling bad and judging herself for causing so much harm. I told that I could identify with everything she had said about *her* Inquisitor because I had been one too. "But," I told her with a dramatic pause, "while I have no trouble with the hypocrisy or the sadism or liking little boys—the gluttony, now *that's* disgusting!" We had a good laugh over where we draw the line in our judgments of ourselves.

I shared with her the lessons I've learned of how to own one's dark power. The key is not to repress or deny it, but to embrace and transmute it with commitment and will, through the heart and into the light. I did admit to her that I was impressed with her dark side. She had certainly trumped me in the "seven deadly sins" department.

I didn't consciously access the Persian life until I met my future ex-husband at age thirty-one. He was one of the ones whom I had made a eunuch. He wanted to marry me so I could make a man of him and repair the karmic wound that I had inflicted, though he wasn't conscious of that.

The Spanish life wasn't fully activated (though I could feel it waiting in the wings for many years) until I was thirty-eight, when I was doing regression work on my relationship with my mother. It was revealed that she was one of the martyrs to the faith I had tortured on the rack.

Even in my late teens, I was accessing my karmic sexual orientation. I just didn't know where it was coming from yet. My fantasies of being in a male body were equally as strong as my fantasies of being in a female body. This really came out when I was angry at a lover. Then I would fantasize I was a man brutally raping him. On our good days, I would fantasize about him raping me, with elaborate scenarios both ways. Only in the light of past life recall does my sexual range, or anyone else's for that matter, make any real sense.

## Expanding My Range

By the time Woody and I broke up around the Christmas holidays, I was already fooling around on the side. Basically, I had very little impulse control. If a cute guy at a party propositioned me—I really didn't see why not. It has been a very hard-earned lesson that I don't have to act out with any attractive guy who wants to sleep with me. My mindset about sex has always been more naturally that of a male in our culture. This developed even further through my twenties and thirties as I got more comfortable with my male energies on different levels.

I was smoking a lot of grass during this period, and I did some pretty insane things. One night in the West End Bar and Grill, a Morningside Heights Columbia/Barnard institution for partying, I let this really weird-looking guy pick me up. Some of my girlfriends warned me there were rumors that a rapist was prowling the West End and preying on Barnard freshmen. My dorm roommate begged me not to go with him, which just fueled my rebellious nature.

Of course, he was a wacko. Back at his apartment, he tied me up and screwed me, while he kept begging me to hold his balls, which was very difficult, considering that my hands were tied. The next morning (yes, I stayed over, being too lazy and hung over to leave), he whacked off and came in my hair. I went to my 9:00 AM French class with this weirdo's come in my hair, thinking *that was an interesting and kinky night, although not necessarily one I need to repeat.* I seemed to have no fear or sexual aversion. Everything in this area seemed like a big adventure to me.

I had many of these adventures, and I learned something from each of them. I seemed to go with different categories of men each time so that I could explore energetically what their particular type was about. Over time, I developed my own convoluted repertoire of experience. Then I could just look at a guy and be able to sort him by energy type. As my repertoire of types grew, I naturally became more discriminating (thank god!). I could just look at most men and think: *"Been there, done that, have the T-shirt."*

Obviously, during this period my consciousness was still very much asleep, and my heart was still kept tightly under wraps. I was operating mostly from a slowly developing discriminating mind, based solely on personal experience. I was only interested in the novelty and excitement of each new sensual experience. If some of the encounters were disappointing, I was so stoned and into my own world of perceptions and sensual gratification that I never let any disappointment slow me down. I was committed to my budding hedonism and had no time for regrets—pushing ever onward to the next man, the next conquest, the next adventure.

Once in the cold and dark of December, after smoking hash for the first time at some guy's dorm, I was walking back at 3:00 AM across the Columbia quadrangle when I experienced an epiphany of my primal animal nature. I had only dreamt of and written poems about this aspect of my being in high school. I felt the freedom of being an animal with senses fully alive to experience the wonders of the earth—and that has never left me.

I had one more adventure, one more semi-transformational encounter, over Christmas break. It was the last encounter before my life was to change forever. It was with a guy I met at a Columbia dorm Christmas party. He was a senior named Larry and drop-dead gorgeous in a Robert Redford/Sundance Kid kind of way. We hit it off and had a very hot romantic week, fueled by the holidays and my appreciation of his visual perfection—always a turn on.

After the first of the year, Larry made a confession to me. He was only with me because I reminded him of this girl back home that had broken his heart. However, it stopped working for him when he came to the realization that she was irreplaceable.

I was hurt and then I got enraged. I got raging drunk and picked a fight with him. I had twenty shots of tequila at some dorm party and was running up and down the male dorm on every floor screaming and bouncing off the walls. Larry tried to calm me down, as he was one of the floor residence managers, but I was out of control. He fucked me in my virgin ass—that hurt enough to get my attention. Then he threw me in a cold shower where I lay curled up in the fetal position—thus ending my first season away at college.

## *The Road Almost Taken*

In between Woody and Larry, among others, I went home for the first time over Thanksgiving break. First I had to get through midterms, which was a problem because I had been partying so much I had to cram the night before, staying up all night and boosting my energy with candy bars and coffee.

By the time I arrived in Chicago, I was completely toasted from lack of sleep and crashing from all the sugar and caffeine. A friend gave me some angel dust (elephant tranquilizer) to help me get through the big "welcome home" dinner my father was throwing for me at this Bavarian theme restaurant that served wild game.

Unfortunately, I had an extremely bad reaction to the angel dust—a really bad trip. I had to go home in the middle of the celebration. A cousin of mine, around my age and a hippie as well, escorted me. To thank him and just for the kinky hell of it, I gave him a friendly blow job. All in all, not a night of very sober decisions.

A few years after this fiasco, I heard that this same cousin had tripped out so badly on acid that he had walked through a plate glass window and has never been the same since. His personality had disintegrated so completely that in a reaction mode he eventually became a devout Hasidic Jew. I guess he needed a very rigid external religious structure to govern his life as all of his internal structures got fried.

Fortunately, I stopped my drug use just short of this happening to me, about nine years after this trip. I got off that road just in time. I was so close to losing myself by the time I stopped that I could read the coming attractions. They looked a lot like what happened to my cousin and some other school friends of mine.

# PART III
## *FINDING IT*

# 7

## *Meeting My Soulmate*

### *First Sight*

When I went to the West End Bar on February 19, 1972, I had no idea my life was about to change forever. I guess we never do. I was looking for a good time, as usual, but inside I was feeling pretty lonely and demoralized by the whole college scene. School wasn't doing it for me. My social life and friends weren't doing it for me. Certainly all the grass I was smoking and the dorm food, chocolate and after-hours meatball heroes I was wolfing down weren't doing it for me.

I was definitely feeling empty on the inside, and nothing I was doing to fill up the void, that black hole in me, was working. Sometime in my thirties, I finally got, and not just theoretically, that nothing was going to fill me up and make me whole except a conscious relationship with some form of Higher Power—the Creative Forces, the Divine, the Tao, or whatever you want to call it. But at eighteen, I didn't have a clue. I was totally asleep. As usual, I was looking for adventure.

I was sitting at a booth drinking a soda with a girlfriend, when two guys, uninvited, sat down with us and started coming on pretty strong. I wanted out, but the guy next to me wouldn't move, so I had to crawl under the table to escape from the booth. I ended up standing at the bar, which I had never done before, next to this big old guy who looked like a scruffy Mexican bandito.

"Want a drink?" he drawled.

"Sure," I said, boldly, considering I had never ordered a real drink before.

"What'll you have?"

"You decide for me."

He ordered me something called a margarita straight up. I gulped it down, licking the rim, thinking sugar was on it. I got a rude shock from the taste of salt. I thought he was trying to play a joke on me so I threw the rest of the drink in his

29

face. He laughed, as he explained away my confusion, and promptly whisked me out of the bar and into a cab.

"Where are we going?' I asked nervously, as we cruised downtown on Broadway.

"My place," he responded with absolute confidence.

"Can't we stop somewhere for coffee first?" I pleaded, thinking this was going a little too fast, even for me, considering I had only known him about ten minutes.

"Nope," he said. And *that* was it.

His name was Rush and he has been in my life ever since. He was thirty-five when I met him, a professional high-level grass dealer and man about town. From the time we met, no other human being has ever made me feel as intensely alive or as enthusiastic about being alive.

Rush passed over in 1998 at the age of sixty from a heart attack brought on by complications from cancer. At that time, our relationship moved to another level that is just as open and present as it ever was—although he is easier to get a hold of now. All of that aliveness and enthusiasm which he activated in me is mine now. It always was, I just forgot. That's what a twin soul or soulmate does for you. If you ever think you've met someone who makes you feel *that* alive—just jump!

## *Thirty-Six Days*

Our first night together was sexually intense in a way I had not experienced before. On the one hand, I found Rush scary as hell. His sexual energy and demeanor were very yang, very assertive. He was 6' 3", about 220 pounds, handsome in a rugged way with almost black hair, a drooping mustache and a half beard. He had some Native American blood, so he had almost no body hair, except in the usual places, and his hands and feet (13EEE), as well as his penis were enormous. And since I was barely 5'1", although voluptuously built, we were an uneven, almost physically impossible match from the start. His place scared me too. It was a six-room, dimly lit railroad flat, overflowing with large black garbage bags full of grass in every room. There was minimal furniture and what was there was scruffy like him.

On the other hand, there was something about how we came together in the rhythm of our fucking, as well as in our cuddling through the night, that made me feel very comfortable with him, very safe and protected. His energy was very bear-like. Since he had a jovial sense of humor, I started thinking of him as Yogi the Bear and me as Boo-Boo—so much for deep first thoughts. He was also very demanding. He asked me to give him head in a way that didn't brook "no" for an answer. I had to ask him what that was, as I had never heard that terminology before.

I remember he took me to a French crepe place the next day for brunch and then we were off and running. He took me out to expensive steak restaurants around town, gave me money to buy clothes, introduced me to lots of strange people and taught me how to drink vodka sours in bars from the Upper West Side all the way down to the Village. But most importantly of all, he introduced me to S&M—sadomasochism, in case you're as innocent as I was. I was clueless.

The first time Rush had me dress up in the classic black garter belt ensemble and tied me up, while I was on my hands and knees, and started spanking me, it was a bit of a fiasco. He kept spanking me harder and harder, demanding that I beg him to fuck me. Except I didn't *get* that we were just playing a game. No one had *told* me. I considered the whole thing an assault on my dignity and adamantly refused to play. "I will never beg anyone to fuck me," I exclaimed proudly as he spanked me harder. Finally, he just threw up his hands and admitted defeat. We went to bed and had sex our usual way.

Rush explained the game aspect to me later. We tried it a few more times, but I just couldn't get into it. I wasn't screwed on tight enough on the inside; this made me tighter on the outside as a defense—not a good combination for such game playing. It took a few more years until I got the hang of it. Even then, I could only play (both ways, mind you, by my late twenties) if it was with someone I wasn't seriously in love with. Then I could play just about anything—Jupiter in Gemini in the fifth house, for you astrology buffs.

With Rush, I felt it was serious from the beginning. In our second week together, there was banging on the door in the middle of the night and then some high pitched screaming. I asked Rush who it was. He told me it was his old girlfriend, Lena, a crazy, 28-year-old, Maltese spitfire. I asked him what she was doing here. He said she had been living with him, and he had just kicked her out after he met me. She must have heard from the neighborhood bar that he had a new girl. It sounded like she wanted back in.

Rush said the best thing to do was to ignore her because she was probably drunk and possibly violent. But she was so persistent, and Rush was afraid she would bring down the police on him—not a good idea in his line of work. He opened the door to calm her down, and she came blazing past him with a 12″ knife heading right for me in the bedroom. Rush had to tackle her (he'd been a linebacker at UCLA, thank god) and then knock her out. Rush certainly lived a volatile life.

This was my first taste of real-life drama, and I fell in love with it and Rush with my whole being, as only a true co-dependent type with no center can.

This volatility continued over the next month. We had lots of sex, rich food, booze and grass, and lots of bar hopping around town hooking up with some very odd characters wherever we went. Rush moved in his own subterranean world like a king (Scorpio sun, Leo rising, Sag moon), complete with his own entourage, strange subjects and unusual customs. I felt as if I was traveling in a foreign land.

After we were together for five weeks, Rush announced that he was leaving the next day for the West Coast on a grass run, his last big score, before retiring from the business. We talked about a spring getaway in the sun upon his return the following week.

He had me sew $10,000 in hundreds into the lining of his coat, which was no small feat, considering that I had never attempted any serious sewing without failing miserably. My mother had not equipped me with any practical skills before I left for college. She preferred to do everything herself so she could enjoy wallowing in her karmic rut of long-suffering martyr, a typical Piscean lament. Not only did I throw favorite wool sweaters into dryers at my dorm that came out the right size for infants, I also had to let Rush finish the sewing, so the money wouldn't fall out en route.

I wasn't a very good first-time accomplice, and worse yet, Rush didn't come back from his last big deal. He was planning to go out with a bang—and he did, but not in the way he had planned. It turned out to be a set-up. One of the buyers turned state's evidence to get out of a former rap and informed on the deal. Rush was busted in San Diego with over a ton of marijuana. It was a federal bust. All five co-defendants turned on him, and he was left literally holding the bag, with several priors and outstanding warrants from Illinois adding to the mess.

I was devastated when I got the news of Rush's bust from a couple of his seedy friends. We only had thirty-six days together, and the romance was over already. I was disconsolate.

# 8

## *On the Run*

### *Busted*

The way I dealt with the loss of Rush, during the three months I had left in the spring semester, was to eat and fuck, smoke (grass and Kools) and drink. Probably in that order most of the time. It didn't take the pain away, but I tried to enjoy the anesthesia of sensory and perceptual distraction. Attending classes was just a way to fill my time until I could party at night.

Something had happened to me during the time I was with Rush. Who he was to me and how his energy affected me catalyzed an opening in my sleeping consciousness. I got a peek at another way of being. He'd talk to me about reincarnation, karma, the nature of soul development, earth changes and Edgar Cayce. I felt as if he was preaching, and I wasn't having any of it. It reminded me too much of my mother who believed in past lives and communicating with angels.

Sometimes, when he talked to me, my perceptions would soften and shift. His face would change into an old grandmotherly face, which was confusing to me, as we were in the middle of a hot romance. For whatever reason, I was in mourning that spring. Our romance had come to an untimely end for an indefinite period.

I went home to Chicago for two weeks before my summer job started as a canoeing instructor and counselor at an exclusive girls' camp in Maine. Then I got a shocking phone call. It was Rush. He had escaped from the San Diego County Jail.

Well, it was not, technically, an escape. He had been released by computer error—some other prisoner had his exact name. He figured he had about twenty-four hours before they discovered the mistake. He wanted me to wire him $400, at least, so he could rent a private plane to get out of town fast. I didn't have that kind of money, but my brother (another soft-hearted Pisces), bless his soul, loaned it to me, even though he knew it was a crazy scheme for me to be involved in. He didn't judge. He just supported me and had faith that if it was important to me, then, ultimately, it would be all right.

I wired Rush the money and he got out of town fast. He came back to New York to hide out with friends and wait for me to come back to him after my summer obligations were over. We met up in Cambridge, Massachusetts, as a midpoint, for four days in the middle of my eight-week counseling gig. It was a very strange interlude.

Not only had I ballooned up to 140 pounds, I also confessed to him that eating wasn't the only way I consoled myself while he was in jail. I named names and some of the guys I had slept with he knew from around the neighborhood. I could tell I was upsetting him, but I just couldn't stop myself once I started my confessional jag. Unbelievably, he forgave me, with no resentful residue. I think he grasped that I had no concept of fidelity, much less monogamy, and he decided our connection was too important to hold my unfaithfulness against me. Rush was one of the most nonjudgmental human beings I have ever met—and I tested him often.

## *Hiding Out*

That fall, when I got back from Maine, Rush and I moved into an illegal sublet up in the Kingsbridge Heights section of the Bronx. I was still enrolled at Barnard, still ostensibly staying at a dorm, still going to classes. I was leading a double life.

Most days, I would take the train down from the Bronx for classes, and once or twice a week, I would stay over at the dorm. The rest of the time, Rush and I were bonding, and our commitment to be together was growing deeper. I remember daydreaming about him during a sociology course on changing male and female roles in society. I was envisioning him standing naked at the front of the class with everyone concurring that he was an absolutely perfect male specimen. I was so in love; I could see no flaws in him. I was even learning how to cook. Rush would roll his eyes with each new culinary disaster; medium-rare shake-and-bake chicken comes to mind.

I began a series of odd jobs to make money for sustaining our lifestyle in hiding. The first of these was door-to-door polling for different surveys: TV polls, Lou Harris, Yankelovich. These jobs were subcontracted out from this sleazy little Jewish guy who advertised for Barnard co-eds at the student center bulletin board. He always tried to seduce me when I went to pick up my money.

My assignments took me knocking on strangers' doors all over the five boroughs. I learned a lot about human nature and how to fake TV diaries when no one would open their doors for me. Most of all, I discovered a lifelong tendency to get seriously, and at times, dangerously lost in any area that was unfamiliar to me like the Lower East Side or the South Bronx. Fortunately, even when wandering through vacant lots and dark streets, map in hand, nothing ever happened to me. I was never too fearful. In fact, I got lost so often, I started to experience each new job as an adventure into the unknown.

Regrettably, the polling work wasn't making us enough money to live on. Rush suggested it would be good for me to become a barmaid in a topless bar. He figured it would expand my horizons beyond the sheltered life and mindset I grew up with and still carried inside of me. Besides, there were lots of ads for these barmaids, even with no experience. By that time I had slimmed down considerably to 105 pounds so getting one of these jobs was no problem. Staying out of trouble was. After six weeks or so, my bartending job became the vehicle for the destruction of our safe haven.

At my first barmaid job in Chelsea the uniform was a leotard and tights. The atmosphere was such that very horny guys were there to watch topless dancers and have a couple of drinks, in that order. Even though I was properly dressed under the circumstances, I never got hit on so much in my life. I had to develop a pretty tough act.

If a guy confronted me from his side of the bar and announced, "I want to fuck you!" I would very calmly say, "Oh, really? Step back from the bar and turn around so I can have a look at you." Once the guy did this, so *he* could feel like a piece of meat, I would disdainfully say, "I don't think so." This hard persona worked for me most nights.

But one night this really cute guy started giving me the eye. After a couple of nights of this, I started reciprocating. We got to know each other a little. He was an Italian construction worker from Brooklyn named Tony. We ended up doing it in the back seat of his car one night; then he drove me home to the Bronx.

I walked in late smelling like sex. Rush looked at me with disgust, as I sheepishly said that I needed to take a bath. Nothing more was said about it, but at least I had the decency to look sheepish. Slow progress was being made.

After I was on this job about six weeks, I got friendly with this mulatto guy, Ray, who was an ambulance driver. Rush got friendly with him too, as he had started coming down to the bar to pick me up more often. Rush invited Ray up to our apartment for dinner one night. That's when the seeds of disaster were sown.

After Rush got a bit stoned or had a couple of beers, he always enjoyed telling stories about his life. He told Ray about his bust in California and how we were on the run. Within a couple of days, we got a knock on the door at 6:00 AM.

I went to get it. When I asked who it was, the guy said, "FBI."

I sleepily headed back to bed, and Rush asked me who was at the door. I told him it was the FBI. He said to go back and ask what they wanted. I did. When I got back to the bed, Rush asked me what they wanted, and I said, "You."

He said to go back and tell them he wasn't there, which I did. I demanded to see ID and informed the agent that the picture he showed me didn't look like him. Then I acted really hysterical and exclaimed that not only did they have the wrong house, but they were probably all rapists, robbers and murderers, and I was going to call the police. I figured this would give us a little time.

It did. The agent seemed to go away from the door. Rush and I got dressed. He told me to go out and reconnoiter to see if the coast was clear. I went down to the lobby and out onto the street, but I didn't see anyone. When I got back to the apartment, the door was unlocked, and Rush was gone.

I immediately went into shock. I figured he'd been nabbed him while I was gone, and I would never see him again. I grabbed the cash and grass stash, fed the cats and aimlessly started wandering by subway down to the Village by subway, getting off every few stops to make sure I wasn't being followed.

I ended up, by accident, in front of a bar on Christopher Street that Rush had taken me to once, called the "55." I walked through the door and there, sitting at the bar, was Rush, calmly drinking a beer. I went into shock again. I thought I was having some kind of hallucination. He must have been in shock too, because he didn't say anything to me either, reinforcing my impression that he was a sur-real apparition. I sat down at the other end of the bar from him and ordered a drink.

We eyed each other suspiciously for a while. Then he sauntered over and whispered to me, "What are you doing here?" I told him that I didn't know. He asked me if I had been followed. I said no. He breathed a sigh of relief and sat down next to me.

"I thought I would never see you again," he said.

"Me too," I said.

"I thought you had picked this place to lead the FBI off my trail and bungled into me," he said.

"I didn't know you had escaped," I said. "I though they had gotten you."

Then he told me his side of the story, which became famous in the annals of stories he liked to tell about how we were destined to be together. He said that when I left the apartment, he felt these great waves of energy with the message that he should split right then and not wait for me to come back.

He started walking down the hallway. As he passed a neighbor's door, he heard an FBI guy say on his walkie-talkie: "He's leaving now." Instead of going down to the street, Rush went up to the roof, jumped over to another building and climbed down the fire escape to the street. In shock, he wandered aimlessly down to the "55," thinking he would never see me again because he would definitely have to leave town. Then I walked in!

Talk about synchronicity. We left town together that very day.

# 9

## *The Real Adventure Begins*

It was Rush's idea to go to Virginia Beach, Virginia, to be near Edgar Cayce's spiritual center, the Association of Research and Enlightenment, (ARE). He had read that the psychic energy there was very high frequency and pure, and that was good enough for him. I didn't have any better ideas, so off we went.

En route, we decided to stop off overnight in Kutztown, Pennsylvania, to visit Kathleen, a friend I had made during my summer in Maine. We got there in the afternoon on a snowy Saturday in February, just about a year after our original meeting.

Rush had procured some windowpane acid, LSD, before we left New York. That night, Rush, Kathleen and I decided to do a trip together. Rush had done hundreds of trips over the years and Kathleen was no novice either. It was the first time for me; I was a little nervous. Rush was very encouraging and promised to look after me so that nothing bad would happen. It was a night that changed my life forever—in a very good way.

Until I dropped acid, I hadn't really understood how incredibly speedy my metabolism was. Rush had said it would take a while for the effects to kick in, but as soon as I ate it, I started tripping instantaneously. It didn't help that it felt as if it were laced with speed, which was contraindicated for my super-sensitive nervous system.

We were sitting at a dining room table with a bunch of people eating salad and spaghetti and meatballs, a dish I have had a fondness for ever since. That's when my perceptual universe cracked open. I looked at Rush and saw and viscerally experienced our eternal nature and intuitively felt the eternal nature of all souls undeniably. As I looked at Rush's face, it split in two as if it had been struck by a lightening bolt. I saw how our souls had originally been one.

I communicated to him: "We are at the seventh level. This is the highest plane at which we are separate entities before merging with the whole. This experience has no purpose except for us to remember our original connection and intention." This was my first experience of spontaneous channeling. I didn't have a clue, at the time, of the meaning of what I was saying. The rest of this event is ineffable.

The big news is that once my perceptual universe cracked open—it never closed back up. In other words, I have never come back from that trip.

After this experience I went to pee, and Rush warning me not to look in any mirrors. Of course, I got stuck looking in a large mirror for what seemed like hours, completely mesmerized, until Rush came and rescued me. Then, we went to see a local college production of "How to Succeed in Business Without Really Trying." The cast kicked only once in unison during the whole show, which Rush thought was hysterical. In all the dance numbers, everyone was so out of sync that when they all finally kicked simultaneously it seemed like some kind of miracle. Then I got stuck in a mirror again in the bathroom.

My next memory was in the middle of the night in Kathleen's living room, just the three of us, all tripping up a storm. Kathleen, who was quite a beauty, kept trying to convince me to leave Rush and stay with her. She kept saying, "Look at him, he's not even human." Truth be told, Rush did look like he was from some other solar system. The closest I can describe it was that he looked canine and alternately equine, as if he was from far beyond the orbit of Pluto.

Even though I could see Kathleen's point, I unequivocally exclaimed, "But I love him!" Then Rush and I went to bed in the attic of this old house. Rush wanted to make love—but I was afraid to. I was pretty sure that if I had an orgasm, I would explode and disintegrate into a million pieces and never be reformed—quite a legitimate fear at the time.

Because we were still tripping, we couldn't sleep. We toddled off to a local diner and had a big Pennsylvania Dutch breakfast, country sausage and all. Then we boarded the bus for Virginia Beach, with our hopes high for new adventures.

# 10

## *Virginia Beach*

When we arrived in Virginia Beach on the Greyhound bus, it was snowing, a rare occurrence there. We stayed in a tiny, cheap motel near the bus station with a silly name, like the Dilly Dally, for a few days until we got our bearings and hunted for more permanent accommodations.

We found a great deal a block and a half from the ocean, a rundown furnished apartment house with six units and cheap as hell off-season. The furniture was especially tacky. The owner, an ancient, Jewish, cronelike widow named Sylvia, offered us a deal we couldn't refuse. If Rush agreed to be the resident manager, we could continue paying our low rent of $200 during the high season, when our two bedroom would go for at least $600.

Rush thought this was perfect. He could stay home and manage the place, while he was working on the next great American novel. I went out and got a waitress gig at one of the respectable seafood restaurants downtown on the tourist strip. We settled down in our first real home together. Completely broke, on the run, but very much in love. I would never again be so young, innocent and happy, all at the same time.

I learned my waitress skills from an old timer named Ann, who labored next door in the adjoining counter-only coffee shop. Ann would actually go up to a table, while she was teaching me the ropes, and take an order with a doughnut sticking out of the side of her mouth like a cigar. I had never seen anything like it and was very impressed with her nonchalance.

I was paid $2 a day plus tips and had to vacuum the joint after closing, as there was no bus boy off-season. I got to eat all the greasy fried chicken and spaghetti and meatballs I could, as well as all the fried seafood that the black cook used to sneak to me, by way of being friendly.

When hiring for the season began in May, two months after I'd arrived, I was promoted to head waitress over all the college girls hired for the summer. As a seasoned pro at nineteen, I got my first taste of being a worker among workers, and I liked it.

During this period, I could eat around 10,000 calories a day and still weigh 100 pounds. You name it—pizza, hot fudge sundaes, doughnuts—I could eat all I wanted. I was in speedy metabolism heaven. It's a time in my life I still long for—and not just for the romance. My metabolism would never be this efficient again. Similarly to when I was pre-adolescent, before the hormones kicked in, I could eat huge quantities of food and naturally burn it off and still weigh less than 80 pounds.

It's easier for me to wax nostalgic for those days of carefree eating than to deal with the loss of emotional innocence I had with Rush then. I would have done *anything* for him. I worked six days a week, double shifts. I paid for everything. Whatever I had was his; I didn't think twice. I had no emotional or financial boundaries with Rush. All the love I had to give was his—and everything else.

# 11

# *The True Nature of Our Interchange*

Rush and I would go for long walks along the nature trails at Seashore State Park, just north of the ARE, which we visited for lectures. On some of these walks, time would fall away. Then space would fall away. Then the dimensions would open up and we were everywhere and everyone and everything—with no boundaries. These experiences began to set the tone for our dynamic.

At night, we would smoke some pot after dinner and sit in the living room and do what we came to call "faces" for hours. We didn't need a TV or any other entertainment because what we were doing was so alive.

We rearranged the living room furniture, which was very shiny and boxy, into a rectangle. There was a couch I sat on, and across from me, Rush sat in one of the squared-off arm chairs. It looked and felt as if we were in a space capsule. As our energy rose, the furniture became iridescent and our auras filled the room with bright colors and lights.

As we continued to rev our energy upwards with the intent of our minds, we began operating at a psychic frequency akin to Kutztown and our times in the woods. We would look at each other's faces as they morphed as fast as flipping cards. Then, the energy in the room would become so intense in its frequency that the room would fall away, and we became continuously flowing light beings in space.

Sometimes, we would speak of what we were experiencing, but usually it was beyond words. Everything in our life became the backdrop for this level of interchange.

Once we dropped some acid in Virginia. It was quite a trip, especially since we seemed to be on a continuous trip that we never came down from.

Rush took two hits of the acid because he thought it might have lost some of its potency. He was wrong—and ended up lying down for eight hours. When I tried to rouse him because Sylvia unexpectedly arrived to discuss some business with him, he told me with a smile that he was in Egypt and I would have to deal with her myself.

I also got lost for a while on that trip. I guess that's why they call it a trip. I was making a kidney bean salad at the time I took the acid, thinking I would be finished before the acid hit. I was wrong. Somewhere in the course of stirring together the ingredients, the acid hit. Three hours later, I was still stirring the beans—they had become the primordial ooze—and I was still in it.

Except for that one lapse on acid, Rush and I continued our interchange on the psychic plane as our normal, daily operating trip, no more hallucinogens needed. Of course, we still smoked pot daily.

My experiences of seeing Rush's face morph into an almost infinite variety of images—some from this dimension, some from others—began to spread out into my perceptions of everyone. When I looked at friends' faces, they would also break down into their flowing energy components and continuously transform, as would the scenes behind them. I was starting to get coherent information simultaneously with these mutating facial images and scenes. I was getting spontaneous soul readings of past lives, while witnessing them. So it began.

I found it incredibly powerful and consuming to perceive reality and other people this way. Rush suggested that I get a sketchbook and try to draw whatever I was seeing, which I did. This began a period of almost ten years of trying to capture my psychic visions through art. While I had some success, my psychic vision kept expanding, as did the range of information coming with the visions. Over time, I slowly realized that art was becoming too small a vehicle to contain all that I was receiving from other dimensions.

Rush and I stabilized at the psychic plane, the soul level of being, by the fall of 1973. The summer season was over. My restaurant's business waned, and our money was running out. We decided to return to New York City, hoping it had cooled off for us.

# 12

## *Survival Mode*

We stayed in a studio apartment with an old friend of Rush's while we went looking for a cheap place. The guy was sweet but a little strange. After a week, with dwindling resources, we moved into the old Albert Hotel on University and 10th Street.

The Albert had seen better days. It was a dingy residence hotel, home to pushers and hookers, but we couldn't afford anything better. We got two rooms on the ground floor with very depressing energy, which didn't help our moods. We were definitely in survival mode, and our psychic level of interchange got lost in the desperation of our circumstances.

The first job I got through an agency was as a waitress at the Alpine Cellar Restaurant in the basement of the McAlpine Hotel, a middle-range relic in Herald Square. I lasted about an hour. Someone showed me what to do on the floor in a very cursory way and then disappeared. It was between lunch and dinner shifts, and I was left to sink or swim. I sunk.

Because of a sudden thunderstorm, the whole cavernous restaurant filled up instantaneously with hungry, demanding German tourists. I ran up so many checks that needed to be stamped at different places and delivered to so many different stations in the kitchen. At a certain point, I just froze in frustration with about thirty checks in my hand.

Then, in the middle of the dining room, the manager appeared out of nowhere and started screaming at me. I threw up several dozen checks in the air and, with a great sense of liberation, yelled, "I quit!" and stormed out, leaving the manager with his mouth hanging open, surrounded by angry Germans. This was not the best career move with our money nearly gone. Rush wasn't thrilled, but he was, as always, understanding.

The next job the agency sent me on was a lunch gig in a busy midtown joint. I went out and got 3″ platform shoes for the job. I didn't have a clue. The other waitresses looked at me like I was crazy, because the kitchen was up a steep flight of stairs from the dining room. That job lasted less than a week, and I was lucky I didn't break an ankle.

Then I started pounding the pavement on my own, because the agency and I gave up on each other. I lucked out right away at the Billy Budd, a piano bar and restaurant in the Shelburne Hotel, at 37th and Lex. The owner, a guy named Mike, hired me as the cocktail waitress and as a fill-in for the lunch shift. He hired me because he liked my looks so much that I had to constantly ward off his horny, married, middle-aged advances. But I got used to that, and it was good practice for warding off all the other similar-type advances occurring continuously through my shifts, from 4:00 PM 'til past midnight most nights. It just went with the territory. The money was the best I had ever made. Lonely, drunken men, ever hopeful, were very generous tippers.

At home at the Albert, things were getting rockier by the day. I came home one time and found Rush passed out on the floor. He admitted that passing out had almost happened to him several times on the street when he was out walking. He said he had a rare blood disorder that was diagnosed when he was nineteen and an MP in the Army stationed in Germany. He said it flared up from time to time; there was no cure or treatment for it.

This information freaked me out so much that I became emotionally unstable. I never knew, when I came home from work, what condition I would find Rush in, or even if he would make it home from his walks. I tried to get him to see a doctor, but he resisted. He was on the run, after all. Plus, he had very little faith in allopathic medicine and said there was nothing left that he hadn't already tried. I began feeling more and more powerless and unhappy over our depressing circumstances.

A friend of Mike's at work, after listening to a semi-cleaned-up version of my troubles, convinced me to go home to my family in Chicago until I could sort out my feelings, as I seemed so confused. That seemed to make as much sense as anything at the time. I informed Rush that I was leaving him temporarily, until I could figure out what I wanted to do with my life.

I was on the run with a sick bandito boyfriend and no cash flow holed up in a funky hellhole eating Kraft macaroni and cheese. I had hit my limit.

# 13

## *Confusion*

As soon as I got back to Chicago, to stay with my dad and step-mom and one of my stepbrothers, I started missing Rush terribly. My dad lived in a beautiful, luxurious high-rise overlooking the lake on the 33rd floor. The discrepancy between my circumstances with Rush and my family situation was absurd. To top it off, the FBI found out I was back. I had to meet with them, with a family attorney present, and give a deposition so that I could be granted immunity for aiding and abetting a fugitive.

Of course, I lied through the whole thing. I swore I didn't know where Rush was; we were not in contact and were completely through anyway. As a term of my immunity, I promised, if Rush contacted me, I would notify them immediately. In the meantime, Rush and I were in weekly communication through a pay phone in a nearby park that I would sneak to late at night.

During this two-month period, I had a one-night stand that was so emotionally wrong for me, I developed a chronic urinary tract infection that I was eventually hospitalized for several years later. I'm sure my psychological state was so confused about Rush that I somatized this condition to keep me from using sex to deny my true feelings.

I got a very straight job as a secretary at an executive consulting firm in the Loop. My Mom helped me dress for success by buying me a bunch of little wool knit dresses for the office. By this time I was about a size 4, weighing 90 pounds. My emotional distress was taking its toll. Working in the nine-to-five world in an office and commuting everyday on the bus really flipped me out. Even though I only did it for two months, I knew this type of work structure would be the death of my spirit.

I explored going back to college, as I was on extended leave from Barnard with good grades on my transcript, Dean's List and all. Since I was so drawn to the criminal element, I looked into the School of Criminology at Berkeley. My thinking was that I could make a living helping outlaws more directly and not just through the law, which was my original intention after college.

Then I had the realization that while I wanted to help mankind, I really preferred doing it one man at a time—and Rush was still my man. My personality predisposition as a Libra meant I desired the personal touch of a one-on-one relationship rather than humanitarian idealism.

I called Rush to let him know that I planned to return to him as soon as I had saved at least a $1000, enough for an apartment security deposit. We missed each other terribly. I felt only half full without him.

I tried to slip out one night, leaving my dad a note explaining my departure. He caught me in the act, and I had to sit down with him and try to get him to understand why I was going back to New York. He didn't like it, but he accepted that I was an adult and had to make up my own mind.

# 14

## *Busted Again*

When I arrived back in New York, Rush was staying with another old buddy. Norman was an alcoholic parole officer with a taste for black women and a sweet but resigned disposition.

Rush and I had a torrid reunion. Feeling whole again, we set out in search of a home. We found a small two-room walk-up on East 9th Street. It was only $150 a month because it had fire damage from downstairs, and we had to paint it ourselves. However, the landlady was nice and friendly, with very good vibes. We painted and moved into our new home, very much in love and happy to be together again.

Then I got another barmaid job in a leotard again at a topless bar named The Blue Rooster in Long Island City. It was a pretty rowdy place. Sometimes the dancers would get so drunk they would remove their g-strings and lie down on stage and dry-hump the air to the cheers of crowds of beer-guzzling men. Sometimes the cops would be called and demand to see whoever was in charge. Usually it was me. Who knew? I was too short to see over the men standing at the bar to supervise the girls.

After a month, I got fired from that job because my register would never come out right at the end of the shift. I wasn't stealing, just not too competent making change. Another career opportunity bit the dust. But, before I left, I befriended this really cute cabdriver, who came in for a beer after his shift, as the bar was near the taxi garages. He had a live-in girlfriend who was a nurse. I invited them over for dinner; it was Rush and my first couple's thing.

At this time, we had a mattress on the floor and milk crates for tables, but it was still our first dinner party—chili and sangria. It was a very pleasant evening. I was fucking the cute cabdriver on the side, but only recreationally, as by now it was finally clear that Rush was the love of my life. Obviously, scruples were not my strong point, but I did hide it from Rush anyway.

My next job, a waitress gig at a joint on East 34th Street, was what I think that brought the FBI down on us. I'm not sure exactly how. Maybe they traced my address through my social security number to my job. I also suspected that one of the waitresses was jealous of me and when questioned, informed the FBI of my whereabouts. But, I wasn't making a very good effort at covering my tracks with Rush. For some reason he also let it all slide. It seemed as if he didn't care anymore and was surrendering to the inevitable.

One morning in June, about three months after my return, there was a pounding at the door at 6:00 AM. It was the FBI again. This time they nailed us, even though our nice landlady tried to steer them away. I hid in the bathroom, trying to flush a lid of grass down the toilet—but I forgot to take it out of the baggy, and the toilet was backing up.

When I came out, after repeated poundings on the door, I caught a last glimpse of Rush being led away in handcuffs by two FBI guys. Another FBI guy gave me a lecture: "Don't you remember what you promised us in Chicago?" I said I didn't know what he was talking about and acted all shocked and innocent. They just walked away with Rush and let me go.

We had been on the run for sixteen months. I knew in my heart that my time with Rush was over—at least for an indefinite period.

# 15

## *The Prison Years*

When the shock wore off a little from our dawn FBI raid, I called a lawyer acquaintance of Rush's from a pay phone on the corner. The lawyer, Russell Dwayne, was a sort of legal jack-of-all-trades and drinking buddy from Rush's crowd on the Upper West Side. He was 50ish, with a crumpled, shiny suit and slicked back hair from a receding hairline. But having a friend in need and being broke meant that Russell was a true godsend.

Russell agreed to represent Rush without a retainer after I promised him $5,000. $2,500 down, as soon as possible from my waitress wages and the other half from Rush whenever—which Russell never saw. He held my hand through the arraignment and was good-natured throughout the entire ordeal, involving numerous court appearances over the next four months. First, Rush was sent to the Tombs. Then after a couple of weeks, he was transferred to the old federal jail on West Street because he was busted on a federal warrant.

After that, Illinois chimed in with extradition papers from an old grass bust. Things started getting messy. Rush was transferred to Sing-Sing, a state facility in Ossining, New York, while awaiting an extradition hearing. It was turning into a very long, hot summer.

In the wake of Attica, there were near riots at Sing-Sing that summer due to the conditions, the heat and the general climate of the times in 1974. When I came to visit, Rush was just about the only white face in a sea of black and Hispanic faces. Thank God, he was a big guy and could take care of himself physically. But emotionally and psychically he was getting extremely depressed and suicidal over the stalled extradition hearing. He begged me to get him out of there. At one point, I had to draw him a portrait of himself so he could see how close he was to leaving his body. He got the message and stabilized somewhat.

I visited him whenever I could, usually once a week on my only day off. The other six days, I was working double shifts with overtime to pay Russell his retainer. I also managed to get together another $3,000 to send Russell to Illinois to work out a deal with the DA there, so Rush's case could be settled out of court.

Amazingly, Russell succeeded in Illinois and the extradition was dropped. We got a federal court date for October. Rush and I prayed for a miracle. Russell did the best he could under the circumstances—but it *was* a ton of grass. Rush was sentenced to three years, with five months off for time served.

I went into shock again after the sentence was read, but Russell was there to hold my hand and walk me through it. I knew I had to stay strong for Rush, because he was losing his will to live. I was only twenty-one, but I had to gather up all my reserves of inner strength to keep psyching up Rush when I visited him.

Fortunately, Rush got transferred to a minimum security prison in Danbury, Connecticut, which was considered a country club compared to the state prisons. There were many high-profile inmates there, such as Gordon Liddy and Meyer Kahan. After a while, Rush got a white-collar job in the office, so that released some of the pressure and anxiety.

I visited him once a week with gourmet food, spending money and entertaining stories to keep his spirits up. He told me later that, during the entire time he was in prison, all the long, rambling letters I wrote him were almost completely illegible. He never told me he couldn't read them since he didn't want me to stop writing. Every year since then, my writing has gotten even more illegible, even to me.

After Rush was in Danbury about six months, in the spring of 1975, he told me during a weekly visit that he wanted me to stop visiting him and get on with my life. He knew I had done my absolute best to help him. He was grateful and would always love me, but he didn't want me to wait for him for another year and a half.

He said, at my age, life should as sweet as an ice cream cone. He freed me from any further obligation to him. He pushed me out of the prison bondage we were in together. He released me fully. I didn't realize at the time what a great gift and sacrifice he was making for my happiness.

Instead, I felt dazed, lost, confused and somehow rejected after my last visit. All my energies had been focused on Rush for so long. I didn't know what to do with myself. But, within days, relief started to well up inside. I didn't need to stay on "crisis alert" about Rush's state of mind anymore.

Not being focused on Rush meant I could focus my energies on me. Since I was not prone to contemplation or being alone, I went out looking for adventure again. It was what I knew how to do best.

Rush only ended up serving about a year and a half of his sentence, but for both of us, it felt like a lifetime. Neither of us would ever be the same again; we changed in different ways and in different directions. In terms of our romance, that phase of our relationship would never return again—at least for me, even though I tried after he got out. The romance had lasted about two and a half years. It doesn't sound like much time now. But then, it was the only period in my life that I had felt truly alive.

## *In the Interim*

Part of my relief at Rush's release of me—he wanted no communication on any level—was so I could swing into higher gear in party girl mode. This had always been my modus operandi in general, but especially when uncomfortable emotions were present.

Not that I hadn't gotten into various forms of trouble in the interim. I had four minor affairs in the ten months since Rush had been gone. They were minor because my heart belonged to Rush completely, until he released me. These affairs didn't count for much more than periodic entertainment on the sensual level—mostly drunken, sexually primitive and, definitely, no heart.

I didn't feel I deserved more while Rush was suffering in jail. I picked men, or let them pick me, just so we could use each other. Emotionally and psychically suffering in empathy with Rush was my own form of karmic bondage. Obviously it wasn't the highest road I could have taken during this period, but I didn't know any other way to be.

# PART IV

## *THE ROARING TWENTIES*

# 16

## *The Zen of Eating and Fucking*

By the time Rush had released me from serving his term with him, I had gotten a pretty good, steady waitress gig at a midtown steak house catering to business-men. One of my new girlfriends from work, Carol, became my bar-hopping, men-hunting, drinking buddy after work. She turned me on to a bar in Gramercy Park, the Honeytree, that catered to cops and doctors who worked in the neighborhood.

One night, I decided to try the place on my own, which I preferred anyway. I got lucky right away. That's the night I met Donnie. He was a thirty-three-year old surgical intern at a local hospital, and he was gorgeous in a swarthy Italian way that I liked, with a thick bushy mustache, stocky bullish frame and dreamy eyes. He was a Taurus with Pisces rising and had played football in college on Long Island.

We hit it off instantaneously and fit together like two peas in a pod. I fell head over heels for him the first week we were together, and the feeling was mutual. We fell into a mutual karmic rut of eating and fucking, smoking grass and drink-ing that was unparalleled in my life to date. Taurus is an even more sensual sign than Libra; both are ruled by Venus, planet of love and all good hedonistic plea-sures.

Donnie had gone to medical school in Bologna, Italy, and being a total party animal, it had taken him more than twice the normal time to graduate. His years there weren't a total waste because, not only did he manage to scrape together a med school degree, he also acquired a taste for Northern Italian cuisine, learned to cook it expertly and taught me how.

We moved through different levels of culinary and sexual heaven together. Veal francese, spaghetti carbonara, fettuccini Alfredo—our dining was as rich as our lovemaking, with lots of eye contact and moaning. On alternate weekends, when he wasn't on call, we would smoke pot and make love, cook and eat and then make love again—all weekend long. The richness of our indulgences had a unique flavor because, for our first six months together, it felt as if we were absolutely equal partners in terms of our capacity to experience pleasure together in almost all our waking hours.

In fact, on the psychic plane, I could see that my karmic connections with Donnie were primarily from lives of experiencing sensual pleasure. I saw us both as women in a plush harem, alternating with visions of us as high-class Babylonian "ladies of the evening." When I looked at Donnie with my psychic sight, especially when we were in bed together in the afterglow, I saw him as a "her"—all rouged up, with full red lips and voluminous breasts. Simultaneously, I would see, with my normal sight that he was a very hirsute muscular man. This took some getting used to. I found it slightly disconcerting at first to have this double vision, but it was all very intriguing.

Donnie's astrological make-up was similar to mine in that we both had Mars, the planet of male energies, and Venus, the planet of female energies, conjunct, or working synergistically together in the flexible signs of Gemini for him and Virgo for me. This meant we were comfortable playing with the full range of our yin and yang energies together—and play we did.

My stepfather had tried to get me interested in Zen mindfulness meditation when I was nineteen, but I was too young and frisky to meditate while sitting and counting my breaths or even walking peacefully in nature. However, the idea of bringing my full conscious awareness into the present moment, so that it became the only moment which existed, appealed to me. I could get a little taste of this with Donnie in a sort of stoned, half-assed way that definitely had a ceiling on it. It was the best I could do at the time. However, I did get momentary glimpses of the sexual act becoming a spiritual one.

During this period, I also started taking a drawing class from the model at the Art Students League. On the very first day of class, the teacher was so impressed with my sketches, he assumed I was a third-year student. When he found out I was a new student, he hung my drawings on the wall for all to see. I seemed to have a knack. I felt as if I was starting to be on the right track.

Then, in late August 1975, just when everything seemed to be coming together with Donnie and my art, I received a letter from Rush. He asked for my help with his upcoming parole hearing. He needed me to get someone to offer him a job, at least on paper. In addition, he needed me to state I was his common-law wife with a home residence he could be released to.

I did these things by mail, convincing our landlady to get her husband to offer Rush a job, on paper only, in his construction business. Then I called Rush and told him I had done everything he had asked of me. He said his chances of getting paroled, with the help I gave him, looked very promising. He asked me if we could pick up where we left off when he got out. I said I would think about it and let him know in a week.

I didn't tell Rush about Donnie because I didn't want him to get depressed again, especially when he sounded so hopeful about his release. Furthermore, I didn't want to tell Donnie about Rush before I thought the whole thing through. Obviously, I had to keep these two relationships separate until I could come to a decision. I was in a pickle.

I decided to go to Virginia Beach for a week and stay with a friend while I sorted through my feelings. I walked the beach a lot and was as contemplative as I was capable of.

What it came down to for me was that Rush needed my support and not just on paper. I felt that since he was still the love of my life, to date, I owed it to both of us to play it out. Even though I was in love with Donnie on the personality level, my feelings for Rush ran much deeper on the more essential level of our soul connection. I could not discount what I knew from Kutztown. It was very confusing.

I made the decision to break-up with Donnie. Then, I told Rush that I would be there for him when he was released. His parole date was set for October, with the first month in a half-way house on most nights.

Donnie was upset and heart-broken, Rush was released, and I felt sort of grim and obligated through it all. I was happy for Rush when his parole came through, but I was not personally joyful about his release. All I felt was trepidation.

# 17

## *Perfect Balance*

Rush had changed a lot in prison, or rather, prison had changed Rush a lot. He wasn't rehabilitated exactly. It was as if his free-spirited outlaw nature was wounded on some very deep level.

Since the job I got for him was on paper only, it wasn't going to cut it with his parole officer. Rush got a job as a waiter in a midtown deli. Having to work for others further demoralized his free spirit, especially after his time in prison.

Our sex life turned pretty grim for me as well. Rush was sexually voracious after a year and a half of deprivation and was wearing me out. He was going down on me all the time, and I didn't feel the natural generosity of spirit to reciprocate. Instead, I complained that his dick was so big I was getting lockjaw whenever I gave him head. My vaginal opening became very sore; I actually went to my gynecologist to see if I could be made larger surgically. I was beginning to feel burdened by what used to be sheer joy.

What had happened? After all we had been through, I couldn't see Rush in the same romantic light as the ideal man for me anymore. In fact, his energies felt very androgynous, as did his appearance, and not in a way that turned me on at all. The love was still very much there and the soul connection, but the sexual chemistry had completely vanished—unfortunately, from my side only.

To complicate matters, I started missing Donnie and our light-hearted sensual hijinks more and more. Being true to my nature, I started seeing Donnie on the sly. After all, I didn't want to break Rush's heart or spirit when he was still on the mend from prison.

After a couple of weeks of sneaking around, a girlfriend of mine invited Rush and me to a holiday party. I made a point of having Donnie invited too. I guess I wanted Rush to meet the man I told him I'd had a fling with for six months prior to his parole. I didn't tell him the rest.

But he had eyes and he could see. Even more, he could feel the energy running between Donnie and me. To make matters more byzantine, Rush and Donnie really hit it off. They were peers in more than just age; they seemed to have an almost instantaneous soul connection. I was astonished at Rush's emotional flexibility and range.

After we got home that night, Rush asked me if I wanted to keep seeing Donnie as a lover. I said I did. He said it was all right with him as long as it was just sex. I told him it wasn't—I was in love with Donnie, and I couldn't help it. The bond was already formed before he got out of prison. Rush said he understood, because he really liked Donnie too.

Then Rush was quiet for a moment. "I guess I'll be moving on then," he said. I responded, "Well, there's no rush. Take your time."

Rush never did move out; he took me at my word. Not only did he take his time, we continued to live together for another two and a half years. We even moved into a larger place together, in more ways than one. Over time, Rush and my relationship evolved to a soul-level friendship that was very loving, as we moved to the next level of our psychic development together.

My lover relationship with Donnie continued for another year and a half. I saw him on Tuesdays, Thursdays and alternate weekends, when he wasn't on call for his surgical residency. Amazingly, Rush's relationship with Donnie evolved into a beer-drinking, sports-watching buddy friendship that endured for twenty-three years.

During the couple of years when I was alternating between Rush and Donnie, I went to the New School for painting classes. I activated and honed my skills as a painter—they seemed to emerge almost intact from my karmic cellular memory.

Since Rush and I lived on 9th Street and Donnie and I lived on 19th Street, sometimes on my way to school, I would hit a moment of perfect balance on 14th Street. It was always fleeting, always exquisite, those moments of balance, and I couldn't seem to get them any other way.

With Rush, I received nourishment from our spiritual and psychic bond; with Donnie, it was from the sensual. Both had heart. But it was only on 14th Street that I caught a glimpse of the integration of my being which I was slowly moving toward.

# 18

## *The Next Level*

As Rush and I settled into the next phase of our personal dynamic, the stage became set for the next level of our soul relationship. In our daily life, we became very affectionate best friends. We still slept together and cuddled all night doing "spoonsies," but the sex part had fallen away.

Rush and I joined a small spiritual group led by a psychic, Angus, which met once a week in a suite in the Ansonia Hotel. We met several old karmic friends in that group. After Angus did my astrology chart and saw my latent psychic abilities in it (a stellium of planets in the eight house), he decided to test me after our group meeting.

We were sitting in a Howard Johnson's restaurant in Time's Square drinking manhattans. Angus gave me a set of keys and asked me to do a reading of what I was picking up using psychometry, which involves tuning into vibrational energies through an object. I closed my eyes. A whole story unfolded in my inner vision as if I was watching a movie. I described what I was seeing. When I opened my eyes, Angus's jaw had dropped open. He was astounded by my accuracy. So was I.

Rush wasn't. He always knew who I was on the soul level and what my potentials were. He also knew it was time for us to start accessing that level of communication. We started at home with an Ouija board. That didn't even last ten minutes; it just made me impatient. Without further delay, I put pen to paper and began writing automatically. This was my first formal reading. It was in the winter of 1976.

Throughout that year, I channeled readings by automatic writing, with Rush there to ask questions and stabilize me. At a certain point, I just let the inner words start to come through, using my vocal chords. Rush took dictation. This was better than having to maintain a strong physical focus for eye/hand coordination, but it was still too slow. The energy behind the words was so fast and intense that slowing down the delivery process, so Rush could write, was painful to my system. It wasn't until 1981 that my channels wised me up and I began using a tape recorder.

Through 1976, I continued painting school, waitressing and seeing Donnie. Rush studied astrology and switched to bartending, which suited his disposition much more than being a waiter.

That winter, Donnie and I took a winter holiday in Jamaica together. I was taking a break from the pill, and I got pregnant. Diaphragms never worked properly for me: they seemed to get stuck inside me. Whenever I tried to pull one out, the suction was so intense, I felt as if I was either scraping myself raw trying to pry it free or pulling my insides out. Donnie hated wearing rubbers; the rest is an old story. What with Jamaican weed and dark rum, contraception got moved down the list of priorities.

When I decided on an abortion, Rush went with me to the clinic. Even though it was Donnie's baby, Rush kept trying to convince me to have it. He promised to help me raise the child because he thought it might be the soul of his dead father reincarnating through me. I declined unequivocally, without giving it a second thought. I was twenty-three and there was no way I was interested in getting tied down that way. I knew I wanted to have kids, but I also knew I had a lot more living and growing up to do first.

In the spring of 1977, Rush and I moved into the larger apartment together. It had a small painting studio for me and separate bedrooms for us, which we soon acclimated to. We started a psychic group one night a week that I led and an astrology group another night that Rush led. It was an exciting time. I also started doing some readings for friends in our ever-widening circle of psychic acquaintances.

We were stoned all the time, even smoking in our groups. It was our way of life, and we didn't know any other way to be. Everyone we knew smoked grass and drank. It was the 1970s, after all, and we had dinner parties, garden parties and drinking parties, at home and in restaurants, clubs and bars.

It was a very social time and there was much buoyancy in the air. Our philosophy was "Be Here Now!" There was so much hope for the future. As always, that which rises must ultimately fall away.

# 19

## *Unraveling*

After our first year together, I realized that the only time I got Donnie's unqualified attention was when I was his patient in the hospital. This happened when I needed an emergency surgical procedure for a strictured urethra due to chronic cystitis, and Donnie assisted the urologist. When he was not on call, he was getting stoned or drunk to unwind before he passed out. Since I didn't want to resent Donnie, or implode my emotions and somatize them into an illness to get his attention again, I started sneaking out on him by the late fall of 1976. At least that was my rational.

Early in the evening, Donnie would pass out from exhaustion and the grueling hours of his surgical residency schedule. Then, I would tiptoe out to the same local bar where I had met him, looking for mischief, as usual.

One night, I met an actor/carpenter, a Leo, with piercing blue eyes. He looked like a young Richard Burton with an ego to match. His wife was hugely pregnant at home, and he was out sniffing around. We had a small affair. The only problem was the only place we could have it was in the apartment I shared with Rush.

Rush got home early from work one day and caught us in bed together. I asked him if he could come back later. I was truly incorrigible. I knew I was hurting Rush, but my lust was stronger than my sensitivity to his feelings. That was a low point.

I was just getting warmed up. I'd go to a party with Rush, then Donnie would arrive, and we'd be a social threesome for a while. After that, Rush would leave, and I would remain with Donnie. Simultaneously, during the party, I'd be on the phone trying to arrange an assignation with whoever else I was fucking at the time.

By late fall of 1977, the Zen of eating and fucking with Donnie had reached a point where I asked myself, "Is this all there is?" Accordingly, I went in search of someone new to fuck. As if that was some sort of solution to my metaphysical search for the purpose of life, rather than just another redundant act in my ever-increasing karmic rut of rutting.

This time, I met one of my fantasies come to life. The Lords of Karma were trying to help me bottom out by fulfilling my deepest unconscious desires for annihilation of self through the "other." His name was Nick and he was a burly Bomb Squad detective, age thirty-six, in a three-piece pinstriped suit, with a pronounced dark side. At that time, I had a crush on the TV detective Kojak (don't ask me why), and Nick was as close as I was going to get to Kojak in real life.

I got drunk while we were getting acquainted at the bar. When I went to pee there was a knock at the door. It was Nick. I let him in and he stuck his rather large dick in my mouth while I was sitting on the toilet. I thought it was rude to refuse this gesture of friendship, so I gave him a blowjob. In my drunken state, this seemed like proper manners. Nick took this to be a very romantic and generous gesture. We were off and running.

He picked me up the next morning to take me to tea at the Plaza. He was dressed in his three-piece suit and I was severely underdressed in paint-spattered corduroys and a T-shirt. It was an impromptu date. Nick was an impromptu kind of guy.

On the way to the Plaza, Nick parked on the east side by the river. He thought it was time for another romantic, generous gesture. I obliged, even though it felt decidedly one-sided to me. I hated to form this type of pattern so early in our affair. I had no idea.

Over tea at the Plaza, Nick told me he felt so overwhelmed by my romantic, generous nature, he thought he was falling in love. Ever the romantic pragmatist, I said, "Well, let's see how it goes." I then informed him of my living arrangement with Rush and Donnie. He informed me that he was separated from his second wife and subletting a friend's apartment in Brooklyn.

Our next meeting was a date I will never forget. Nick came to pick me up at my waitress gig, a couple of hours before my shift was over. He sat in my section and ate and drank his fill while staring at me intently with lust. Periodically, he would call me over and inform me of his intentions to ravage me later. I was literally weak in the knees, not to mention soaking wet.

We got back to my place around midnight. Rush wasn't due home until after 4:00 AM. Nick laid his gun, unholstered on the bedside table, as we smoked a joint.

"What's that for?" I asked, pointing to the gun.

"Just to make sure you do everything I want." He said. "And just in case we're disturbed," He added.

"Oh, my God," I exclaimed. "You wouldn't shoot Rush, would you?" I made him promise that the gun was only there as part of our game, which was heating up rapidly.

I thought we were finally going to stop this one-sided nonsense and fuck, which we did, but not in the way I had expected. It turned out that Nick was a backdoor man, and it hurt like hell. Being so aroused for so many hours and drunk and stoned left me not just violated and shocked during and after the act. I felt blown away and impressed by his mastery of me, in what I realized was a truly real game of sadomasochism, which he had been setting me up for all along.

I had to sit in the bath to gather my thoughts, which were totally fucked out of my head. I soaked my aching heiny and tried to reverse my energy flow back to normal, as it had been severely traumatized.

Nick and I lasted a couple of months. It was the sickest ride I have ever chosen to be on. In public, he treated me like a lady: fancy clothes, jeweled cigarette lighters, expensive dinners. He even wanted to set me up in a high-rise apartment, so I could be on call for him full time as his personal slave, rather than just occasionally.

Nick didn't see it the way I did. He truly fell in love with me—as much as he was capable of. I felt no love for him at all. Over time, I realized I didn't even really like him. Nonetheless, something in me needed to play this out and get it out of my system, once and for all.

We would go to his apartment in Brooklyn and play sex games. One time, I remember dropping a tube of KY Jelly into a mailbox (a federal offense), so that he couldn't fuck me in the ass (wishful thinking).

We did have normal intercourse too, and once or twice, he made a gallant effort to go down on me, but I could tell it was a stretch for him. We even went to Hawaii before it was over, but after that it *was* over. We fought through the whole vacation. Whatever we had, it didn't travel well, especially in the light of day.

We ended up one more time together after Hawaii. It was degrading to blow him with a gun pointed at my head and then be pissed on, before he fucked me in the ass with no mercy. This last meeting, which ended with us slapping each other in the face in his car, cleansed me of the need to ever go down such a self-destructive dead-end alley again.

# 20

## *Geographical Cure*

Around the time I was breaking up with Nick, Rush and I did some psilocybin (magic mushrooms) at the Museum of Modern Art. It was the first time I had done any type of hallucinogens in the city; other times I'd been in more natural surroundings, such as in 1973 in Kutztown or Virginia Beach. It was a really intense trip.

I started weeping uncontrollably in a room of Cezanne landscapes. The light and the wind moved over the rocks and trees so realistically that I lost control emotionally at the exquisite beauty I was witnessing. I had no idea human beings could be so talented that they became co-creators with the Divine. I was blown away. Rush had to drag me out of the room sobbing, before the guard, who was eyeing me suspiciously, threw us out.

The trip was just getting started. In a room of German Expressionists, I became transfixed before a portrait of a couple by Oskar Kokoschka. They appeared to be so alive in the picture, not just because I was tripping, but because the artist had used painting knives to etch his subjects' nervous energy into the paint.

I was even more mesmerized by this vision of aliveness in portraiture than I was by the Cézannes because human nature had always interested more than nature itself. This was what I had been searching for. I had to learn how to paint like this, only with a more positive view of human nature than Kokoschka, who portrayed his couple as not very happy. I found out later that he had become a depressive after being shell shocked during World War I.

Our trip continued over hot chocolate at Cafe Figaro on Bleeker and Mac-Dougal. I flipped out over some synthetic whipped cream on top of my cocoa. It seemed to be billowing and growing with a life all its own. "I didn't order this," I screeched to Rush. He helped me tame it by removing it with a spoon, before it expanded into a large alien creature.

Then, I flipped out thinking about my relationship with Nick. The realization hit me irrevocably that I didn't even really like him, and I would have to end our affair posthaste. Just thinking about it made me realize how unhealthy it was for me. Moreover, I could see death at the end of that line. I got the shivers just thinking how close I had been to the abyss.

Finally, after I calmed down from the whipped cream and Nick, I told Rush that my vision at MOMA was a sign pointing to my next move. I had made it a practice since Kutztown to make major life decisions on hallucinogens, which I used ritually once a year as a spiritual accelerator.

I wanted to find Kokoschka and study with him wherever he was. Obviously, I wasn't thinking too practically at the time or I would have realized that Oskar had probably croaked many years before that. Fortunately, I found out from my painting teacher at the New School, who had become somewhat of a mentor, that Oskar had founded a school, the International Academy of Fine Arts, in Salzburg, Austria. That was close enough for me.

With Rush's encouragement, I wrote the school which responded enthusiastically to my request to study there during the upcoming summer semester. I was also offered me a simultaneous translator for the lectures, which were given in German.

My summer plans in place, I decided, again with Rush's encouragement, to travel through Northern Italy and Southern France after summer school. Then, I planned to settle in Southern Portugal to paint until my money ran out; I figured that would last about six months. My father concurred that six months was reasonable, and Portugal was a safe bet for a girl on her own. My brother helped me with a loan, using a small family trust as collateral. I was ready to roll.

Next on my agenda was to formally break up with Donnie. We had agreed to separate for the winter, while I was seeing Nick and he was seeing someone else. We hadn't talked much since the fall. I arranged to meet him one afternoon at a local watering hole, the Grassroots, a cavernous, funky dive with true East Village flavor.

We quite lovingly agreed to part as friends and wished each other well. There were no hard feelings, just fond memories. We both felt it was time to move on.

# 21

## *The Back-up Plan*

I was already pretty schlossed on screwdrivers by the time Donnie left the bar. At that moment, I looked up from my drink and saw the bartender. He was absolutely drop-dead, movie-star gorgeous. He had long dark hair and a beard, bedroom blue-green eyes, and a body that was a ten, with just the right amount of bow in his lean, hard jean-clad legs to look as if he just got off a horse. Moving on was not going to be as painful as I thought. He looked exactly like a pirate in a romance novel.

He was very friendly. He kept feeding me drinks as I wrote him notes about how cute his ass was. I asked him what time he was getting off, and he said, "Soon, darlin', soon," in a husky southern drawl.

By the time he got off at nine, I had consumed at least ten screwdrivers. He ordered me a cheeseburger in the hope that it would sober me up enough so I could walk. When it came, I picked it up and the burger fell out of the bun, leaving a cheesy stain on my new black suede boots.

The next thing I remember, I was in his apartment. It was very eerie, because his place was in the same building Rush and I had lived in, only two floors up from our old apartment. It had the same floor plan and decor—a mattress on the floor. Very déjà vu, but at least I was moving up in the world.

He started serenading me on a classical Spanish guitar. The serenade seemed to go on forever. I was just hoping he would stop wooing and jump me before I passed out. I think he did, but I don't remember much of that first night.

What I do remember is the next morning. I woke up and realized that I had never even asked his name. I wasn't sure I really wanted to know either. I kind of liked the idea of being such a female chauvinist pig that I didn't really care. He told me anyway. It was Van. I said, "You must be kidding." What with the guitar playing and singing and dreamy looks, it felt like a made-up name. But he wasn't kidding; that really was his name. We fell in love, head over heels, within a week.

This is really the only way to go if you're on the rebound for less than twenty-four hours and want to feel no pain.

In addition to being a composer/musician/bartender, Van was also quite a romantic—much more than me, which didn't take much. When he found out I was going to settle in Portugal in the fall, he told me it had always been his dream to live there and compose beautiful music. He was a Sagittarius with Pisces rising and an unfulfilled wanderlust; his background was half-Irish and half-Portuguese.

In the serendipity of the moment, the synchronicity of our meeting and our mutual dream of creative expression, we agreed to meet in Lisbon in early September. Not to mention that we were hot as hell for each other.

Rush was not pleased by this turn of events. His encouragement of my overseas plans was based on the idea that it would help me develop as an independent entity—no longer dependent on men for my identity, including him. Of course, there was the underlying unspoken possibility that I would come back from Europe and we would pick up where we had left off before prison and Donnie. Van appearing on the scene had definitely put a wrench in the works from Rush's side.

I remember the week before I left for Salzburg sitting at a table in the Grassroots with Rush and Van. They toasted me, and Rush said, "To the most beautiful woman in the world." I believed him, because that is how he always made me feel.

Later that week, just before I left, we had one more meeting of our ongoing psychic group. The most powerful psychic in the group, Dagmar, was there, visiting from Bermuda. Dagmar was a round, smiling, black healer in her sixties with a huge and powerful heart. Her readings were always crystal clear and cut through any bullshit. She warned me, "Beware of a man named Gunter; his energy and appearance will be like a fox." Rush and another woman, Lynn, concurred with this warning.

Warning noted, I packed my bags and set off on my travels. It was late June 1978. I was twenty-four and this was my first big solo adventure.

## Psychic Interlude

What was really going on was not just that I wanted to study art and travel and become an independent entity. My psychic abilities were scaring the shit out of me on many levels. I had the illusion that if I ran off to Europe and studied art, I would be able to channel most of my psychic energies creatively and the rest I could just stuff down. I wanted to try to lead a normal life with Van. Marriage and kids, the whole trip, because that's what he wanted. I was willing to try that, to avoid being who I was becoming.

I was becoming someone people were starting to come to who were various sorts of crises. They wanted me to help them by going into trance and doing readings to give them clarity. I did some of this, and it terrified me to have so much responsibility over someone else's life. Rush was there to conduct and help stabilize me in trance. Both he and the readings implied that I wouldn't be able to do the highest level of readings without him.

I knew this was true. I wasn't at home enough inside myself to stabilize the channel in trance. In fact, there was no one home at all. There was just a black hole in my center that I filled with pot smoke. I knew that, if I kept smoking pot and doing readings, even with Rush there, one day soon I would go out of my body during a reading and never come back. I had no internal anchor of a strong and healthy sense of self. I knew I had to choose. Smoking pot or doing readings. So—I stopped doing readings.

I rationalized that I didn't want to be dependent on Rush, even as a psychic stabilizer, but this was only the partial truth. The whole truth was that my gifts had developed psychically before I had time to develop as a person. Rather than put in the work, I chose to run away.

# 22

## *Slip-Sliding Away*

I hadn't realized it yet, but my travel karma sucks, astrologically speaking. I have Saturn in the ninth house of foreign travel. This means that foreign journeys have always turned out to be lessons in endurance and other Saturnian virtues. But this was my first time crossing an ocean, so how was I to know?

Halfway across the Atlantic on British Airways, two of the engines conked out in the middle of a ferocious storm. We started bobbing up and down like a roller coaster and the stewards passed out free booze in coach. This was not a good sign. We were informed that we were heading back to JFK due to engine trouble and weather.

Fortunately, since my Saturn is in the sign of Libra, it gives me enough of an innate sense of equanimity to ameliorate my travel karma by making the most out of any travel disaster. In this case, the guy sitting next to me happened to be the cutest guy on the plane. I had already scoped him out at the boarding gate. He was English, a Celtic stone mason, with long blond hair, a beard and twinkly blue eyes. He was traveling with his adorable young daughter, age five, to visit Mum in London. His estranged wife had run off and joined a commune in upstate New York. He was the perfect traveling companion for a flying fiasco.

He had a bottle of brandy, and I had steak sandwiches. We decided to pool our resources. Cozying up under a blanket, we masturbated each other as the plane rocked and rolled. There was a feeling of terror in the atmosphere and the stewards' eyes that we turned into the excitement of living on the edge.

By the time we got back to JFK and were waiting for another plane, we were having a splendid time. When we finally arrived in London, I had missed my connecting flight to Salzburg, and British Airways wouldn't put me up. Ever the gent, my new friend invited me to spend the night at his Mum's.

He snuck into my room after lights out and we consummated our trans-Atlantic foreplay marathon. I must admit I was a little more demanding than usual, riding him one more time after he was clearly exhausted. I think overseas travel on my own made me a little more nervous and insecure than usual.

I knew I had promised Van fidelity until we met again in Lisbon. However, in my mind, that didn't include foreign affairs. I had the temperament of a diplomat when it came to matters of the heart—and a Machiavellian snakelike one at that. I was born in the Chinese year of the water snake, after all. Besides, this was my first night away from home.

# 23

## *No Edges*

Upon my arrival in Salzburg, I entered into a very strange space/time warp that never really went away the whole time I was there. I just learned ways to adapt to it.

I checked into my humble lodgings, a small room with a shared bathroom in the old city and unpacked. I was homesick already, as I looked out my window at the incredibly beautiful graveyard where Mozart was buried. In this melancholic state, I went wandering the streets. The old part of Salzburg felt very medieval, with dark, narrow cobblestone streets and imposing two-and three-story buildings made of stone. Present time seemed to fall away.

I started holding on to the buildings as I walked to stabilize me, and also because I felt as if they were closing in on me. I needed to hold them up too. These stone buildings looked and felt as if they had harder edges than normal modern buildings. That's when I realized this was the first time, in almost eight years, I wasn't stoned on grass.

Not only was I in withdrawal from the main buffer between me and me and me and reality, I was also bereft of my secondary buffer of having a man to hold onto. Smoking had softened the edges of reality for so long that I had completely forgotten my perceptions were drug-induced on a daily basis. Now the hard edges of reality seemed to be back with a vengeance. The impact of this made me aware of how weak and semi-permeable my own boundaries were. Without any grass or man as internal or external reference points, I was at a loss as to how to relate directly to reality. Fortunately, since I like adventures, acknowledging the fact that reality straight was more surreal to me than reality stoned allowed me to adjust my attitude so I could try and enjoy this new trip.

On my first day at the International Academy of Fine Arts, which was located in an old fortress on a hill overlooking the city, we spent all day drawing from the model. This turned out to be what we did most of the time. I knew this was going to be an excellent opportunity for me to really hone my technical skills of figurative drawing on a deeper level. I started enjoying myself in class and even made a new friend on the second day. Her name was Meredith, and she was my age, from Boston, with curly dark hair, glasses and a friendly nature. This was her second year studying sculpture, with a carryover crush on one of the teachers.

Meredith showed me the ropes: where to eat well but cheaply, where to drink and where to party. I learned the first week that if I joined everyone at lunch with a tumbler of red wine, I was useless for any sustained, focused work in the afternoon. So I abstained until dinner each day.

At the end of the first week, we had a weekly lecture with slides, given by the head professor. One of the assistant professors from Vienna was appointed to simultaneously translate the lecture, as promised. This professor was quite the dapper dresser. He shared a seat with me, smelling of cologne, and whispered the translation into my ear. I couldn't help noticing his well-groomed reddish hair, goatee and silk cravat. I was impressed that I had been assigned a professor as translator, rather than just one of the student assistants.

After class, I asked the professor his name. It was Gunter, of course. That's when I realized he did look like a red fox. Of course, he invited me out to dinner that night in a group. He made eyes at me all night and walked me back to my inn, which conveniently happened to be just a block away from the apartment he was subletting for the summer.

I did remember Dagmar's and the others' warnings, but I didn't feel too concerned. Gunter felt relatively harmless to me. He was charming, and he enjoyed wooing me in a continental fashion, with flowers, perfume, expensive dinners and scenic day trips to bucolic villages.

It turned out that while Gunter was quite vigilant in his courtship techniques and tentative kisses, when it came to any sexual initiative, that was left to me. I quickly understood why. Gunter, at age thirty-five, was married to a domineering older woman whom he called "Madam." She ran him, their two children and the household with an iron hand. This little red fox had no sharp teeth. But I did.

Gunter and I had a lovely summer, in and out of school. I got to enjoy much more of Salzburg and its environs at a much higher level than I could have afforded on my own. Gunter paid for everything and was very sweet about it. There were concerts at the Salzburg Festival, steam baths, boat trips and hikes in the mountains to picturesque country inns. He was the perfect guide for his own country.

I had a picture of Van hanging over the bed in my room that I would moon over and talk to every night, after Gunter dropped me off. I really missed Van but had no guilt about Gunter. I just felt I was doing my best coping with the reality at hand. It didn't mean anything in the larger scheme of things. But then, what did?

One of my fondest memories of Salzburg was with Meredith. We went on a day trip to the most ancient salt mines in Europe. We rode up on a precarious cable car, swinging in the wind, to the top of this mountain. There, after we paid, we were given bright yellow slickers with hoods and matching pants. Once a group had gathered, we went into the mountain in a dark elevator. It seemed as if we were moving downward forever. Then we were instructed to slide down, single file, on these large slides. There were several of these slides, and each one brought us deeper into the core of the mountain. We came out into a dark, cold, damp cavern with salt oozing out of the walls. As we were guided through the mine, Meredith shivered and said, "I don't like it here at all."

But I was in heaven. I started skipping and singing, "Hi ho, hi ho, it's off to work we go. No time to say hello, goodbye ..."

The salt mines had activated memories of my many lives lived underground, some of them as a dwarf. I was perfectly at home deep within this mountain; I felt I'd just located a missing piece of my soul.

## *Dwarf Interlude*

For several years after my trip to the salt mines, my memories of past lives as a dwarf kept popping up in dreams, spontaneous flashbacks and real-life dwarf encounters.

In one dream, which felt very real, there was a ceremony in which a large group of dwarves crowned me queen and presented me with a giant golden key. They placed the key on a heavy golden chain around my neck. Being barely 5'1", I began to realize that inside I was still one of the "little folk," only just sneaking by in this life—passing, if you will, by a few inches.

Upon my return to New York, a hunchback male dwarf with long dark hair and a red cape kept popping up all over the place. I felt as if he were following me. One night, I ran into him in a restaurant, and he bowed, kissed my hand and looked after me longingly. That was definitely a new class of admirer.

Another time, a client came to my place for a reading and informed me there were two middle-aged female twin dwarves, in ornate military overcoats, standing on either side of my front door chatting. I responded impulsively, "They shouldn't be talking on duty!" as if it were the most natural thing in the world to have official dwarf bodyguards.

Most importantly, after the salt mines, I accessed a karmic memory of my life as Maria, a crippled hunchback dwarf in medieval France. I was homeless and abused in that life, powerless over my circumstances and in physical and emotional anguish every day of that mercifully short life.

Maria has stayed with me. Or rather, I keep her close. She reminds me, especially when I see human suffering on the streets or on CNN, that *"There but for the grace of God go I."*

Also, I have always had an aversion, not so irrational in hindsight, to visiting any medieval French towns.

# 24

## *Drifting Through Italy*

When my semester ended, I bid a fond good-bye to Gunter, with promises to keep in touch and meet again someday. Then I boarded a train for Venice.

The night before, under the influence of wine, I seduced the male model I had been sketching nude all summer in class. It was a mindless fuck, just for the hell of it, because Gunter had already left town, but it left me melancholy. Perhaps that's why I didn't notice that the train kept backing up into Austria, every time we attempted to cross the Italian border. I asked some German students on the train what was going on. It turned out we were stuck in the middle of a wildcat Italian trainworkers strike, and they wouldn't let our train cross into Italy.

This went on for thirteen hours, with no food or water on the train or in any of the stations we kept backing in and out of. Fortunately (my mixed travel karma again), I had packed six large meat sandwiches of assorted wursts and salami and bottles of juice, just in case. I shared my provisions with the German students, two couples, who were quite hungry and thirsty and very grateful.

This really paid off when we finally arrived in Venice at 4:00 AM, eight hours late, with the station completely shut down and no porters in sight. My new friends helped me lug my huge duffel onto the right water taxi to get me to my pensione, which was several blocks from the canal. Without their help, I might have been in some trouble, as I was too groggy to think clearly. I probably would have just crashed for the rest of the night in the empty station.

I spent two days in Venice, four days in Ravenna, two days in Bologna and a week in Florence. My primary focus was to enjoy the art of each town and explore all the different flavors. Without fail, I managed to get lost on every stop of my itinerary. My sense of direction in unfamiliar places is atrocious, combined with an uncannily inaccurate, but assertive sense of being right when I'm wrong and willfully never asking for directions until I'm too exhausted to move or speak. I thought just guys had that problem.

I especially fell in love with Florence and started hanging out on the Ponte Vecchio with a group of young troubadours from Ireland. I was homesick and lonely; it felt like a hard stretch being on my own. We drank cheap wine and talked until all hours. I envied their carefree lifestyle.

The only girl in the group asked me if she could shower in my room, as they were living on the streets and, of course, I said yes. While we chatted, as she was dressing after her shower, I realized that, as poor and close to the bone as I was traveling, student class, her vagabond lifestyle was a whole other level of carefree that I was probably not too well suited for.

On the train to Naples, en route to the Italian and French Riviera for a week, I missed my connection. The trains was so insanely crowded in August, with everyone on holiday, that I couldn't hear or see when to get off. Even if I could have, I had no room to move. I ended up in Milan. I was so demoralized by this turn of events; I called Van and asked him if he could meet me in Lisbon a week earlier. He could, and I was thrilled.

I was tired of traveling on my own. My sense of bravado and adventure had been overridden by an almost overwhelming sense of being alone and adrift. Van would anchor me.

# 25

## *Intermezzo in Portugal*

My plane trip from Milan to Lisbon was another travel fiasco. I flew Alitalia, a name that still sends shivers up my spine. They lost the huge duffel I'd been lugging around Europe all summer. In it were the art supplies from New York that I had been saving for my work in Portugal, as well as all my clothes and sketchbooks from Salzburg. I must have angered the travel gods by attaching a cheap, plastic, flowered umbrella to the outside of the carrying straps on my duffel. The lords of travel, in the guise of the Alitalia luggage handlers, were not amused. For this, I paid the ultimate travel nightmare price.

By the time Van's plane arrived from New York, I had had several hours to book a moderately priced hotel room for a week and come to terms with the loss of all my worldly possessions. When Van got off the plane, I barely recognized him, except for the guitar.

Van had shaved off his beautiful beard and mustache and cut his hair very short. The change in his appearance was so drastic, I went into shock. He looked like a shorn, frightened rabbit of a boy, with a less strong chin than I could have imagined. Certainly, he was not the mature man of twenty-seven I had fantasized about since our parting. In that moment, the bottom dropped out of my world.

Still, our room was lovely, the sex was great, and the breakfast in bed of cafe au lait and hot rolls with melting butter and jam felt like the Ritz to me. I finally had someone to enjoy traveling with and, as we explored all the exquisite sights, sounds and tastes of Lisbon, I decided I was still in love, after all. It was harder for me to enjoy traveling alone because I felt like I was continuously yelling into an echo chamber with no sound returning.

Van, being a Sagittarius, turned out to be a great traveling companion. In hindsight, traveling was actually what we did best together. Each day was a new adventure for the senses and the exotic newness of it all enlivened our dynamic. It was a good distraction for what wasn't going on in terms of my inner journey.

Emotionally, Van and I were not quite on the same page. He wanted to marry me as soon as possible; I asked him to give me two years. We compromised on one year. I found out later that Van had flipped out while I was away all summer. He was drinking heavily and getting into fights, one of which involved damaging his hand quite badly with broken glass. Not only that, he had given up his apartment and put his stuff in storage, as some sort of fait au compli to put pressure on moving in with me when we got back. Water does seek its own level after all—only it seemed that Van needed to be filled by me as a longer range proposition. The pressure was definitely on.

The reason I asked Van for two years was because I already knew, after our reunion at the airport, we were not meant to be mated for life. All the same, just because I saw the end of our relationship at the beginning of the middle, that didn't mean I wasn't willing to play it out. Besides, I didn't want to spoil our plans. I wanted us to enjoy playing out the middle in Portugal. I was willing to shoulder the burden of knowing the end, without any clear idea as to how long the middle would be.

After a week in Lisbon, we rented a car and decided to tour the Algarve, the southern coast of Portugal, until we fell in love with some fishing village and rented a house to settle into. I got $400 from Alitalia, which admitted my duffel was irretrievably lost, and off we went.

We bought meats and cheeses, bread, fruit and wine and had picnics during the day, pulling off the road as the whim hit us. One day, we pulled off the main road onto a dirt road we followed for about a quarter mile until we came to a lovely meadow sprinkled with wildflowers. After our picnic, it was time for our siesta, which always involved a prolonged period of lovemaking.

In the midst of our entwined embrace—Van and I tended to coil around each other facing sideways—we heard a volley of gunfire go off very nearby. Van jumped up, buck-naked, with his penis erect and curved liked a scimitar (adding to his pirate persona, I might add), to confront a local quail hunter, who was as surprised to see us as we were him.

I hastily covered myself with a blanket as the confrontation ensued. Van stood there, with his arms crossed, eyes blazing and sword drawn. The hunter backed away into the woods. I was impressed with Van's forbidding stance; it made me feel safe and protected by him. That was a good sign. Maybe the middle wouldn't be so bad after all.

We traveled the coast from Faro in the east to the lighthouse at the westernmost tip of the country. Of all the towns we passed through, we agreed we were most drawn to a little fishing village called Albufeira, an hour or so west of Faro.

Right away, we were befriended by the American expatriate owner of a craft shop, Leigh, who found us a great house to rent for our stay. This was an incredibly good omen.

One night, Leigh and I had a talk about men. She encouraged me to make the most of what I had with Van while I was still young and had the emotional energy for it. I took Leigh's words to heart, being too naive to recognize projection when it hit me over the head, and settled into domestic life with all the enthusiasm of a budding domestic goddess. Our beautiful house, on a hill overlooked the town, had a terrace overflowing with flowers. The rent of $200 a month included the services of a maid/laundress. We were in expatriate heaven.

I went to the market every morning and shopped for food. We smoked the native cigarettes and drank the local vino verde, as well as sherry, port and liqueurs. After lunch, we took our siesta, and then we'd pick up our work from the morning. Van composed and I painted. I tried my hand at landscapes, seascapes, village scenes, portraits of some of the locals and dream visions, most quite nightmarish. One was of me coming out of the ocean, holding my hands up to my father and exclaiming, *"Look! No hands, only nubbies!"*

It seemed an idyllic time on the outer levels—but things are not always what they seem. On the inner levels, I was not just having bad dreams, I was starting to experience severe migraines that were excruciatingly incapacitating. My psychic energies were getting dammed up with a vengeance.

Also, I was discovering, once the visuals wore off a bit, that Van wasn't much of a talker. It wasn't that noticeable when we had travel sights to activate an exchange of impressions. But now that we were settled in a domestic scene with familiar terrain, Van's true taciturn nature was much in evidence. I shouldn't have been so surprised or disappointed—Van was a composer, not a lyricist, after all. I was tired of being the sole entertainment, with no TV or movies available. After a while, I felt as if I was talking to myself; there was so little response.

We started drinking more to pass the time. Then we started fighting more, over stupid things like money. Van had a decidedly more frugal streak than me and didn't like me taking too many baths because we had to pay for gas to heat the water. He went out drinking in the local bars more on his own. I missed him, but I didn't. I missed somebody.

To break things up, we took a trip for a week to Seville and then, by boat, to Tangiers for a few days. That helped. Wandering around the Kasbah, bargaining for caftans, drinking mint tea at cafes and watching a foreign world go by enlivened our relationship again as traveling companions.

Over Thanksgiving week, a married couple we were friendly with came to visit and brought some grass with them. I hadn't smoked in seven months. Stoned, the whole town, and especially the beach, shimmered and sparkled in my perception. I realized that I had been in heaven for months but had forgotten how to see. The grass helped me remember. I wished I could be high all the time; I didn't think I could maintain that sparkle on my own. We traveled to Cordoba as a foursome. Again, Van and I were at our best—bodies in motion, not at rest.

Then, it was time to go home to New York; our money had run out. It was early February, getting very cold, rainy and damp, and we had no heat. I had written Rush a month earlier, as he had requested, to give him time to move out of our apartment. He was pissed because, in his heart of hearts, he still thought I would get tired of Van and come back to our old living arrangement.

Rush was probably right, in my heart of hearts as well, but Van had pulled a fast one by giving up his apartment before he left. He had assumed he would be moving in with me forever. I was forced to choose. I settled on Van over Rush. Why did I do such a stupid thing? I did it because I was indecisive by nature and my relationship with Van was newer, which gave me the illusion of moving forward.

The truth was, I was afraid I couldn't go back to being lovers with Rush, even though my soul connection with him was far deeper than any passing pirate karma with Van—though we were still going pretty hot and heavy in the bedroom, if nowhere else. The crazy glue of our sexual chemistry was ultimately the deciding factor. Who says only men think with their genitals?

We were flying home on TAP, Portugal's national airline. As we got on the plane in Lisbon, I wasn't thinking about my travel karma; I was too preoccupied with going home and dealing with Rush's wrath. Sure enough, just as we were taxiing down the runway, a passenger yelled, "Stop the plane. Part of the wing just fell off!" Fortunately, the pilot was able to stop the plane in time for the mechanics to check that the landing flap on the wing had indeed fallen off. We were put up by the airlines for four days, before they got us another flight out. It was an unexpectedly pleasant last interlude before flying home.

# 26

## *Prelude to a Bottom*

When we arrived at JFK in the early morning, I had a premonition I should call Rush from the airport. Even though I had given him a month's notice, I was afraid if he was still in the apartment there might be violence when we arrived. Van had a very short fuse.

I was right. Rush answered the phone groggily, still half-asleep. I asked him hysterically what he was still doing there. He mumbled something like he had lost track of the time. Besides, he figured I would get over Van as soon as my feet hit U.S. soil, and he never understood what I saw in Van anyway—and so on.

I told him, in my most serious tone of voice, that we would be there in an hour, and it was imperative he vacate the premises immediately because we were exhausted from the trip. When we got to the apartment, Rush had vacated but in the most passive/aggressive manner possible.

The place was filthy; there was clutter everywhere. Mounds of rotting garbage and dirty laundry were scattered in every room. It took us several days to clear out Rush's mess. This did not bode well for our homecoming, or for any kind of friendly or even civil connection with Rush, as we moved forward in our New York life together.

Van and I settled into domestic life in the East Village with the best of intentions—and you know what they say about those. We lasted a little over a year, before I couldn't take it anymore.

On the outside, things appeared to be moving along. We both got lucrative restaurant gigs—me waitressing, Van bartending. I cooked Southern food for Van, and we had lots of friends and dinner parties and were very social. Our act was so good we were the envy of everyone in our circle. Van composed on a piano he bought and put in the den, and I painted in my studio. The sex was never the problem. I was just bored.

Van's dream was that we would get married, move to an isolated small island off the coast of Maine and have a couple of kids. The idea of having to take a boat ride to get a quart of milk was the least of my concerns. It was the picture of us holed up, alone with one another in some rustic cabin and snowed in for months on end, that made me want to scream. Obviously, we had reached the end of our journey together.

The end, once we agreed on it, took six months to implement, because it took Van that long to find an affordable apartment in the city. We both ended up paying the price for his giving up his apartment the year before.

To pass the time, I smoked more dope, and he drank more booze. We started sleeping separately, more and more. It was very civilized. We even made a deal that in ten years or so, if we hadn't met anyone better to settle down with, we would look each other up—so much for the illusion of sexual safety nets. It did help ease the transition of breaking up though. We had been together for two and a half years.

I couldn't wait for him to move out, once the decision was made. Van told me later that the whole time we were together, I never once looked him in the eyes—I was always too stoned. That may have been an exaggeration on his part of the length of time that I never "saw" him, but it was certainly where I was at during the last year and a half. Nonetheless, if that was where I was at by the time he left me—that was nothing compared to where I was going.

# 27

## *One Is the Loneliest Number*

After Van moved out, I was relieved for about twenty-four hours. That's when I realized I was all alone—not just in the apartment but in my own skin. Not only hadn't I ever really lived alone before, except when I was in transit from one man to another, but I had never felt so empty on the inside before. I proceeded to make my best attempt to fill myself up.

I discovered that the Grassroots bar, that same dingy East Village watering hole where I had broken up with Donnie and met Van, was a perfect place to unwind after a hard night painting in the studio. I would arrive there around midnight, stoned and ready to party. Over the course of the next three months, from September through December, I partied myself right through just about every guy hanging out at the bar—and the Grassroots became my whole world.

I had a couple of regular sex partners whom I hung out with a lot during those months. I wouldn't even deem to call them lovers. They were both Vietnam vets whose good looks were scarred from years of drug and alcohol abuse, and whose tender hearts were in permanent shutdown against any more pain. They consumed so much more drugs and booze than me, I never needed to look at my own use. I was still OK compared with them.

I had always known, from the age of nineteen, I was a potential alcoholic. That realization occurred in Virginia Beach when a girlfriend taught me how much fun it was to start off the day with bloody marys and screwdrivers. I liked what alcohol did for me too much in terms of loosening inhibitions. I had controlled my drinking for eight years by just smoking a lot of grass every day (except for my eight months in Europe), but during this three-month slide into hell, I completely lost control.

I switched from drinking vodka gimlets to shots of tequila, to tumblers full of Meyers dark rum with a shot of orange juice (for my health). The dark rum seemed to make me the most insane. As my tolerance expanded, I was shooting for oblivion, drinking up to a dozen tall glasses full of rum every night. I figured I'd end up in an institution somewhere.

Hopefully, if my parents found out and footed the bill, I would be sent to someplace civilized, like Switzerland, where I could paint watercolors in a garden by a lake. In the meantime, I was determined to party as hard as I could in my attempt to feel no pain. But that was all I felt. I wrote in my diary every day during that period, *"I'm in pain. I'm in pain. I'm in pain."* For pages and pages—it was all I wrote for months.

The two main guys I was hanging with, Joe and Mike, lived in almost identical filthy apartments with identical grimy, mostly bare mattresses on the floor. The three of us hung out together or separately, mostly at the 'roots' and, after it closed, at after-hours bars that were usually shooting galleries in the back room. When I got unceremoniously fired from my waitress job for stealing, a low point in my complete loss of control, I thought about getting a job in one of these after-hours heroin dens, since I was there so much of the time anyway.

I proceeded to celebrate the holiday season, after I got fired on December 2, 1980, by sliding further down the slippery slope of addiction. I started doing things I swore I would never do—smoking opium, sniffing heroin and popping any pills given to me—especially Quaaludes. The opium was the best and felt very familiar. Later I put together those feelings with past lives in harems and Byzantine brothels. I had a particularly strong memory of one as a Chinese concubine with bound feet and a wicked life-long opium habit.

Besides becoming a garbage-head with drugs, I also began eyeing guys I wouldn't have even looked at before—and more than just eyeing them. One night, in a blackout, I went home with one of these guys. He was a cute NYU student who fucked like a chipmunk. By this point, I was identifying my "dates" by animal type. That was as deep as I was capable of going with anyone. I trashed his apartment, flailing around in a grayout in an attempt to get up and out. I lost control of my motor functions.

Another time, on a Saturday night near Christmas, I was leaning on a stack of Sunday *New York Times* next to Gem Spa, an all-night newsstand in the East Village. I put too much weight on the stack, and it fell over with me attached, right into the slush and filth of the gutter. I was so drunk, I couldn't even get up.

By the time New Year's 1981 had arrived, I was officially a falling-down drunk, garbage head, and a "manizer," which is somewhat of a euphemism for being a complete female chauvinist pig.

# 28

## *Spiraling Down*

After celebrating New Year's with a week of nonstop partying, I tried to get my act together. When I looked in the mirror, my face had a pale, bloated look with a hint of panic in the eyes. I had spent most of the last month either very stoned or drunk, vomiting, screwing or passed out. I tried to piece together what had happened.

Somewhere in the fog, I vaguely remember Gunter showing up at my door with perfume, cognac, silk scarves and a puppy-dog look in his eyes. He had come for a surprise visit. There was also a hint of longing to jump ship from his restrictive Viennese life. I treated him very shabbily, kicking him out after one night, after making him sleep alone in my back bedroom. I kicked him out to sink or swim in New York City on his own, after he had been such a kind, considerate guide and host on his turf. Dagmar's warning was not about him harming me. In hindsight, it was warning me not to do what I did—incur karma by my insensitive, selfish treatment of him.

I vaguely remember running into Rush at the Grassroots. He said my energy had become so bad, he wanted nothing to do with me. He didn't want to hang out drinking or getting high. In fact, he didn't want to see me or speak to me at all. That should have struck a chord somewhere deep in my soul, but I was so anesthetized at this point, it didn't even make a dent in me—certainly not enough to even consider changing my course.

What was my course at this point? I sat every night at "my" table at the 'roots.' It was the one in the corner, because I was getting paranoid, and at the window, so I could look out at life passing me by while I drank. I engaged in my version of social drinking. If any guy was brave enough to come over and say "hello," I looked him up and down and told him to "fuck off" in a dead tone of voice.

I sat at my table, night after night, with my drinks backed up for security, from midnight until the bar closed, looking down at the carved names of other drunks in the wood of the table. I'd stare down at the table until I couldn't see the table anymore, only an abyss I was spiraling down into, without a clue of how to stop. I was too far gone. I had lost any memory that there was any kind of Higher Power I could pray to for help.

I tried calling some of my restaurant friends to get a job, but I was too far gone to deal with daylight. I wrote in lipstick on my dresser mirror, *"Only one joint a day,"* as I had a faint clue that I might be overdoing the grass—I could never stop at just one.

Stumbling home from the after-hours places at 6 or 7:00 AM, I would see the "straights" heading off for a day at work. I'd look down my nose at them and thought, *"What pathetic losers—thank God I'm not like them."* In the meantime, I had reached a point where I couldn't hold down any food.

My Dad invited me to Miami for a week for a visit with him and my stepmother, as long as I wasn't working anyway. I grabbed at the chance. I thought a geographical cure—getting away from all the people, places and things in the Grassroots—would help me dry out enough to be able to work again.

Two days before my planned departure, I was smoking a joint in bed one night around 8:00 PM and passed out, even though I had just woken up. I had so much smoke and other stuff in my system that it just couldn't tolerate any more. When I came to and looked at that joint in the ashtray, I realized, for the first time in eleven years, that grass was no longer my friend. It couldn't help me do anything—and I didn't even know when it had turned on me.

It had certainly turned though. From expanded perception, all I had left in my view of reality was denial and distortion. From enhanced sensual pleasure, all I had left was the need for immediate gratification like a two-year-old—and even when I got it, it was never enough or never quite right. The grass was always greener around some other corner, with some other guy, in another room at the party of life.

As I was pondering all this, I was so filled with smoke, I knew that one more toke would make me pass out again. I needed to get my act together so I could get to the 'roots' which had become my whole world by this time, and tell all my drinking buddies, who were the only friends I had left, about my trip to Florida. I didn't want them to worry about me being gone—like they cared.

The phone rang. It was my old friend and drinking buddy Mitchell, who was an old friend of Van's as well. He was the one who had inherited Van's apartment. I hadn't seen him on the scene in months. He asked me how I was, and I started sobbing uncontrollably and babbling incoherently about how much pain I was in.

He kindly invited me to lunch at his place the next day. He was transformed. He didn't look anything like the falling-down, pissy, beer-guzzling drunk that I had helped walk home sometime in late August. At that time, his bathroom was filthy, the toilet didn't flush, and he wasn't much cleaner. Now he was serving me a salad with sprouts and raving about the benefits of fresh juice, as he was juicing some carrots. The apartment and he were gleaming.

He told me that he had gotten sober in a spiritually-based recovery program for a little over four months. "Thank God. You really needed it," I exclaimed with all sincerity. He invited me to come with him to a meeting that night. I explained why I couldn't go. I said, "I loved to, Mitchell. But you see, I have to buy a bathing suit because I'm going to Florida in two days to dry out." I actually said this with a straight face. The synapses in my brain were so fried, I couldn't make the connection between Mitchell's program and me.

As I continued to make excuses, my inner voice, which I hadn't heard in what seemed like years, yelled in my head, "*Just go! JUST GO!*"

I didn't analyze—I just went. That voice inside my head was too powerful to ignore. It cut through all my denial, for the moment anyway. I was so lonely and I was enjoying Mitchell's company so much, I told him (and myself) that I guess I would tag along with him to the meeting to keep enjoying his company. It was the most major decision I have ever made in my life—and remains so to this day.

# PART V

## THE ASSASSIN AND THE SOCIOPATH

# 29

## *Sobriety My Way*

The meetings I started going to every day were very social, even friendlier than the bar scene and certainly with a healthier focus. After a few false starts, I fell in love with Mitchell's program of recovery.

The stories about drinking and drugging that people shared were so entertaining. It was better than TV, because it was live. I had always been enraptured by the idiosyncrasies of human nature—every person with their own unique saga. The meetings reminded me of that old TV show intro: "There are a million stories in the naked city and tonight you'll hear one."

Right away, I got the social fellowship part of the program. After meetings we went in groups for coffee and sat around smoozing for hours. It was a good start. It was easy for me to substitute my dependency on the bar scene for the social world of this program. Sure, it was another dependency. But, being a true codependent type, it was at least a step up from making a dingy East Village bar my whole world.

Then the denial kicked in. I was wearing black all the time and officially in mourning. I rationalized: I was only twenty-seven and could've had at least another ten years of partying, if I hadn't hit a bad patch for a couple of months. All my drinking buddies concurred, of course. They were in much worse shape than me, and if *I* felt the need to get sober, it was shining the light a little too brightly on their own situations.

About a month after I went to my first meeting, I went to a rock concert with Rush, who had decided to start hanging out with me again, now that I had cleaned up my act. But maybe I was cleaning up my act a little too much for Rush, or not in a way he approved. He really didn't like the idea of my being in any kind of recovery program, especially one that touted absolute unconditional abstinence from any self-prescribed mood-changing substance as a definition of sobriety. Rush was never a joiner, of any kind of group, unless he was in charge; he was just a renegade by nature.

He had checked out recovery programs in the 1960s in Los Angeles and decided they weren't his cup of tea. Rush didn't like any kind of absolutes or the idea of me becoming some kind of "Moonie." He kept passing me a joint at this concert, and after about the 10th pass, I took a hit. I felt really bad the next day because I had worked so hard at being "clean and dry" for over a month. I had passed on the nightly vodka gimlets on my drying-out trip to Florida. I didn't even pack any grass to take on the trip with me—which was a complete first. Since the age of sixteen, I had never dealt with my family without a chemical buffer—it never would have occurred to me. But Mitchell had explained that I couldn't be high and sober at the same time. What a novel idea!

I got more upset with what Rush had done when I realized his agenda wasn't mine anymore, at least, not on this issue. He had sabotaged my hard-won sobriety and I had let him. This made me feel intensely sad. I decided I had to take space from Rush for awhile.

I asked for more help with my program and got an interim sponsor. I volunteered to make coffee and got a home group where I went regularly and got to know all the other members. And, of course, since I was switching my dependency from the bar scene to the sobriety scene, I started having a few small affairs with guys I met at meetings, who were as newly sober as me and in their early thirties. I knew it was suggested that I not get emotionally involved with anyone the first year, but I wasn't. I was just having some friendly sober sex.

One of my light affairs was with a kindergarten teacher, and the other was with a restaurant owner; both were sweet, nice and mellow guys. I was just grateful that I could have sex without being stoned and enjoy it on the sensual levels without being too inhibited. That was a first, as I had always been high on something before—but there were no sparks with either of these guys.

Old habits die hard. The black hole inside of me, which I used to fill up with grass, drink and men, wasn't getting filled up enough with meetings or men with no edge. True to form, I started hunting for bigger game. Of course, I went back to my old hunting grounds, the Grassroots, where I knew the terrain and had gotten lucky before.

I started going there on Sunday nights in June, with four months of sobriety under my belt. It felt like the safest choice because it was a calm night that just attracted neighborhood locals—not like a Friday or Saturday night, when it became a crazy, jammed, pickup scene. I sat on a stool at the far corner of the bar, at the opposite end from where I used to drink, as a symbolic gesture.

Not so symbolic was the fact that I wasn't getting high anymore before I came to the bar. I was going to my regular Sunday night meeting where I made coffee.

I obviously wasn't drinking alcohol anymore. I was nursing a bottle of Saratoga water and biding my time. I was on the hunt, and I was waiting.

It took a couple of Sundays. He walked in with a friend and sat in the middle of the long bar. He ordered a bottle of Saratoga water and stared at me. I stared back for a long moment. Then I looked away.

He was about 6'3", 185 pounds, with curly, light reddish-blond hair cascading to his shoulders and cold, changeable green-blue eyes. He was my complete visual opposite. He looked like an alien to me—not just from another country, but from another galaxy. It wasn't just because of his looks, though; it was the intense other-worldly energy emanating from his eyes.

He came over and attempted to make small talk. He was drinking Saratoga water and so was I. He was a painter and so was I. I was cool, to say the least, and blew him off. He was coming on way too strong and fast for me to process. He left the bar with his friend shortly after that. I was still waiting.

The next Sunday night, he came in again. This time he was alone. I was sitting on the other end of the bar this time, near the front door. He did a double-take when he saw me looking at him. I could see he was hesitant to come over and be rejected again. So I crooked my finger and motioned for him to come over. I said, "Don't worry. I won't bite you," and smiled. I handed him a Hershey's chocolate kiss that I had picked up at the meeting, to seal the promise. The game I had been waiting for had begun.

# 30

## *The Assassin—Phase I*

His name was Paul and he was of Dutch or, more accurately, Friesian ancestry. He was thirty-three, an Aries, (with a Pisces moon and Gemini rising) and had been recruited by one of the more obscure government agencies when he was sixteen.

Paul had been a poor street kid from the Village in jail for killing a guy in a street fight. The exact resume this type of agency was looking for. If they were going to invest time, money and energy training someone to become a killing machine, he already had to have proven he had the instinct and was OK with it. Being poor was perfect, because he was more susceptible to patriotic indoctrination and the lure of a paid education, travel to exotic places and an especially good benefits package.

By the time I met Paul, he had moved up the ranks to become a senior career officer in this agency. Or so he said. He was basically an assassin, as well as an undercover information gatherer, or spy. He had bullet wound scars on his abdomen, weak kidneys from being beaten there, as well as numerous other physical injuries and scars—including as no feeling in his left arm from nerve damage after having it almost severed. These were all occupational hazards he seemed to accept with no qualms. He had been sent on undercover assignments in many countries that had sometimes lasted for years, and he was not welcome in most of those places anymore. He was travel weary and looking for a soft place to land.

Paul's internal scars were much worse. He was a heavy cocaine addict with a free, unlimited supply from the agency, which kept him on a very short lease. He used the coke because grass wasn't enough to anesthetize himself from the pain of his life anymore, plus it kept him pumped up psychologically so he could keep performing.

Of course, I didn't know any of this when I first met him. All I knew was that he was Viking gorgeous, with the coiled, dangerous energy of a lion ready to spring. I was drawn to his heat and darkness and the danger and challenge of I knew not what.

Paul wore me out our first night together. He was capable of fucking all night, until I had to beg him to stop. I was sore and needed to rest. I didn't know it was cocaine fueling his passion. He was the drug I had been looking for, to fill me up—I didn't need anything else.

He had a sublet in the Village and was separated from his wife and two kids—a marriage of fifteen years and two pre-teens. It was strange to be with a "family man" who was so young and hip. It was even stranger when he dumped a bucket of money over my head to surprise and impress me while I was lying in bed. I did start to get suspicious after that, but I was already hooked. I fell head over heels by the end of our first night together—and in sobriety, no less. I fell even harder because there was no buffer and nothing to fill the black hole inside but him.

A few weeks later, when he confessed, sobbing with his head in my lap, about how many men he had killed, it felt too late for me to get out. He had wooed me too well: picking me up nights at my waitress gig near Carnegie Hall, after making all the other waitresses swoon with his good looks, dreamy eyes (only for me) and $50 tips. At home, he rubbed my feet as he fed me Beluga and pate' from Balducci's and made love to me all night with a hungriness that seemed insatiable. I was being devoured, and I only wanted more.

# 31

## *I Put a Spell on You*

The first few months with Paul were a delirious roller coaster ride of sexual and emotional highs, when we were together, and deprivation lows, when we were apart. This inspired many late-night, poetry-writing catharses unequaled since the bomb squad detective.

Being with Paul was better than any drug I had ever been on. I still qualified as officially sober in my recovery program, as I was off mood-altering substances by *their* definition. What a trickster I thought I was. I had just switched addictions. Similarly to trading deck chairs on the Titanic, the ship was still going down.

Our first summer, Paul gave me a curled, golden 6″ lock of his hair, looked me in the eye, and solemnly said, "You know what to do with it," as if he were performing his part in a ritual ceremony. He was and I did. A piece of our karmic puzzle was a life in which he was a warlock and I was a witch. Not the good kind either, and not one of my better lives in serving the Light, to say the least. We were adversarial peers in that life, with mutual respect, but playing different games on different fields.

Instinctively, I knew he gave me a lock of hair so I would put a spell on him. Intuitively, I knew I shouldn't because I knew the power of it. Especially since whatever spell I put on him would surely be returned to sender and magnified at that. Even more importantly, I was subtly aware that I had made a commitment, before entry into this life, not to misuse my psychic gifts by doing what I was about to do. While I was on temporary hiatus from using these gifts professionally, I knew that didn't exempt me from misusing my powers by casting a spell.

I knew such a self-aggrandizing ego move would probably backfire all over my soul karmically. I knew I had promised not to—but I did it anyway. Not one of my most rational, high-level decisions.

Here's what I did: I bathed Paul's golden lock directly in my vaginal juices as I recited an incantation, visualizing his image in my mind's eye. The idea for this came from somewhere deep inside—in a place that required no thought.

"You will always love me.
You will never leave me.
I will always be all women to you.
And so it is."

The deed was done. The only way to disperse the spell would be to burn his hair with the clear intent to dissolve the spell—which I never did. The closest I came was during one of our breakups, three years later, when I threw his hair out, but never with the firm intent to dissolve the spell. It was more like memento housecleaning, just before I married someone else. I only had to think about him for a moment to bring him to my door, consciously unbidden, after a three-year break and three weeks before my wedding day.

Even after I finally managed to release him, eleven years from the day we met, the spell is not completely broken—either way. I just don't feed it with any thought, emotion or psychic energy—although writing this book isn't helping.

Around the same time I cast my spell, I gave him, at his request, clippings of my pubic hair. I knew he had built some kind of altar or shrine to me in his home that he did his thing on. It serves me right that our love affair became a multilayered, mutual karmic obsession with such force that we were almost obliterated by it several times.

## Karmic Obsession: A Case Study

Rush and Donnie, who were still close buddies, met Paul a few months into our relationship. They were extremely upset about it. They tried to convince me that Paul was dark and evil (not even knowing what he did for a living, just from his energy) and definitely not "one of us." "One of us" meaning the "sons of light": a karmic family of souls committed to the life force and the light in all beings. They were so vehement; it was as if they were trying to deprogram me from the cult of Paul or something.

What they didn't know was that they were the catalysts in helping me realize the true nature of who Paul was to me. The reincarnational drama of our karmic bondage began to unfold, inspired by their urgency and intensity to keep me from it.

It's true that Paul was not in the soul family of the "sons of light" that Rush, Donnie and I had been in for many lives and in many forms. We've all had our slips, and it was during some of these karmic "slips" into the dark side that my karmic bondage with Paul was born.

Paul's soul roots were much darker and more alien, and his purposes on the earth had a lot more shades of gray than ours. My definition of an alien is: any soul whose primary development is more than 51 percent in dimensions other than the earth. As such, when Paul showed me his alien "faces" there was no judgment attached—it just added another level of kink. No wonder he liked to dance to Rick James' song, "Super Freak" while pointing at me.

My primary memories of Paul were from Atlantis and Rome, and the karmic dynamic or inner feeling tone in both of these lives was very similar. In Atlantis, Paul was one of my lovers but not exactly by his choice. He was one of my sex slaves in a life in which he was not considered a real purebred human. He was considered a subhuman in the categories of the time, which I helped to create as one of the genetic scientists of that era. So not only was there double-indemnity karma, but kinky as well, as I was in the male form in that life. Paul was a mix of alien, animal and human components. He was big and powerful but, as one of the ruling elite, I was always in control.

In Rome, similarly, I was one of the ruling elite—this time as a very decadent patrician wife of a centurion who was rarely home. Paul, looking very similar to his image in the present life, was a Germanic tribal chief and warrior, captured in battle, and brought back to Rome in chains with his men. I rescued him from his fate as a gladiator in the arena by making him one of my personal sex slaves. Talk about a rut within a rut within a rut.

Our first meeting was very romantic. He was manacled in a line of prisoners I was examining for potential use. As I weighed his balls in my hand to check their heft, he glared at me with the threatening look of a coiled lion ready to strike if his chains were loosened. I knew it would be fun to tame him—and it was. He became one of my favorites. However, I never loosened his chains completely because, even after he was broken in, he always had that look in his eyes, which I found very tantalizing.

This time, my unfinished business with Paul was to release him from the karmic bondage I had imposed on him—except he just kept coming back for more. Karmic bondages are exceedingly difficult to unwind, and casting a spell that knots things further surely doesn't help.

In the bigger picture, with hindsight, it is no excuse that Paul volunteered to be my sex slave again. It was just irresistible—as most karmic obsessions are. All I could say at the time was: "Let the games begin." Ours certainly had. It was a potentially incendiary karmic auto-da-fe' with the two of us holding a lit match together—almost like a funhouse mirror image of a couple holding a knife to cut their wedding cake.

# 32

## *Surrendering My Will*

Simultaneously with my first fall season with Paul, I visited Rush over Labor Day in Virginia Beach. I had made a new friend at work, Suzie, who became my best friend—and I relapsed on grass and cocaine.

Notice how I slipped that into the sequence of events in the fall of 1981? That's just how I slipped back into my old bad habits of grass and, now, the progression into cocaine. One might think Paul was the instigator of this backward slide. But it wasn't him—it was me. Sobriety was getting too real. I knew I would have to change my act to stay sober and really look at myself. I was scared shitless.

That started when I went over the inventory list of my defects of character with my sponsor in the program. I confessed to her that most of my shortcomings, which I called my "bag of tricks," had to do with manipulation and control, especially in my relationships with men. My sponsor, Kate, asked me if I was entirely ready to give up these defects, and I said emphatically, "No fucking way!"

Within a week, right after my home group meeting where I made coffee, I went out with Rush and Donnie, who were relentlessly trying to dissuade me from being with Paul. They passed me a joint, and I smoked it. The next night, I let myself get into an even more compromising position. Through a friend, I met this fat, sleazy guy who was a professional photographer. He offered to do a photo shoot of me at his loft. Of course, I knew it was a come-on to get in my pants, but I went anyway.

In the course of the shoot, he persuaded me to disrobe more and more as he obviously got hornier and hornier. Then he propositioned me by almost jumping on top of me in a whalelike move on his couch, while passing me the coke spoon. I snorted and ran. Ironically, the photos turned out to be some of the best ever taken of me.

After that, I was off and running again. For the next six months, from October through March, I was smoking grass on the sly that I conveniently got from Rush, who was happy to supply it. I only did coke that once. I was still going to meetings and lying about my sobriety, but only as a sin of omission, because I stopped sharing and just sat there isolating. Even odder, I was hiding my smoking from Paul, although he smoked and snorted all the time.

The paradox was that I was sober when I met him, and he preferred me that way. After I told him my drinking and drugging story, he was more than happy I didn't use anymore, because he liked me just the way I was—loyal to him with no extracurricular bar-hopping or men.

Ultimately, the only person I was honest with about my smoking was me. In hindsight, this doesn't really count because nobody was home. I was still asleep, so there was no one present to be a reliable witness for any semi-objective version of the truth.

For six months, I kept a journal chronicling my controlled weekly experiences getting high. On the evening of April 5, I saw clearly that if the joint I held in my hand was not going to be my last one, then I would fall off the fence of control I was precariously perched on. And the only place for me to go was back into the party scene I had already bottomed out in. All that I saw out there for me was a black void. On the other side of the fence, I saw staying sober in the fellowship. With that vision I saw light, love, joy and, especially, hope.

That night, I surrendered my will and admitted that sobriety my way didn't work. I was not the first person in AA history to be high and sober at the same time, although I gave it my most valiant effort. Nobody could say I wasn't spiritually arrogant.

# 33

## *Breakup*

April 6th, 1982, was my first day completely sober in over seven months. It was also Paul's birthday. There was a freak snowstorm with over a foot accumulation. We went out to play in it and have dinner at our favorite Chinese restaurant. I had told him over dinner he could have anything he wanted from me for his birthday. He asked, "Are you sure?" I said yes, with trepidation.

The next act in this little birthday drama, or farce, took place at his friend Ira's loft. Ira, an amateur photographer, had offered to take some erotic photos of me and Paul "doing it" as a birthday gift for Paul. My participation was my gift. I am sober one day, Paul is coked up, and Ira, a nebbishy kind of guy, is getting excited as he calls out directions. It turns out that Ira is the only one who's getting excited, because Paul is too high on coke and has performance anxiety. I am just going through the motions, not being overly fond of X-rated public displays of attention. It was a disaster. In the short run, it put Paul in a bad mood with blue balls, and in the long run, those photos would come back to haunt me.

As I started cleaning up my sobriety act again, my relationship with Paul became tense. We had declared our undying love for each other over Thanksgiving. However, by June, I realized that despite our intense karmic/primal crazy glue, we were incompatible on just about every level. Even more than the fact that our personalities were polar opposites, the reality was that, spiritually, we seemed to be moving in different directions. What had initially inspired me as a challenge had gotten old fast. I was more likely to get worn down and become cynical like Paul before I was going to get him to "see the light."

I tried to break it off. One time, I attempted to end it on the stoop of my apartment building. I was afraid that, if I let him inside, the crazy glue would take hold. He managed to persuade me to go inside and make love one more time, as he was agreeing with me about how incompatible we were. Who was the trickster now?

He did disappear from my life for eight months after that. Even though I had initiated our parting, I still felt wrenched in two by it. The fact that I left my rose-colored glasses (literally) on the front stoop, as he persuaded me to go inside with him, was a fascinating symbolic—or not so symbolic—reminder of how blind I became in his energy field. Without my glasses, I am legally blind, and while the weight of this symbol was not lost on me, it didn't help ease the pain either.

The winter before the breakup, I had gotten a little beagle pup I named Luna (her middle name was sea). After Paul left, I went for long walks with Luna in the West Village, sat at cafes and watched the world go by. I went to my meetings daily. I tried to have a sober relationship with myself for the first time ever. It was so hard.

I called it the summer that Leela spent alone with Leela. I was twenty-eight and just getting to know myself for the first time without the mirror of a man or the buffer of grass. I even made it through a whole season with only a minor sexual skirmish or two. That was progress.

By the fall, many things started falling into place. I got even more serious about my sobriety and got a new sponsor who laughed a lot (something I wanted) to help me with my spiritual program of recovery. I took two new lovers, both sober, who were not too serious and not too light. One was a Waspy Wall Street type—a good-looking, fast-talking manic-depressive with a penchant for mild S & M games. The other was a very sweet, very mellow giant of a black jazz saxophone player. Having two such different lovers helped me feel more in balance with my different sides—and it satisfied my cravings for chocolate and vanilla for a season or two.

# 34

## *The Readings Begin Again*

In the winter of 1982, I started having some physical symptoms that precipitated a psychic crisis of faith. At the time, I had already started doing a series of short informal karmic readings for my new friend Suzie about her troubled relationship with her mother. However, I was not officially back to work as a professional psychic yet.

I felt that waitressing was all I could handle during my first year of trying to stay sober. Doing readings for souls in crisis was just too much responsibility, given my fragile sense of self. My migraines were getting worse each month, and weekly chiropractic adjustments and acupuncture treatments were only slightly relieving the growing pressure in my head. In addition, my left leg started swelling up and becoming numb so I could barely walk on it at all. With my livelihood threatened and Donnie saying I might need surgery, if it was phlebitis, I was inspired to do a health reading for myself. With my back up against the wall and Suzie supporting me as conductor, I went back into a formal trance for the first time since 1978 when I ran away to Europe. I had never done a reading sober or without Rush present to stabilize me.

What the reading basically said was: *"You're a very stubborn girl, and this is the only way we could get your attention. If you make a commitment to do psychic work again, we guarantee that all your earthly needs will be met."*

Sure enough, after a day of soul searching and, once I made the mental commitment to hang out my shingle professionally again by June, my physical symptoms disappeared overnight. I have not had a return of leg numbness or migraines ever since. I also found out, through my brother, about a small family trust that could help me out until my private practice took off. In June, I hung up my waitress apron after ten years and retired with honor from the field. I felt I had learned a lot by being a worker among workers and by trying to spread joy and humor mindfully to all those I encountered on the job—from my fellow employees to the customers.

This really paid off karmically in a very direct and concrete way. Most of the earliest clients for my readings, as well as for my paintings, came from this restaurant job—and the referrals continue to this day.

By March 1983, as I finished unwinding from waitressing and was fully back in my chosen field, Paul turned up after an eight-month separation. My readings informed me that we were at a midpoint in our karmic cycle of healing, and we still had much to learn from each other.

For me, it said, *"Giving of self, letting go in the giving and being fully replenished from within."* This was my first taste of what I call "reversing the flow," where I am fed by the Higher Forces vertically and don't need to feed off others horizontally. Then I can give from this inner fullness without becoming drained or affected by negative energy.

Reversing the flow became one of the most powerful lessons I ever received, even though it took another nine years to fully lock in so it became second nature. I was finally beginning to remember from past lives how to fill the void in me with Universal Energy, rather than anything that was ephemeral—such as people, places or things.

The reading also said that while there are *"different stages of influence at play here, mutual reciprocity is really more on a soul level of endless circles balancing each other."*

This time, Paul was more committed to moving toward the Light. He quit the "company," divorced his wife and got off cocaine for good (but not yet grass). He was afraid that the karma he had already incurred was so bad he would not be allowed into the Light. I felt it was my job to encourage him on his new path, without absorbing any of his negative energy or karma, or lowering my tone to meet him. My job was to help him raise his tone. It's a tricky business when you've deluded yourself into thinking you're Mother Teresa of the bedroom—committed to helping mankind—only doing it one man at a time.

# 35

# *The Retired Assassin—Phase II: The Big Split*

Paul and I had another year together after the first breakup. Then we split up for three years before the last go-round, which lasted five years. That three-year split was not the biggest split that was going on. The really big split was inside of me.

Once I was back "on line" psychically and seeing Paul simultaneously, it became crystal clear that I was literally split in two internally. Not just my male/female split, not just my mind/heart split, not just my matter/spirit split, or even my light/dark split—but the essential karmic split in my soul that I came into this life to bring into balance. This split was between my spiritual nature and my desire nature—epitomized by my psychic path and the karmic pleasure rut Paul activated in me so well.

I had an inkling of this split for years, but now it was definitely coming up to be healed in a way that was increasingly uncomfortable in terms of my identity. I had so many lives as a spiritual being and so many lives as a sensual being that it felt as if both of these cycles of development had very little meeting place in me.

I knew that healing this split would make me feel more whole and integrated than I had ever felt before, but I didn't have a karmic memory of how to fuse these two halves—because there wasn't one. Or, at least, I couldn't access any.

All my highly evolved lives of psychic development were as some form of priestess, oracle, seer or wizard. They were predominantly either celibate or, if there was sexual energy utilized, it was usually through ritual, rather than on any personal level. These were lives governed primarily by the higher chakras and focused on being a verbal channel for Source energies, through discriminating mind and direct energy transmissions.

All my especially enjoyable lives of sensual development in my karmic pleasure rut were governed primarily from the lower chakras which focused on ego power, creative/sensual energy and security/survival themes.

*"What was the missing link from these two cycles?"* I asked myself. I saw that what was missing was a more personalized level of heart development that would allow me to commune with others with unconditional love, compassion and support for their spiritual growth. The trick was to focus on developing this missing link in me without losing the higher octave of heart development that was more transpersonal or universal—or losing the lower levels of my development, which were an essential and integral part of my human experience. I had an irrational fear that, if I moved to the next level of development, all my enjoyment of the senses would fall away and I would turn into some kind of ascetic or nun—highly unlikely.

What my readings were telling me is that this new level would be *"a new aspect of not needing other human beings for security, as the self's possessions in any sense, but letting go of the definitions of what makes a relationship with another human being."*

I tried this with Paul, who continually pressured me with his need for commitment and security. He wanted marriage, children and making a home together. I'd look him in the eyes and say, with as much energy and mindfulness as I was capable of transmitting, "All we have is right now." And he would just flip out.

Paul didn't want to experience the eternal *now* with me, he wanted the *rest* of this life together. It became a real karmic tug of war—with him trying to place me in karmic bondage—exactly as I had repeatedly done to him. That'll teach me—it just took awhile for me to learn. I found out later that he was even punching pin holes in the condoms we were using, hoping to trap me—one way or the other.

By April 1984, I couldn't take Paul's pressuring me anymore. My internal split manifested as a split with him. I didn't see how I could heal this split internally if I stayed with him any longer. I wasn't strong enough yet to stand my ground, with him pulling me down vibrationally into our mutual karmic desire rut. It was so hard to do because, if anything, the sex just kept getting better and better, hotter and more intense, the more we realized that the inevitable split, based on our true incompatibility, was coming up fast.

Two months before this second split, a personal reading spelled it out for me: *"Need is not the issue here, desire is not the issue here, fear is not the issue here. The issue here is freedom in aloneness, openness without vulnerability in the negative sense, and integrity of beingness based on this open flow."* When I got this reading, my initial response, even before I was counted out of trance, was, *"Oh, shit. I don't like this reading one bit."* This was my usual response to personal readings for many years.

I felt my channel guides, my Higher Self, my soul, were leading me into a primary relationship with the Higher Forces that I was resistant to on the personality levels. Even with this ambivalence, I was willing to start on this path by breaking up with Paul.

I didn't feel as if I had a choice; the internal split was becoming too painful. So much for free will. This primary relationship with the Divine would take many more years to lock in. My personal preference was for juicy tangible relationships that my ego still had the illusion of controlling, instead of the intangible fruits of merging with the Divine. I knew I needed to cultivate this in theory but, at age thirty-one, I still didn't know how.

It wasn't until my midthirties, when I became a serious student of internal energy arts, such as water method chi gong, wu style tai chi and ba gua that I had the daily physical and energetic structure with which to commune with the Divine or the Tao. But, even at age thirty-one, I was given a glimmer of how this path I was starting on would ultimately infuse all my relationships—even the most intimate ones—with Divine communion, which was much more on the soul level and universal in tone.

## Psychic Interlude to a Prelude

Even though my readings had informed me that the karmic music with Paul would be played again, I felt the need to focus more on myself, for awhile at least.

I had the first solo show of my artwork, paintings and pastels in Soho, called "Visions and Dreamworks." I continued doing soul readings with clients and, most importantly, developed a new form of therapy which utilized altered states, past life regression and dream work. It was an exhilarating time, creatively and psychically.

I slowly started to feel as if I was giving birth to myself, and my life was becoming my canvas. Up until this point, I had always been sure that one day I would have children, even twins, as they run in my family. I even felt, at times, the souls of my unborn children waiting for me to give them the go-ahead so they would know when I was ready for them to come through me.

Now the probabilities in this area were beginning to shift inside of me. If I truly wanted to be a psychic therapist and healer at the highest levels I was capable of, in terms of vibration and focus, having children would pull me down to a necessary physical level of attention. As a trance channel for many lifetimes, I knew my primary focus needed to be nonphysical.

True to form, I manifested this shift as another health crisis. The realization that I was at a major crossroad put me into a state of mourning. I developed a large ovarian cyst (exacerbated by going off the pill) that made me look and feel as if I was about eight months pregnant. My doctor said it could burst at any time and warned me that, if I started to bleed, I needed to rush to an emergency room for surgery, as I might start hemorrhaging.

I'd had enough experience by this point to know I was just somatizing my emotional state. I asked Rush, who had come into his own as an extremely powerful psychic healer, to help me process and heal the deeper levels of the cyst's physical symptom.

Rush placed his hands over the area of the cyst, one above it and one below it as I was lying on my back, and had me feel what it was saying to me. I wept as I told him about the choice I felt pressured to make: life as a priestess or being a mother. He pointed out my extreme nature and reminded me it didn't have to be one or the other at this time. I didn't have to slam the door and seal the probability yet.

In my heart of hearts, I knew I had already made the choice. Nonetheless, Rush was right; I did tend to get ahead of myself. Because I can see future probabilities so well, I speed through the more gradual nature of the emotional process. Rush suggested I keep this probability open in my mind and body and allow it to naturally close over time in a more flowing way. He helped me see how my extreme nature had precipitated this particular crisis.

At the time of this healing session, I consciously made the choice of the priestess path—but only as an initiate—and I resolved to keep the other door open. The cyst dissolved completely with no residue within 24 hours after the healing.

I kept the door open until I was thirty-nine. At that time, in a very flowing way on all levels, I had a tubal ligation to formally express my commitment to the priestess path. Later that same year, on a trip to Egypt, Rush officially initiated me at Karnak in Luxor and in the sarcophagus at the King's chamber of the Great Pyramid in Giza. The full story of that trip is described chronologically in the chapter, "Time Falls Away."

During this second interlude from Paul, my primary focus was the psychic/spiritual side of my development. But true to form, my secondary focus was my desire nature; I had four minor affairs that first year.

All these affairs were with guys whom I met through my recovery program. One was with adorable twenty-four-year-old with a sweet disposition and a perfect body. But there was no real heart connection on a personal or deep karmic level, even though I felt my heart was opening, in general. Another was a Brooklyn cabdriver in his late twenties, with a playful disposition, handsome dark Italian looks and a perfect body, who was especially hot in bed. But there was no real heart connection on a personal or deep karmic level. They both were named Ronnie, and I saw them during the same fall/winter period. This was fun, although I felt a bit too young to be having twin boy-toys yet. I guess I was determined to have twins, one way or the other.

In the spring, I met an Australian, a dapper dresser in his mid-thirties, who worked in advertising on Madison Avenue. I nicknamed him the Dingo for his particular brand of energy in and out of the bedroom. But there was no real heart connection. I could feel a regressive theme developing.

At the same time as the Dingo, I had a brief affair with a good-looking accountant named Bob, but he turned out be such a depressive that his energy quickly became oppressive and I had to break it off. Besides, as with the others, it just wasn't clicking for me on a deep enough karmic or heart level.

By the summer of 1985, my heart was opening more, but I didn't seem to be connecting with anyone deeper. I had done a lot of work on myself spiritually and emotionally, even if my affairs that year didn't reflect it. I felt ready to meet someone with whom I could play out all the levels with—spiritual/psychic, mind/heart, soul/personality and of course, let's not forget, the sensual.

I was overripe for meeting Peter. I first heard him speak at one of my home group meetings. He was 6′ 3″, with fair hair, gray-green eyes, a lanky, sinewy, athletic body and an arrogant but charming double-Leo disposition. In his upper-class English accent, he told a story, which he thought was amusing, about being deported from Switzerland after beating a wealthy woman who was keeping him as her gigolo.

Instead of this story warning me off Peter, as he seemed rather proud of it, I found it intriguing. In hindsight, I can see that the karmic winds were blowing us together, as I remember thinking, "*I'd like to bring this one down a peg or two.*" He was so full of himself. Fate brought us together two more times over the next week at his home group, and then at mine, where he heard me speak. He came up to me after the meeting to shake my hand and thank me. I suggested we have coffee some time. He said, "How about right now?"

# 36

## *Karmic Marriage in Hell: A Case Study*

On our first date, Peter and I talked all night over coffee in the outdoor garden of a cafe near my apartment in the East Village. He told me of his dreams of becoming a fiction writer, even though he had only dabbled in journalism in Africa and made his living now as a carpenter.

I was encouraging and supportive and mirrored back to him visually and energetically his potentials. He was mesmerized by his own performance and by his attentive audience of one. He asked, "Are you always this positive and supportive?" I spontaneously replied, "Only in the beginning." If you subscribe to the idea that you can tell the whole story of a relationship by what occurs within the first twenty-four hours after meeting, this surely was the case based on what unfolded between us.

After the cafe closed around 1:00 AM, we wandered around, walking and talking. Neither of us wanted to part. Finally, around 3:00 AM, I hesitantly invited him over to my place. Since Peter was such a sensual being (he had made his living from it) and since I was such a sensual being (it was my karmic rut, after all), one would think that things would go off in bed without a hitch. But the twenty-four hour rule was in effect, and it was a complete disaster.

First, he was completely passive and left it to me to initiate everything. Once I did get him started, his kisses were too wet and not to my taste. He had such huge, oversized lips and such a big mouth that engulfed my mouth, I felt as if I was being drowned in a sea of saliva. His penis, which was donkey-sized and uncircumcised, I found visually unappealing.

His shaft under his foreskin was so sensitive that he came almost immediately once I straddled and slid him inside me. He apologized, and said he hadn't had sex in quite awhile. It wasn't just the quickness that upset me; it was that we were such a bad fit. It felt as if we were trying to ram a square peg into a round whole and, not just physically, but on more subtle energetic and emotional levels.

I'd had this square-peg/round-hole problem once before, during a brief fling in the early 1980s with a darkly good-looking parole officer I'd met at a New Agey party. He also had a large, thick, uncircumcised penis. After a few tries, Joe and I agreed that as much as we were attracted to each other, it just wasn't working out sexually. The head of his penis could fit in, but his foreskin would get stuck around the opening of my vagina. It was very unpleasant for both of us. We stopped seeing each other because, besides the visual attraction, there just wasn't enough rapport or inclination there for a friendship—a wise decision.

With Peter, because we had such an incredible mental affinity right from the get-go, and because we were both so sensually experienced, we decided to try it again to see if we could make it work.

The good news was that Peter was the first man who not only supported my sobriety, and was sober several years himself, he also really supported my psychic work. In fact, that side of me seemed to turn him on the most. This was a good sign in a potential friend, client and/or channel groupie, but not necessarily enough to balance out our poor chemistry on the primal levels. The X factor was definitely missing.

After Peter's mother abandoned him at age seven and ran off with another man, he was raised by his granny, a psychic healer in London. Thus, he found my presence emotionally and energetically comforting, just like the good, safe side of his home life.

The down side of being "granny" to him was that, while he wanted to marry me because of my spiritual and mental development, which he believed would continue to evolve (I was a good investment), he also thought I was short and funny looking and he never quite seemed to get my sense of humor.

Now, I have always been considered a classically attractive if not beautiful woman—at the least cute and perky, with a bawdy sense of humor. While I may be short, I have always had high self-esteem about who I am and how I present myself. But two and a half years of being the object of Peter's critical and emotionally skewed view of me left its marks. He called me "dog-tooth" affectionately in private; in public he made excuses for my appearance, as if he were escorting the "elephant lady."

Being spiritually evolved enough to transcend his verbal and psychological assaults most of the time, and even resorting to the old "sticks and stones" at others became exhausting. Even worse, his abuse became insidiously debilitating to my self-esteem in ways I didn't fully realize until after he was gone—and *that* was what he wanted. I may have karmically and semiconsciously wanted to bring him down a peg or two, but boomerang karma was in effect for the duration of this relationship—and has been ever since for me.

Boomerang karma is a term I originated. It means that if one is operating at a high enough psychic speed to cut through the density of the physical plane and manifest quicker through one's thoughts, intent and will, then the corollary is that the karmic law of cause and effect comes back so fast, it hits you in the back of the head. It's a sign of how high a speed one is operating from. Manifestation from desire doesn't need to take years or lifetimes. It essentially means that you get exactly what you put out—just faster.

Since Peter, I have experienced that the reverse is also true. Whatever good I put out into the world, in thought, deed or even intent, usually comes back to me within twenty-four to forty-eight hours—although not necessarily from the same direction. However, at this stage with Peter, I was just learning how to throw the boomerang and wasn't too skillful yet at using it in a positive way.

Peter became very possessive of my time and space within weeks of our first date. He insisted on moving in with me, even though I knew it was better for me and the relationship if we took it slow and had at least one night a week on our own. However, he bullied me and fell into a rage until I relented and let him have whatever he was raging about—a very dangerous precedent to set up.

We compromised. He agreed to pay rent on a raw dump of a loft space he shared with a roommate. He didn't slept there once and just used it for storage. It was a symbolic gesture of $600 a month to show he wasn't officially living with me. But he *was* living with me, as an ever-present space invader in my small one-bedroom apartment. The only privacy I had from him was in the bath. I became slowly water-logged again, just like my pre-adolescent days, only not for such a fun reason.

When we were in bed, we slowly came to an accommodation so that sex became more pleasurable if not ecstatic. His body odor started to bother me. I swear he started smelling literally like shit to me. Maybe it was his hygiene. I knew he had hemorrhoids and was English, but I took it to my therapist anyway. I considered it an extremely ill omen that Peter's smell, especially after sex, was such a turn-off.

I became aware that his body odor was just the tip of the karmic iceberg or, in this case, the karmic shit pile. I started accessing memories when I was in bed with him of a life in Persia. I was a male court astrologer, and he was one of many boys I had castrated and made into eunuchs for my pleasure and control. Oh-oh.

When I got a whiff of what I owed him karmically, it confirmed I was in for a rocky ride.

During our second year together, we got formally engaged, with a ring and a date. I thought I was marrying him to give him his balls back by letting him wear the pants, be in charge, in control and that whole package—to help bring into balance and heal our karma. However, I also had the feeling that once you make someone a eunuch, just marrying him might not be *quite* enough to balance the scales so he chooses to forgive unconditionally.

Then, I started accessing memories of two other lives with Peter. One was in China. I was his concubine, and he enjoyed torturing me sexually. In the other, he was a sadistic SS officer who was especially cruel to me. Gee, and the honeymoon hadn't even started yet.

Peter epitomized my repressed dark side and all the power it contained. I projected all that darkness and power onto him—similarly to Paul—and they both played their parts impeccably. Timing is everything. I was thirty-three and he was thirty-five. We figured tying the knot was the only thing we hadn't tried in the relationship arena. Besides, I rationalized that if Jesus could get crucified at my age, then getting married was the least I could do. Not the best attitude.

I also had memories of one lovely life in Ancient Lemuria where we frolicked about like twin souls, only half-immersed in the physical plane. This created a nostalgic undertone of spiritual and mental communion that wafted like false advertising through the present dynamic. I had a feeling that our marriage was going to be an attempt to heal all the harm we had done to each other. That is, if we didn't kill each other in the process in an idealistic attempt to recapture that lovely Lemurian energy again.

My father had the same kind of energy: dark and demanding, emotionally cool and critical, and like a south-seas pirate in his business practices. While I was growing up, I got to witness the power of his well-developed dark side in his interactions with others, especially his employees and my mother and brother. With me, he was as loving and affectionate as he was capable of.

Peter's dark side was totally directed at me. I was finally home. My karma with Peter felt as if it was hitting all the right daddy chords. By the time we got married, about two years after the first date, we had already been in individual therapy, pre-marital counseling and even chaired a group of couples in recovery for a year. Our relationship had become all work and little or no play. I felt imprisoned in karmic bondage with no doors, windows or hope of escape.

Peter was becoming more verbally abusive toward me as the wedding date approached. In public, people were shocked by what he said about me and about women in general—being "controlling bitches and he hated all of them" and so forth. Sometimes after our sobriety meetings, so many people would come up to hug me, shake my hand or commiserate with me, I felt as if I was a one-woman receiving line at my own funeral of autonomy.

When Peter wasn't raging, his depressed nature would flare up, and he would take to his bed for weeks at a time. I couldn't tell if he was really sick or just incredibly lazy. As time went on, my diagnosis became more multilayered: he was a rageaholic, manic-depressive and, in the winter, he had a legitimate case of the flu and seasonal affective disorder.

By the time we got married, he had piled up so many debts that I had to pay all the wedding and honeymoon bills. I found out his true financial status the night before the wedding, when he confessed to me that he had been lying about his finances for over a year. I agreed to go ahead with the wedding for two reasons. First, all our relatives were already flying in from Chicago, Miami and London and, second, he promised to enter a recovery program for debting and signed a note to pay me back everything I put out. Still, not the best omen.

Peter was adamant about having a big, expensive wedding reception, something I could have cared less about. He had insisted I cook and clean for him all along. When I hired a housekeeper and ordered in food, he went into a rage, because he wanted his granny. He was his happiest when, once a week on Sunday, I served him poached eggs on toast and fresh orange juice in bed. That was the day I felt the most oppressed.

The only thing that seemed to keep him relatively calm was when I did psychic readings with him as the conductor, especially when he got to ask personal questions about himself. When we operated psychically, our souls connected and there were glimmers of hope. I remember seeing his angelic nature *once* early in the relationship, as well as his hurt little boy, when he was telling me how his mother abandoned him while he was recovering from knee surgery in the hospital. In hindsight, it's what I call the classic "bait and switch;" it hooks us into karmic relationships that need healing.

Those glimpses of our soul connection, plus his angelic face and hurt little boy, were the false advertising that kept us locked in a karmic prison which took on the false outer structure of a marriage. The night before the wedding, my psychic channels told me to view the whole wedding as a farce and to maintain an emotionally detached, witnessing perspective as I played out my role of the bride with no attachment. A portentous dream the morning of the wedding confirmed this, among other things.

Premonitions of disaster abounded. Our couple's counselor fired us months before the wedding. She said she couldn't figure out why we stayed together because we fought so much and so venomously. We said we loved each other, and she said that obviously, in our case, it wasn't going to be enough. We just didn't want to hear her.

When Peter attacked me, if he worked on me long enough, I allowed myself to be lowered to his level and rage back. I hated the side of me he was activating. I didn't even know I had that side before him, and I started hating who I was with him. Not the best sign.

Our friends, on both sides, begged us not to get married. They were unanimous. Not only were they afraid we would end up hurting each other, they pointed out that if we had to work so hard at our relationship—maybe it wasn't meant to be. Shouldn't it be easier? We hadn't even hit the honeymoon yet. Attitudes, omens, signs, undisputed feedback—all negative. What's a psychic with blinkers in the romantic area to do?

My stepmother, who was divorced by my father after eighteen years, said that Peter reminded her of my dad's cold, critical nature. Other friends said that Peter looked so much like Paul, they got confused.

Only Peter didn't treat me one-tenth as well as Paul. Paul had loved me more than I loved him. I was the beloved. With Peter, it was becoming a pure love/hate affair—and not in that order. He had escalated from verbal and psychological attacks to pushing and pulling me around, and he was twice my size. What would you predict would be the outcome?

As one who reads signs and portents for a living, what was I thinking? The karmic bondage felt so intense, I felt as if the only way out was through. Ladies and gentlemen of the jury, I married him. I married a man with whom I had no sexual chemistry whatsoever. The sex was barely tolerable. Maybe, in some twisted way, I though I could kill a couple of karmic birds with one stone—if it didn't kill me first. Sure, I was trying to heal my karma with Peter. But if I was trying to get out of my desire rut, wasn't marrying someone for whom I had no desire a balancing karma? I kept forgetting my extreme nature.

# 37

## *Untying the Knot*

The unraveling of our marriage began on our honeymoon to Hawaii. Which is to say, we never really had a marriage at all. While we did travel well together, taking on the roles of husband and wife brought up with a vengeance those parts of us that needed to be healed. The commitment of the marriage vows was the trigger, making it feel safe enough for the deeper karmic wounds to arise.

Being a wife to Peter brought out an absolute cessation of any vestige of sexual desire for him or, it felt like, for anyone else ever. My sexual energies felt completely dead. This absence of desire for Peter was probably there from the beginning. I just stopped making any effort to play along once the ring was on my finger. This, of course, enraged him, as he wanted to have sex all the time. After all, it was our honeymoon. I felt burdened by having sex once a week—much less several times a day, which was his wont.

My sexual shutdown perfectly activated his karmic issues of feeling like a eunuch. As for his emotional abandonment by his mother, I became the great castrating mother archetype. It was a complete karmic lock.

I was determined to stay the course in karmic hell; it felt like just punishment. Peter needed to do something pretty horrible to force me to abandon him physically like his mother did—but he managed it.

Right after the honeymoon, he started having a very hot sexual affair with an old girlfriend he still obsessed over. After about three months, I confronted him in bed one night. Looking him in the eyes, lying side by side, I said, "Are you fucking someone else?"

Peter didn't even attempt to deny it. On some level, he seemed completely relieved that I had called him on it and brought it out in the open. Now, the final scene in the karmic unraveling could commence.

I told him I was unwilling to be his warden, keeping tabs on him at all times and turning our marriage into a prison, which it felt like anyway. I told him he needed to make a clear choice to recommit to monogamy with me, which meant our once a week duty fuck. Not surprisingly, he said he would like to have a more European marriage and have a mistress for hot sex (he liked to fuck her in the ass) and keep me as his wife. He still got off on the fact that I was a professional psychic, therapist and spiritual teacher.

I agreed to Peter's suggestion of an open marriage, on the condition that I could take a lover as well. After all it was the 1980s, so it was only fair. I also warned him that in most cases, unless there was an extremely solid emotional commitment to make the marriage relationship the primary one (which wasn't the case), most open marriages spelled the beginning of the end.

The reason I was amenable to opening up the marriage was because Paul had been sniffing around for several months. I let him take me to lunch and give me a book on the benefits of adultery. My hot backup was already in place, just waiting to be activated.

We were off and running. For two months, the fact that we had other lovers actually made our sex life more fun in a kinky, twisted way. Mostly because my sexual energies got activated again almost immediately with Paul and there was a juice overflow back into the marriage bed. We had agreed to see our lovers once a week. I, of course, started sneaking out and seeing Paul in motels or friends' apartments almost every afternoon while Peter was at work.

My therapist, who was also our marriage counselor, was not too concerned about my ability to juggle Peter and Paul emotionally or sexually as he knew my history. He was more concerned about when I would find time to paint. I shrugged and told him I would paint when I was eighty; I was having too much fun now.

By September, six months into our farce of a marriage, Peter informed me that he was bored with his ex-girlfriend and wanted to know what I thought about that. I asked him if he wanted to renegotiate our marriage back to a monogamous one, and he said, "Not really. I just want you to stop seeing Paul, at least until I find someone new. I don't want you having fun if I'm not." A typical Leo statement. In fact, he further implied that he would prefer I got another lover instead of Paul, one I was not so enamored with, as it was making him jealous.

I replied, "I would be happy to stop seeing Paul, but only if you are willing to recommit to monotony—oops, I meant monogamy." I explained that I refused to be cruel to Paul because his emotions wouldn't just snap back like a rubber band if Peter changed his mind again. At this point, Peter asked me, "Well, how long do you think it will take you to become bored with Paul, like I am now with Lisa?"

I thought about it, and replied, "At the rate things are presently going, I predict at least ten more years." I admit this was a provocative remark, so it was no surprise when Peter hit the ball back with some nastiness. I got upset and threw my cup of warm tea in his face. Then, all hell broke loose.

Peter went into a rage. With tea dripping off him, his face became transformed into a red mask of glaring eyes and a pulsing vein in his temple. He lunged and attacked me with such force it knocked me off my chair and onto the floor. He went for my throat throttling me as he banged my head on the carpet. I thought he was going to kill me. He stopped, just in time, before I fully blacked out.

Afterwards, Peter went to a meeting. I got ready to see a client for a soul reading. Then a fortuitous chain of events occurred which prevented me from rationalizing his violent outburst—and probably saved my life.

The client I saw that afternoon had been abused by her husband so badly that she came into my office in a neckbrace. He had beaten her head against the wall so often that she had been hospitalized for depression. She had received a series of shock treatments before she was willing to leave him. I got the message.

That night, at my home group, Sadie and Sam, two close friends and clients visiting from Florida, wandered into the meeting. It was raining torrentially out, and they almost didn't make it because of the weather. They said they felt compelled to come.

They asked me how I was, and I told them over dinner. They insisted I not go home because it wasn't safe. They wanted me to stay with them overnight to give me time to gather my thoughts.

I was up all night talking to them, pacing the floor, and remembering my client's story that day, as well as the progression of events leading up to Peter's assault. By morning, I called Peter and asked him to move out immediately. Later that day, I went home and had the locks changed.

During that night of soul searching, Sadie reminded me that in one of her readings, years earlier, the channels had warned her, in relation to her own karmic drama at the time, *"Don't fuck with the eunuchs. They can be vicious."* After the karmic ball was hit back into my court, so to speak, I conceded defeat. I could not continue to try to heal Peter's woundedness at the expense of my own life, even if I was the one who had helped inflict the karmic wounds. I had taken it as far as possible. I had to surrender to the truth that all I could do now was free myself from karmic bondage.

After seeing Peter go into a rage and lunge at me violently, because he wasn't getting his way during a marriage counseling session, our therapist told me that

Peter's journey of healing from this type of violent abuser pattern might take many more years. The violence would more than likely escalate, if I stayed with him. He told me it was no longer safe to be alone with Peter. He recommended filing for divorce immediately, which I did.

I came to realize that I had to start owning my own power, especially through my dark side, and stop projecting it on the men in my life. I had to forgive myself for any harm I had done to Peter, and I had to forgive him for any harm he had done to me in all our past lives. I had to get on with my life.

I had to finally admit to myself that I had indeed married a man with socio-pathic tendencies. All the signs were there before the marriage; I had just chosen not to read them. Because … because … because … karmic marriages in hell have no "because." They are not rational. They exist for bringing up deeply ingrained karmic patterns that could not come up in any lesser way to be healed. At least I survived.

# 38

## *The Assassin—Phase III: Taking It to the Limit*

When I told Peter it would take me at least ten years to have my fill of Paul, I was estimating it based on the levels of emotional and sexual intensity that Paul and I were operating at during our first few months back together. I should have known that once Peter was out of the picture, Paul and my mutually obsessive natures would exponentially increase the intensity of our interaction. It only took us five more years to completely max out—but, oh, what a lovely slide. Until we hit bottom, that is.

I ran into Paul about six weeks after the honeymoon. I was eating my favorite dish, prawns with black bean sauce, at my favorite Szechwan restaurant in Gramercy Park. It also happened to be Paul's favorite Chinese place; we considered it ours. He ran in, his car double-parked, to get some sesame noodles to go. Our eyes locked, and I felt shivers down my spine. I hadn't felt that alive since we parted three years earlier.

He sat down across from me and asked how I was. I was neutral about married life. He told me that after he had come to my door unannounced three weeks before my wedding day and heard the news of my impending nuptials, he cried for a week and couldn't sleep or work.

He informed me of his new job as a vice-president of art investments at a major Wall Street securities firm. He wanted to take me for a ride in his new Mercedes and show off his new office with a view of the East River. I didn't quite believe him, because when we split up, he was floundering between being a freelance journalist, a limo driver and making art. I figured if the job involved travel (which it did), it was probably some kind of cover, which he denied, of course.

I passed on the invite. I was a married lady, after all. It was all too sudden for me anyway. I've never been that quick at switching gears emotionally. Besides, I knew he would be back. I could see and feel the excitement in his eyes. He loved the hunt as much as I.

His excitement was contagious. After I left the restaurant, I was strolling along 14th Street which, at that time, was a bawdy Puerto Rican shopping haven of sidewalk hawkers selling cheap clothes, bright scarves and inexpensive baubles. It looked like heaven to me—which was quite a stretch. Everything and everyone glittered with energy and light. Usually, I avoided 14th Street because I found it so depressing. My inner gyroscope was shifting.

When I got to my therapist for our weekly session, I told him all the colors in the world were brighter since seeing Paul. He just listened in his usual way, smiling and nodding. Internally, I was saying, *"Uh-oh!"* I realized that the colors of my life had become progressively muddier shades of gray since Paul had left.

After that first sighting, Paul started calling me almost daily, repeatedly insisting on taking me out to lunch and to see his new office. I didn't stop his phone calls; I took all of them. I let him seduce me because I wanted him back in my life. I just wasn't ready to take responsibility for that decision yet. He wooed me diligently, with all the right endearing words. When we did see each other, he pleaded with me, cried and laid his head in my lap. I welcomed his soft caresses. He gave me everything I never got from Peter, and I realized how much I missed being appreciated for just being me.

By the time Peter confessed his infidelities to me, I was more than ready to let Paul know I wanted to become lovers again. The week before I came to that decision, Paul had taken me to a seafood place in Sheepshead Bay. After lunch, we were lying on a blanket at the beach when he made a confession.

He told me that, about a year after our breakup, he had met a woman named Ricki, and they had fallen in love. She had had an emotionally and sexually dead marriage for many years that had ended in divorce about two years before she met Paul at a party. She was a few years older, about forty at the time they met, and she was more than ripe for what Paul had to offer. He was an extremely passionate and romantic lover.

About six months after they got together, Ricki was diagnosed with breast cancer. The next year was a hell of surgery, chemo and radiation, with Paul sticking by her side, until she died in his arms. When Paul turned up at my door, it was just a few months after Ricki's death. He was in so much pain. In his grief, he didn't know where else to turn.

When I told him that I was getting married in three weeks, he felt his world completely disintegrate. That's why he swore he would never let me go again after he ran into me at the Chinese restaurant.

Paul was more than willing to get his foot back in the door as my lover, even accepting, at least verbally, that Peter and I were going to stay married. At our first lunch date, he gave me a book on the benefits of adultery, slyly planting seeds any way he could.

On our first night as lovers again, Paul picked me up and was planning to drive us to a motel, just over the George Washington Bridge, in New Jersey. Peter was out with his lover that night, as our new agreement meant we could both see our respective lovers one night a week. I was so nervous; I felt like a virgin. It is truly a gift that my imagination works so well in my favor.

Earlier that week, Paul had rung my door unexpectedly late one afternoon. I let him in, even though I knew Peter could come home from work early. We quickly lost control, with Paul fixating on my breasts because they'd gotten larger since he'd last seen them, and also because of the trauma of Rick's double mastectomy. Besides, Paul had always been a "breast man" anyway, because he wasn't breastfed. He loved to fondle them, play with my nipples and suckle them for extended periods.

I had to stop him after he went down on me, because I was afraid if we started having intercourse, we probably wouldn't be able to stop. If Peter walked in on us, there would probably be violence, knowing them as I did. Paul left with such a hard-on bulging in his pants, his eyes looked as if they were going to pop out of his head.

By the time he picked me up for our first tryst, things were as sexually on edge as they could possibly be. My reaction to the sexual tension was to insist on picking up a rack of babyback ribs to eat at the motel. I had developed an insatiable craving for some meat on a bone. When I'm sexually hungry, I get physically hungry—somehow I get very confused. It's a weird form of displacement that I occasionally lose control of. And it happened that night.

When we got to the motel—the kind with three-hour rates and mirrors on the ceiling—I was gnawing on the ribs, while Paul was working his way up my body with his mouth. Finally, the moment arrived for him to enter me after a half-hour of foreplay—he with me and me with the babybacks. We locked eyes and fell right back into our karmic sexual rut of mutual obsessive desire. I felt as if I was his home energetically, and when he filled me up to perfection for hours, there was no place on earth we would rather be—ever.

We made love face to face, kissing deeply with our eyes smiling. I was coming every few minutes with my legs braced on Paul's shoulders, or held up by his strong arms. Then we had our usual interval of oral sex. We finished doggy style, as we had always done, coming together, our cries in unison. It was the only position Paul could ejaculate in, as he needed to be upright on his knees because of kidney damage.

When we came together, it was so powerful that it momentarily blew our fuses, and we passed out. On the ride home to Peter, I realized that nothing in my life compared to what Paul and I had together. If Peter had hammered the first nails in the coffin of our marriage with his adultery, then this night with Paul just finished the job. We just let it set awhile before we buried it.

# 39

## *Looking Through the Eyes of Erotic Love*

I knew I would always have a predisposition to identify myself as a sexual being, once I understood my astrological make-up in my midtwenties. Having a Libra sun, or ego energy, focused through the eighth house of sex and/or metaphysics meant that my baseline identity would always prefer to commune with the Divine through the physical senses.

What I didn't know in my twenties was that, as I evolved psychically, my sexual energies could be transmuted into spiritual energies. The energetic continuum between sexual and psychic energies has always been clear to me. But, I also knew that I couldn't skip the sexual (as if I'd want to) to get to the higher frequencies. I could only choose to transmute these energies while playing out my karmic evolution. If I repressed my baseline sexual nature, I knew it would hold me back later and put a ceiling on how far I could develop spiritually.

Once my sexual energies became fully activated in my teens, repression has never been a problem for me—in fact, it's been the opposite. My karmic attachment to my sexual identity actually slowed down psychic development considerably, based on readings I received in my midtwenties. Even before I stopped drinking and drugging, these readings informed me that I wouldn't be able to fulfill my potential psychically unless I stopped being a "party girl." Not surprisingly, based on my karmic rut, I chose not to listen to those readings for a long time. In fact, I'm still working out some of the ramifications.

In my late twenties, when I was so intensely involved with Paul, I actually pitied people who seemed to be sexually repressed, or asexual, or just too old or too something to get it on. I saw all beings through the lens of my 2nd chakra sexual identity and judged them as lacking something essential if they didn't appear to have any sexual juice. Since I was having so much fun with my karmic rut, I naturally assumed that it was the best and only way to be fully alive and human.

By my late forties, I had evolved to a point where I didn't see human beings through such a skewed, subjective lens of perception. Now, I try to accept all stages of life, ranges of development and karmic unfoldment without judgment. However, it is important for me to remember how limiting my perception of self and others was. I have empathy for those who are as blinkered as I was, whether for ego or karmic identity protection. I feel special compassion for those who are the objects of their judgment.

## Nostalgia for the Good Old Days

I have always enjoyed the scent of danger and adventure of that moment when a new lover's penis is entering me for the very first time. Not just the sense of being invaded and filled, consumed and vulnerably open—but the aesthetic sensual thrill of how it looks and feels, its heft and depth inside me. Just the idea of another being, through his shaft, moving inside of me and filling me with his unique energy—if it's the right kind—is wonderful.

What I have not mentioned until now is the handful of times when I went to bed with good-looking men, with good bodies and big, hard cocks (whether thick or long or both), who left me completely untouched, no matter how far they drilled inside me. They left me invaded but bored, because there was no chemistry, or what I call the X factor between us. If this chemistry on the primal sexual levels is missing and, even worse, if there is no emotional juice from the heart running between us, then I could never be with this man more than once. It feels like living death to be sexually invaded—but not touched.

Sex is completely pointless to me unless there is an open-hearted, mutual emotional spark and primal sexual chemistry—and the bar keeps rising as I evolve. As my sexual energies have transmuted more and more toward the psychic levels of communion, my erotic priorities have shifted as well. What I now look for in a perspective lover is a clear and open energetic channel for communion with the Divine. An open heart is implicit, as is minimal emotional baggage which can clog the channel. Personal attraction is secondary to vibrational soul affinity.

However, the transmutation of my sexual energies didn't occur until almost seven years after my final breakup with Paul—and then only after much internal emotional and karmic housecleaning.

With Paul, I had the best, most intense, mutual, reciprocal love I had ever experienced. It did not diminish over time but just kept getting better, with more intensity and deeper levels of emotional and sexual intimacy moving into our dynamic every few months. We would gaze into each other's eyes and kiss and make love for hours. Since I had a seemingly unlimited capacity for orgasms, our sex felt like the ultimate roller-coaster, amusement-park ride that life had to offer. I could take this ride almost anytime I wanted to, with no waiting in line. Paul even developed the capacity to separate his orgasms from his ejaculation so he could keep up with me on the ride—with multiple mutual orgasms all the way home.

Why couldn't I have this with Peter? I knew from our first time together that the chemistry was off. It was a warning that I failed to heed. The pheromone levels, and the karmic bondage and the personality dissonance all came later—or maybe not. Maybe all of that—pheromones, bondage and dissonance—is contained within that elusive X factor that's either there or it's not. When it's not there, I have learned to trust my primal instinctual wisdom and see the lack of chemistry (with no potential for alchemy) as a warning sign that says: "Enter at your own risk."

The first week that Paul and I became lovers again is a high watermark in my memories. After experiencing so much emotional pain for more than two years with Peter, it was a relief to surrender to my feelings with Paul, which were not tainted with the karmic baggage of animosity and abuse that had accumulated in my rapidly disintegrating marriage.

In fact, since this was the first time I had ever let Paul know I unconditionally loved, appreciated and cherished him, he was deliriously happy. I had never seen him so happy. On the ride home, from a day of making love outdoors on a friend's luxurious country estate, Steve Winwood's song," The Finer Things" a song came on the radio. The lyrics epitomized our feelings in that moment:

*Time is a river*
*flowing into nowhere*
*we must live while we can*
*and we'll drink our cup of laughter*
*The finer things keep shining through*
*the way my soul gets lost in you*
*the finer things I see in me*
*the golden dance life could be*

Paul started dancing and singing riotously in his seat while driving down the FDR Drive. I looked in his eyes and knew I had never made anyone else this ecstatically happy—and probably never would again. Being a classic codependent type, making Paul happy made me happier than anything I could think of.

That afternoon, we had made love in the pool house, in the pool and alongside the pool. We didn't want to miss doing it everywhere possible—it was like sexual circuit training. I remember one particular vision. It was of Paul, standing on the diving board, grinning at me before he dived into the water. In that moment, I saw how he had aged in the three years we had been apart. He had put on at least thirty pounds and developed quite a paunch. He looked bloated, white and puffy—not at all like the golden Adonis I had met five years before. But I had aged and put on weight, too. I realized that I loved Paul all the more in that moment in his imperfect humanness. Love truly is blind, especially the adulterous kind.

By the time Peter and I split in September, Paul and I were a couple again. My old pattern of having a backup firmly in place was rock solid and failsafe. At the same time, I was going through a lot of painful emotional fallout. My worst fear, since my parents divorced when I was twelve, was of letting someone get close enough to stab me in the heart metaphorically and feeling powerless to stop them. I had actualized my worst fear with Peter.

During the six-month separation process after I threw Peter out, I realized that my fear of emotional pain was much worse than the actual pain itself. What I actually felt was an incredible reservoir of emotional strength—survivor strength, if you will—that I never knew I had. After this insight, my predominant feeling was relief that I had gotten this lesson in six months rather than six years. The old saying that scar tissue, especially of the heart, heals stronger than the original was certainly true in my case.

I thought I might be blocking something, since my overriding emotion about the end of my marriage was relief. I took this concern to my therapist, as the Kubler-Ross model of the mourning process—denial, anger, bargaining, sadness and acceptance—didn't seem to apply to me. Horace told me not to worry about it; emotions naturally arose in their own intrinsic order. In hindsight, maybe I had all those emotions from the beginning of the relationship anyway.

Any feelings of sadness were not really over Peter. It was more over the realization that marriage, as an external structured institution, was not exactly tailormade for my particular type of soul development. Horace concurred. Even though he was a Ph.D. and psychoanalytically trained, and even though he believed in general that the optimal model in which to mature emotionally was marriage and children—in my case he was wise enough to offer another option.

He saw me on the "path of the mystic." Any marriage would be directly with the Divine. He encouraged me to honor and validate my path. Similarly, several years prior, he had advised me against going back to school to become a Jungian psychoanalyst. At that time, I felt I needed some sort of external degree as validation of my inner gifts. He pointed out that it was just insecurity on the ego levels, and I needed to internally validate the path I was on as worthy. He saw that the psychic therapy I was developing at the time (with past life regression as its core) would be cutting edge by the time my training as a Jungian was complete. Thank God for Horace. I am so grateful I chose to accept his wisdom and to use his guidance to empower myself.

## Karmic Interlude with an Old Soul Friend

My relationship with Horace as my psychotherapist is just the tip of the karmic iceberg. But then I see just about everything in any given incarnation as the tip of some karmic iceberg. Except when a cigar is just a cigar—as I also believe that randomness and chaos, contradiction and paradox are woven into the Divine tapestry.

The reason I trust Horace implicitly for his sage wisdom is because I remember him from a life in China, where he imparted a philosophy and perspective on life that served me well then. In that life, I was a well-kept concubine to a wealthy merchant, who didn't treat me particularly poorly, considering the conditions of the time. My feet were bound, I was sexually his slave, and I wasn't allowed to leave my elaborate set of rooms that were part of my master's compound of residences, all protected behind thick outer walls. But, at least, I was fed, had a roof over my head, servants to wait on me and wasn't beaten, except in sport.

As a bird in a gilded cage, the only haven I had was an exquisitely beautiful walled garden. It had elaborately manicured grounds, fountains, reflecting pools, flowers blooming in all seasons and a living Buddhalike figure who resided there. This embodiment of enlightenment was the gardener—Horace, of course. Just to round things out, my master happened to be Peter in that particular Chinese incarnation.

Horace taught me how to accept and surrender gracefully to the reality of what is and to embrace the beauty and aliveness of life without condition. He showed me how to be free within my own being, even though I was a prisoner in my external circumstances. He groomed and maintained the garden in ever-evolving perfection through its changing seasons and taught me how to do that with my mind. He empowered me then, as he has continued to empower me this time around. He is what I call an old soul friend, and having him in my life is a blessing.

I knew all this from the first time I met him. We were interviewing each other to see whether we were a good fit as therapist and client. He was already Peter's therapist, referred by a friend of mine. I told him, after a year with Peter, I didn't seem to have a blueprint to go deeper into intimacy and commitment because I had never been willing to do it with anybody. Horace asked me, "Do you know how to receive love?" I knew he had hit the nail on the head. I was great at giving love and caretaking, but I was afraid of being open and vulnerable enough to receive love. He had my number, and we were off and running.

My relationship continues with Horace to this day. It has evolved over more than two decades to being friends and peers. We have tea and chat occasionally, catching up on old friends and clients and helping each other out where and when we can.

## *Phase III continues*

Paul was much more accepting of my "all-we-have-is-right-now" philosophy after our three-year break. After what he had been through, he had mellowed in his need for external structured security with me.

Our routine settled in to seeing each other three to four times a week for very hot and lengthy love-making sessions. After all, it was the core foundation of our primal glue as a couple. We were always lovers first; friendship was not even a close second. There were still too many differences on multiple levels for us to have that simpatico vibe that friends need to have. Ironically, it was that same polarity that kept us coming back for more.

If we had time after our love-making sessions, we took luxurious baths together. We chatted and caught up on our weeks in my old-fashioned tub built for two. We would even do "faces," from time to time. Most of the faces I saw with Paul were always variations on the alien or extraterrestrial ones that I saw when we first met.

Occasionally, we would go to local restaurants for dinner or lunch, and on special occasions, to fancier ones. Paul's career was really taking off in the art boom of the late 1980s, so he didn't have much time to spare. He also had joint custody of his two children, but they were teenagers now and didn't require as much time or attention, except on weekends.

We worked out a schedule that allowed maximum quality time together, without interfering with our careers. Sometimes in the early morning, Paul would let himself in while I was still sleeping and make love to me for an hour or so while I was still dozy. Then he would kiss me goodbye and go off to work with hardly a word, except the usual whispered endearments.

This system worked perfectly for the first couple of years. Because Paul was so busy, with long work days, business dinners and trips and caring for his children on weekends, it made our times together all the more precious. Not only did it take the pressure off of feeling emotionally smothered by Paul's desire to be with me, which had been a problem in the past, it also allowed me ample time to invest in developing my private practice, which grew exponentially during those years, as did my social life.

# 40

## *Life as Theater in the Round*

I developed a client base composed primarily of therapists, healers, bodyworkers, creative types and teachers. Most clients started coming to me for the ten-session psychic therapy that I had created over the years. This therapy was an eclectic mix of modalities, including everything I felt that could help move my clients to the soul level of consciousness and beyond. I called it the vertical journey, back to Source, to distinguish it from traditional psychotherapy, which focuses more on healthy ego development, which I consider the horizontal path.

Just doing soul readings and karmic astrology consults wasn't enough for the type of self-realized client I seemed to be manifesting. Most had already done the horizontal trip, were usually older than thirty-five and were ready to take off psychically and spiritually. Their ego functioning needed to be stabilized internally as well as externally stabilized as a prerequisite for this type of intense, accelerated inner work.

My therapy included such experiential modalities as: meditation, energy and mind/body practices, mirror work for self-love and for cracking open the psychic perceptions by learning to do "faces," dreamwork, chakra and emotional clearing and hands-on healing for toning, energizing and activating the psychic circuitry. The core of the therapy was past life regression work. Beyond that we worked on the development of channeling capabilities, and for more advanced clients, we explored other dimensions and activated the galactic light body.

Most of this work was done in altered states—for me and the client—and I was having the time of my life. I was never bored because I was utilizing so many of my gifts. I had so many interesting and evolved clients; I had to keep working on myself just to keep up with them. They, in turn, appreciated my work so much that I had to turn away quite a few clients, as my waiting list at times was between three and six months for an initial appointment.

I also had time to do a very prolific series of paintings of alternate realities and had my third solo show in Soho in the fall of 1990. I was riding higher professionally than ever before. My relationship with Paul was equally as important to me and going just as well, although he did start to become more cynical about my work as he got more involved in the big-money scene downtown.

I started hanging out with a group of buddies, mostly male, from my recovery program. We would all go out in groups for Chinese or Italian food after our Saturday night meetings. I was more social than I had ever been, which is saying a lot.

My special buddies, who were also close friends, were David and Larry. We were as close as boyfriends and girlfriends can be, without actually doing it—although they did try in the beginning, as boys will be boys. The reason my relationship with them was so cozy, comfortable and naturally intimate was, of course, because I knew them in past lives. While these were minor lives, in terms of their significance to my soul development now, they were major relationships in the past.

David and I had been mates in several lives, but none of them quite human. We had lived underground as dwarves and had frolicked in the woods as elf and hobbit—that one was a bit of a mixed marriage.

David was a professional nature photographer at the time. One early spring, we went on a trip to West Virginia to shoot waterfalls. We camped out in the woods, went white water rafting and were perfectly at ease with each other. No sexual tension, (once he got a girlfriend), just perfect compatibility. Not that we didn't enjoy each other's minds, as well. David was quite a wiz and later became a computer genius.

Larry was in the shoe biz in this life, and he had a thing for feet. Fortunately for both of us, I just happened to be a perfect sample size 6 at the time. Larry had rooms in his apartment filled with mountains of shoes and boots, all in size 6. I was in shoe heaven when I visited him. He would help me try them on, with some moaning and sighing—but that's as far as we ever got in that direction. Then I would leave with huge bags of footwear, both of us happy with the exchange.

Larry had been my husband in a minor Middle Eastern life in which he was a rug dealer. I'm not exactly sure what we did on the rugs in that life when he wasn't selling them, but the karmic residue was just complete and utter smoozy comfortability under just about any circumstance.

There was no sexual charge or tension with either of these friends. They were just a joy to hang out with, which I did for many years. My life with Paul was sexually fulfilling and seemingly endlessly exciting, but we weren't exactly what I would call friends. David and Larry helped round out my life immeasurably.

As the years went by, I realized more and more that not only couldn't Paul travel with me into the psychic and spiritual realms where I lived most of the time, he couldn't really provide me with the kind of comfort, support and companionship my friends did. We were just lovers—but at least we were lovers who never seemed to cool off. Not only did Paul's busy schedule give me enough room to breathe, professionally and socially, it also gave me the opportunity to start taking some vacations on my own.

At first, I was hesitant to go off on my own for ten days in the Caribbean during the winter, but Paul was traveling for weeks at a time on business all over the world. My friend Laura inspired and encouraged me. We first met during my years with Peter, when she gave me a solo show in her gallery space. Then she became a therapy client and finally a traveling companion and role model, in more ways than one.

For my first trip during the holidays in 1988, I went with Laura to Vieques, an island off the coast of Puerto Rico. The next year, I went to St. John, in the U.S. Virgin Islands. It was there that I fell madly in love with the world under the surface of the ocean. I prepared for this by getting a prescription snorkeling mask before the trip, so I could see all of the fish before they hit me in the head, as I am so nearsighted.

I was so exhilaratingly in love with my new sport that I spent at least six to eight hours every day underwater, swimming from reef to reef, until I exhausted all the reefs I could get to by swimming or walking. Then I started taking day trips to all of the other reefs on the island. I had discovered a never-ending wonderland of visual bliss for my soul and all my senses. I had no fear of exploring the reefs on my own, as I have always been a strong swimmer and very confident, if not at times foolhardy in the water and whenever I am sailing, whitewater rafting, canoeing or kayaking. Water just seems to bring out the devil-may-care adventuress in me—as do pirates.

More fear inducing than traveling alone, was my fear of driving automobiles. I had failed all attempts to learn to drive in high school; everyone had given up on me. When I was fifteen, my biology teacher, who was also my driver's ed teacher, told me he had never seen anyone who was so smart in class be so incredibly stupid behind the wheel of a car. I seemed to be mechanically dyslexic—I confused the accelerator with the brake. When sailing solo, I'd turn the rudder the wrong way, jibbing when I meant to come about, causing a capsize on a sailfish in Lake Michigan around the same time.

My father tried to teach me as well, in a large, empty parking lot at Soldier's Field. He gave up after I couldn't master the power brakes whatsoever. I am not mechanically inclined, to say the least. I have no depth perception either, so I resigned myself to the fact that operating heavy machine would always be a dangerous activity for me—and for any others with me or in the vicinity.

The year after Paul and I got back together, when I was thirty-four, I had a reading that directed me to take driving lessons (in Manhattan no less) as well as weight training exercises. I had been doing so much trance work that I was loosing my grip on physical reality—both through being in my body and in terms of my ability to focus in the physical plane. I had been using Paul as an anchor through his very primal sexual energy, plus I was eating a pound or two of meat a day.

In fact, Paul enjoyed seeing me just as soon as I finished doing trance work with a client. He'd wait outside in his Mercedes until I beeped him. Then he would come running in and literally nail me to the earth, fucking me to get me back in my body. My channels didn't think that using sex and meat to ground me was the most empowering or spiritually uplifting way to go.

I started taking driving lessons in the spring of 1988, but only on the days when I didn't do any trance work. I knew that would be contraindicated. I also started working out with some hand and ankle weights. The weight training was fine and dandy, but, boy, did sitting behind the wheel of a car in Times Square or on the Belt Parkway bring up all of my worst fears! Being physical was my weak area, and operating a car was downright terrifying.

I had some pretty trippy semipermeable perceptual and energetic boundaries with the world around me. I couldn't really tell where I or the car ended and other objects, like people or other cars, began. If the car was an extension of me, I was in big trouble. It really forced me to get some discriminating boundaries in my physical focus, because I had been drifting too far the other way. In fact, I used to joke that I had lost my "drift control" years before and had just accepted this as one of the occupational hazards of being a trance channel. Driving helped pull me back from that perceptual edge of "no boundaries."

I got my driver's license on my second try, as a birthday gift of empowerment for my thirty-fifth birthday. I'm sure getting that license gave me the inner jumpstart I needed to become a world traveler on my own—even though I haven't really used my driving skills much since. I have confidence, with a few brush-up lessons, I will be able to activate those motor skills and focus once again, when the need arises. But for now, I have shelved the driving. I still can't do it automatically enough to enjoy it when I'm on vacation.

By our third year together, Paul's business began peaking in the bull art market of 1990. My business went into a strange lull, after being inundated for several years with clients. That's when I got in touch with my baseline worst fear—and it wasn't of having no business. It was of having no relationship. I knew that, some day, I would have to work through that fear and be more than all right with being on my own.

Through our third and fourth years together, Paul was making money and I was making Paul. He was getting very puffed up on the ego levels about how well he was doing. He strutted around the house proclaiming to me, "You have no idea what an important man I am" as he peacocked around, he snapped his suspenders and showed off his custom made shirts and suits. Being a Taoist by nature, I knew that whatever rises must ultimately fall away. I would remind him, although I loved him with money, that I would love him equally as much if he had none.

I really didn't care about money and business all that much. For me, being raised in a well-to-do family, I knew, by the time I was a teenager, that money could never really buy me anything truly important—like happiness, peace of mind or love. And *love*, especially sexual love, was still how I primarily validated and identified myself. Having a lull in business didn't affect me that much; I had enough confidence in my psychic gift to not need a continuous supply of external validation in that area. Besides, I was still making enough money to pay my monthly nut.

I used all my freed-up time to paint more and work on my first book in the psychic field. I was even instrumental in starting a recovery program for marijuana addicts, in addition to being more active in giving service in my 12-step recovery program, which was more focused on alcohol. I hadn't smoked any grass in over eight years, but Paul was still smoking, although I wouldn't let him smoke in the house. He had warned me, when I took him back, that he was never planning to stop smoking grass. I needed to accept that about him up front. Which I did. But my response to it was to help others quit. In doing so, it kept my memory green as to how screwed-up pot smoking had made me over the years.

By our fifth year together, Paul and I had moved to an ever deeper level of emotional intimacy through the vehicle of our love-making. I had finally surpassed the two-and-a-half-year monogamy record I had attained with Van in my twenties, and I still wasn't bored sexually. I had learned how to take care of my needs for spiritual, psychic and social communion through my relationships with friends, clients and groups I was involved with.

Just as Paul and I were moving deeper together, the bottom dropped out of Paul's world. He lost his job for a variety of factors, one of them being a change in the tax shelter laws involving art consortiums, which was one of his specialties.

As his money started running out, Paul stopped smoking grass, started smoking cigarettes and became increasingly despondent. I was ambivalent about this because, on the one hand, I knew how much it would change him for the good and, on the other hand, because I knew how much it would change him. I had been through that tunnel.

I knew the first year or two of recovery could be brutal, especially since he was "white-knuckling it" without a spiritual support group or program. At least he had set up trust funds for his kid's college education as a tax shelter during the good years. But his ego took a terrible blow. As high as he had been on life when I took him back was equal to how low he felt about himself now.

Our last spring together, just months after Paul lost his job, we went on our semi-annual pilgrimage to the Catskills, where we spent the day at Haines Falls. Every spring and fall of our seven years together, as a ritual, we'd bask in the sun at the top of this majestic waterfall. Then, we'd hike into the woods and made love. In the afterglow, we went to Woodstock to eat at our favorite Chinese restaurant, the Little Bear, overlooking a bubbling brook.

This time, I realized, as we were finishing doggy-style, that Paul and I had hit an emotional wall. We didn't seem to be moving deeper into intimacy anymore. After our love-making, as Paul wandered along the banks of the creek and I sat sunning myself, I felt, for the first time, the beginnings of our estrangement. I knew we could still go on for years together, but we had gone as far into emotional depth and intimacy as was possible for us. This saddened me. Yet at the same time, I was philosophical. I figured we'd had a good long run of more than ten years, off and on, and I was willing to coast indefinitely toward our bittersweet unwinding. But it was not to be.

After that trip, Paul continued to get stranger and more estranged, not just from me, but from life in general. As he got more depressed and angrier, it got harder to be around him. He was struggling to make ends meet, just at the time my business starting booming again. He began to be cynical about my work in a way that was extremely unsupportive of me, and it started undermining our relationship.

I knew that his grass and cash withdrawal were major factors in his situational depression. I was willing to cut him some slack. As things slid further downhill, he became increasingly hostile and uncommunicative. I told him how much I loved him, whether he had money or not, but that was not the real issue here. He felt like shit about himself. Nothing I said or did was going to help, even loaning him money—which I did.

As his self-esteem got increasingly shaky and his self-loathing escalated, he started getting irrationally touchy about how I treated him.

One day, he arrived two hours late for a date. By that time, I had made other plans because he hadn't called; I just figured something had come up. He completely erupted and screamed at me that I took him for granted and didn't appreciate him as much as I used to. All true, unfortunately. He stormed out. Then he left a message on my machine a short while later—the gist was to not contact him. "I am just too pissed off."

He disappeared from my life forever. Well, almost. Five months later, he showed up on my doorstep. Just like I knew he would—but I had prepared myself for that eventuality. I had gone back to work with Horace to get strong enough so I wouldn't take him back when he showed up again.

Paul and I had been on this karmic merry-go-round for eleven years, and I was ready to get off. Horace said that we needed to, metaphorically, tie me to the mast and plug my ears, so that, like Odysseus, I could sail past the island of the sirens without being seduced by their singing. Good old Horace. He knew how to make life bigger than life.

Horace had faith in me. Even if Paul seduced me back with our old karmic tune, he knew that I would eventually escape, although I might be marooned on that island of desire for another ten years. Horace was good. He knew his words would get me thinking. Did I have another ten years to waste dissipating my creative energies in my karmic desire rut with Paul? I think not.

With that decision, I felt bigger, fuller and more complete alone than I had ever allowed myself to be before. When Paul told me plaintively that I was the love of his life, I told him that he was the love of my life too—at least to date. I wished him well on his journey. We both knew we could never be just friends. We had as much closure as we were capable of. I felt as I had gone as far as I could go, without karmically disempowering myself. It was the hardest door I ever had to close.

# PART VI

## *ONE DOOR CLOSES …*
## *AND ANOTHER OPENS*

# 41

## *Celibacy Sucks—But You Get a Lot of Work Done*

I was thirty-eight when I closed the door on Paul, and it took another year for me to seal it. I may have been stronger and wiser, but I was not a particularly happy camper. I knew what was coming up for me. It's what I call an FGO: a fucking growth opportunity.

I realized that the reason it's so hard to close a door, like I did with Paul (and not even try to keep my foot in it), is because another door usually doesn't open right away. In the first few months after Paul disappeared, while I was working with Horace, I discovered the reason the hallway feels so cold, dark and drafty. It's because it isn't really a hallway—it's an elevator shaft—and the elevator was taking me up to the next level of soul evolution.

It was an express elevator. When it stopped, there was a door. When I opened it, I screamed and slammed it shut. I demanded to see the psychic equivalent of Monty Hall: I wanted to play "let's make a deal" to trade this door. I wanted to go for what was behind the door marked "new relationship." I was informed by my guides that the new door was nonnegotiable. It was the door I was ready for.

What was on the other side of the door? It actually was a new relationship—of direct communion with the Divine. No middlemen. It was what my being had been preparing for through my readings and inner work for years, and now it was here. I didn't recall ordering this particular relationship from the menu of life, at least not on the personality levels. Talk about growing pains—clean, sharp, deep.

I knew I needed more help, beside Horace, to acclimate me to this new relationship. My readings kept reminding me: *"Being fed by the intangible fruits of Source energy was going to be an acquired taste for me, because my ego would have absolutely no illusion of control."* With a decade of sobriety, I started a new relationship with a sponsor in my recovery program that had gone through similar growing pains at ten years. I figured since this new relationship with the Divine was nonnegotiable, I might as well learn to surrender to it as gracefully as possible.

When I was thirty-nine, I decided to have the tubal ligation I'd wanted for over seven years. It was a symbolic act as well, preparing me for my more formal initiation in Egypt when I was forty. I committed myself to at least eleven months of celibacy—one month for every year I was involved with Paul. Then I hunkered down to finish my book, which had been on the back burner for as long as I could avoid finishing it.

I even got a computer to help me write more easily, though I had been phobic about what I called the C word for years. When friends started talking about their computers, it immediately made me feel queasy; I had to change the subject or leave the room.

My friend David helped me set up my first computer and offered to give me a few rudimentary lessons in DOS to get me started, in exchange for a soul reading. During the first lesson, he said that he had never heard anyone ask so many stupid questions. I felt just as much like an imbecile as when I had attempted to learn to drive in high school and, basically, gotten the same response from my teacher.

I have semisuccessfully used a computer ever since, although I have learned not to go directly from trance work to computer work, as my post-trance energy makes most electronic equipment jam or go crazy, as if I'm passing a magnet over it. I call all my computers Calibur; I got Calibur IV in 2007. I anthropomorphize my computers, as well as other electronic or mechanical devices, such as my vibrator, Lil' Oscar. I have a better relationship if I treat them like living entities.

## Karmic Interlude—Popping the Cork

One of the reasons I was able to close the door with Paul was because of some deep karmic work I did with my old friend Rush about a year before the split. Ever since I divorced Peter, who had been my primary conductor for personal and universal readings, my relationship with Rush had evolved to being primarily psychic partners on the soul levels. Rush had disappeared from my life while I was with Peter because he didn't approve of the relationship. In fact, he sent us champagne flutes as a wedding gift, as a back-handed comment on our union, since Peter and I had been sober for years.

Ironically, as soon as Paul was back on the scene, so was Rush. It was as if, after Peter, Paul didn't seem so bad to him. Or maybe, it was just time for us to work together again. At any rate, Rush and I kept our bimonthly psychic meetings separate from Paul.

We did readings together, just like in the old days with Rush conducting, and then we did hands-on healing sessions with me receiving. Afterwards, we would go out for dinner. It became an important part of both our lives for the next ten years. When we were together, it automatically activated our highest levels of psychic and energetic interchange.

At my request, Rush conducted a past life therapy session to help me resolve some karmic issues with my mother. I had been getting in touch with my dark side more and more, and it seemed to be specifically coming out in relation to my mother. I was cold, detached and critical with her—just like I had seen my father with her (and just about everybody else) when I was growing up. I was getting progressively kinder, gentler and more compassionate with everyone, except her. The dichotomy was becoming increasingly clear and more uncomfortable.

I had already done a lot of step work in my program, as well as emotional childhood work, to clear that level. I had discovered that, as a child, I had chosen my father as a more positive role model than my mother because he was more powerful. My mother was passive, resigned and inactive—whereas my father was exactly the opposite. The down side was that my father treated her heartlessly and that was part of his package—which had a ripple effect outward into all my relationships.

While being emotionally detached was an asset in my line of work (so a client's energy wouldn't back up into me), it was a liability in more intimate relationships. I was ready to get in touch with my mother karma and fully own my dark side. I had become aware that my father had helped me activate it—it was inside me all along. There was no blame or judgment of my father, just a desire to get on with the next level of coming into my full power potentials. Dealing with my mother felt like the cork that would pop open my third chakra, so that I could begin to transmute all of that power to a higher level of operation.

Rush had to keep canceling our appointment because of business abroad. Over several weeks, I became increasingly frustrated as I waited to clear this level formally with him. In the meantime, I was walking around muttering to myself, as past life stuff kept bubbling up from deep within my psyche.

By the time Rush finally arrived to do the session, I had been waiting impatiently for three weeks. I was more than ready to begin. After I gave Rush the basic outline of what we needed to do in trance and prepared myself energetically, he started counting me into the altered state. I abruptly sat up from my prone position and said, "I really don't want to do this!"

Rush laughed and said, "All right now. Just lie down and let's get started."

I will never forget that moment. My ego resistance came up so strongly that it overpowered my desire to release the karmic pressure I had been under for weeks. That memory has helped me when I work with resistance in clients ever since. I do with them exactly what Rush did with me. I acknowledge their conflicted feelings as the last gasp of their ego fears before the new level begins to move in. I always insist on going through with the session, because I know they wouldn't have shown up to do the work unless they were more than 51 percent ready.

My session with Rush reviewed two primary lives in the karmic chain with my mother. In one, I was a Jewish male prophet in ancient Palestine. My mother, then as now, encouraged me to use my psychic gifts to aid our people, who were politically oppressed. I started preaching rebellion from the street corners, and I liked the way it made me feel. Then I was imprisoned for inciting an insurrection and punished by having my eyes put out by fire.

After I was blinded, I was released and spent the rest of that life embittered. I blamed my mother for encouraging me to use my gifts. Therein lays the first karmic linkup. I blamed her, instead of taking full responsibility for right use of my psychic powers. I misused the gift for ego aggrandizement. I enjoyed the power of being a prophet, forgot I was just a channel and got whacked. At the time of this work with Rush, I was afraid of going public with my psychic gifts and extremely apolitical. The key to healing my karma here was not just in forgiving my mother, but in an even deeper commitment to right use of my gifts and the power that comes with them.

Around this time, I had two medical crisis connected to this reincarnational drama. In the first, I was diagnosed with a hole in my left retina and warned it could become detached at any time. If my vision ever became blurry, I would need emergency laser surgery to correct it. I passed on that one. No more fire near the eyes—thank you. I had just gotten over the lifelong need to wear large, tinted dark glasses to protect my eyes as they always felt so vulnerable.

The other crisis was that a rare benign bone tumor was growing out of my left cheek into my sinus cavity. It was causing a lot of pressure and pain. The specialists were very excited about operating on it by removing my cheekbone completely and reconstructing my face from one of my ribs. I decided to pass on that as well, even though the doctors warned me that if the tumor kept growing I could end up looking like the elephant lady. I decided to heal, or at least shrink the tumor, with magnet therapy and visualization. I stabilized the condition over several months (confirmed by CAT scans), as I knew from my readings it was a test of my healing abilities to develop faith in them—close to the bone.

In the second life in the karmic chain with my mother, I was a Spanish Inquisitor. This was the one where, in addition to being a religious hypocrite and closet pederast, I was also a sadist who enjoyed personally torturing potential heretics.

When I was torturing my mother on the rack, she turned out to be a true martyr to the faith. As she was suffering, she looked at me with unconditional love, compassion and forgiveness. Her eyes seared into my soul. She saw all of my darkness and forgave me utterly as I was slowly killing her. This was too much for me. I had to hit her over the head and put her out of her misery. That was the exact thought I have had in this life from time to time! At least now I realized it would be regressive—to say the least.

What I needed was to forgive myself for who I was then. I was soooo *bad.* I had to have compassion for all my suffering, underneath all of that darkness and misuse of power. I had never fully owned before how much darkness I had in me. This was very hard to do. Even harder was to forgive myself for the harm I had done, epitomized by what I had done to my mother.

I was able to do that with much cathartic sobbing and with Rush's help and encouragement to just let it all go. It was the most powerful work I had ever done on myself. I knew if I could integrate my dark side by owning it fully and no longer repressing it, then I wouldn't need to have a Peter or a Paul to play out my dark side for me. I could just play with my own—transmuted to the heart level or higher, of course.

As I felt myself becoming more whole and comfortable with my power and as my heart opened as a channel for this, I visited my father in the Philippines, where he lived as a sort of modern-day South Seas pirate. I hadn't seen him in many years.

Beside the fact that he had invited me, which was a sign in itself, my purpose for this journey was for karmic healing with him. Before I went, I did past life work with Rush, which revealed there were many lessons to learn from this five-week visit with my father, who lived in the middle of nowhere, on the island of Mindanao in the Sulu Sea, just north of Borneo.

In some past lives with him, I saw that I had condoned and even encouraged his dark side, as it served my purposes. But it was never directed back at me—just as in this life. So who was I to judge?

I needed to love and accept him just as he is, dark side and all. I no longer needed to create separation from him on the heart levels by judging how he chose to live his life. What a relief. I no longer needed to be his—or anyone else's—karmic judge or jury. Each soul is their own anyway, and I was more than ready to relinquish the role.

Now I don't need to question why someone is the way they are. I only need to see clearly exactly what *I am* doing with them. As I released this judging role, I started feeling more connected on the heart levels with my father. I didn't need to seek his energy elsewhere to connect with him by proxy.

This healing journey to visit my father popped something open in my heart that just wasn't ready to be opened until then. When I returned, I started feeling more connected to everyone.

I had always protected my heart because it felt so incredibly vulnerable. After surviving my relationships with Peter, Paul and my father, my heart started to feel strong enough to open more fully. My relationships with these very dark male energies had activated my own dark side in a way that I could own without judgment of myself or anyone else's dark side. Most importantly, I didn't need to be drawn to complete myself by magnetizing dark energy in a mate. I had my own.

Traveling to Mindanao was a four-day ordeal, with my usual horrific travel karma of missed connections every step of the way. I was walking with a cane from a recent Achilles' tendon sprain, which was quite painful and debilitating—some dramatic symbolism for my journey.

As soon as I got to Mindanao, supposedly for a cruise on Dad's new yacht, I was tested. The boat was only half-built and lying like a beached whale on stilts in dry dock. I asked my Dad, "How could you invite me on a cruise when there is no boat?"

His reply, which was so impeccably him, was, "Wishful thinking?" I realized, after spending some time with him, that he was lonely and wanted my company, but he was afraid I wouldn't come *just* to spend time with him. Sadly, he was probably right in his tactics before the visit, but only partially right after it.

Although I still have a residue of being attracted to darkly good-looking con artists, big talkers and snake-oil salesmen as lovers, it's not nearly as compelling as it used to be. After all, now that I have healed my heart connection within myself and directly with my Dad, projection is redundant. I can just look in the mirror.

Rush saw the earth plane as a giant oasis in the middle of a vast desert with many caravans passing through it. My job was to find those journeyers who were moving in the same direction and speaking the same language I was. I didn't need to dissipate my energies or distract myself by focusing on any of the others. I didn't need to judge them either.

All I have to do now is to be open to meeting my karmic family of fellow travelers at each stage in the journey. I call it "connecting the dots."

# 42

## *Spring Fling*

Even though I had lived in a garden apartment since 1977, I never really got into gardening until Paul left in the spring of 1992. Propitiously, at around the same time, my long-time next-door neighbors whom I shared the backyard moved out, further inspiring me to claim this outdoor space as more my own, before the next neighbors moved in.

Just as I was reclaiming my inner space as all my own for the first time ever, I also claimed my outdoor private space. As I started to expand psychically, my outer garden began blooming beautifully as well.

I knew I needed to find a teacher to study the internal energy arts with, as a way to ground and energize myself in my body. I had almost burnt out my nervous system and fried myself from running so much psychic juice through me over the last decade or so. I had even contracted Lyme disease the previous fall, which further debilitated me.

Having regular hands-on healing sessions with Rush, as well as weekly bodywork sessions and monthly acupuncture, became a necessity just to keep myself going psychically. I needed to find a way to regenerate myself and become my own generator of energy—not just a channel for it—as my readings kept suggesting. My nervous system, which was the physical equivalent of my psychic circuitry, was becoming increasingly frayed.

Chi gong seemed to fit the bill. These are ancient mind/body energy exercises from China which allow fresh life force energy, chi, to circulate through the body for vitality and health. I started studying spontaneous healing chi gong, with a fire method teacher who was originally from Shanghai. After a year, I realized that fire method, even though I loved it and had a natural affinity for it, was fraying my wiring even more. I found a water method teacher for chi gong and tai chi, Franz, whose system was a much gentler modality for all levels of my body. This helped root me to the earth and strengthen my nervous system gradually without strain. I knew that I was finally on the right path to empower and ground myself without using meat or men.

By that fall, I felt as if I had a lot of plates spinning simultaneously in my life. The book was coming along, as was my private practice. I was enjoying being in my garden and doing chi gong daily, as well as swimming a mile three times a week for aerobics and circuit training for developing more muscle mass. I had lost twenty pounds and felt great.

I decided to go on my first scuba vacation in February 1993, after being certified that fall. Paul had never wanted me to dive, as he thought it was too dangerous, plus anything as equipment-intensive as scuba was a challenge for my energy system. Getting certified was a real accomplishment, equally as fear-inducing as learning to drive.

I went to Bonaire for ten days and enjoyed the diving, especially the sensations of floating under water like a fish. I discovered that snorkeling, my first love, was just as visually exciting and a lot easier to do on my own, with no buddy necessary (or dive master) and no major equipment challenges. I enjoyed my holiday underwater. On land, it was a different story. I was stoic about it—not the best tone to have on vacation. I became lonely, tired of traveling and being on my own.

When I got back in early March, I had been celibate for eleven months. A new world's record, beating my old record of six weeks from the summer I spent alone in the early eighties. My first week back, I received my monthly seltzer delivery—the old-fashioned kind, in glass bottles with metal nozzles, so it never goes flat. I drank about a case a month, twelve bottles, and considered it a real treat. When the bell rang, I opened the door with my bathrobe on. It wasn't the old delivery guy. It was a new one.

This seltzer man was 6'3", with shoulder-length blond hair, twinkling green eyes and a very mischievous grin. He had the body of a super heavy-weight wrestler and looked like a Viking out of a romance novel. Oh, my. After I paid him for the seltzer, he started flirting with me, and I hadn't even given him a tip. He invited me to keep him company on his delivery route around the city, but I declined. Still, I couldn't get him out of my mind after he left.

I knew I was operating on a higher plane psychically than ever before, but simultaneously I was aware that spring was in the air and that, as Cyndi Lauper sang, "Girls just wanna have fun!" I needed to talk it through with my friend Laura, who's my role-model for all things adventurous and free-spirited. Laura concurred that it would be good for me to have a spring fling, especially since the guy was literally delivered to my door. It was some kind of sign. Even if it wasn't serious, she reminded me that at least the seltzer he delivers will never go flat. We had quite a hoot about that.

I called the seltzer company the next day and left a message for my delivery guy to call me. I didn't say why. But the wise-ass who took the message told my guy, "Some lady has the hots for you." When he called, I found out his name was Jake and I invited him over ASAP. He came over the next day, and we had a reasonably hot time. Jake was very friendly and generous with his tongue and cock, which was long and hard, like his torso, and exceptionally thick, as was his mind, unfortunately.

Jake was in his early thirties, extremely easy-going and good-natured. He was an airplane mechanic, in between jobs, a bit down on his luck, with some ongoing beer and recreational drug use thrown into his story. I couldn't come up with any deep karmic bond with him, even though I tried. The most I could intuit was that he had fixed the wheels of my chariot in ancient Rome. Obviously, there was nothing too heavy going on here, which was just fine after my nearly year-long drought.

Not only did Jake look like a storybook Viking, he ate, drank and fucked like one as well. We had a couple of good months together. He'd come down from his place in Connecticut and spend weekends with me, and I'd barbecue rare meat in the garden and replenish his beer supply as needed. He reminded me of one of the guys I had been seeing when I hit bottom in 1980 (only his act was cleaned up a little), big and sweet, with cartoon watching his entertainment of choice.

We had virtually nothing in common, except for the sexual chemistry and the visual aesthetic. It fizzled out after a couple of months, when we ran out of absolutely anything to talk about. It concerned me though. I had this weak area when it came to visual attraction overriding any higher level of interaction. This was one I was really getting ready to get over, once and for all. I was getting tired, as well, of the concern of well-meaning friends who were afraid that my choice of men was regressive to my spiritual and psychic growth. While I assured them that my affair with the seltzer man (whom I never let anyone meet) was just the "pause that refreshes," I was aware that I wasn't being scrupulously honest with myself.

# Sexual Interlude—Looking Through the Eyes of the Visual Aesthetic

What is beauty? When I looked into the eyes of any client after I channeled a soul reading for them, all I saw as I was coming out of trance was the unique beauty of their soul. This was true of every client, even those who appeared exceptionally unattractive by cultural, aesthetic or even personal standards when they first walked through my door.

I could even raise the level of my visual perspective when I was looking around sobriety meetings, spiritual retreats or watching people go by from a sidewalk cafe. So why couldn't I do it with a potential lover?

I started realizing, during my time with Jake, that I was hitting a new level of bottoming out—an all-time low—in how I related to men. My priorities sucked. For someone who now prided herself on always putting her spiritual evolution first, this appeared to be a weak link in my developmental chain.

At a distance, my perspective with other human beings was soul to soul. I saw them from a very detached, objective, witnessing perspective with minimal personal coloring. But let anyone into my potential sexual range, and it was as if I was looking at them under a visual aesthetic magnifying glass in which all I could see, in great detail, was the surface.

This character defect really bugged me when I saw it in operation with men. I found it positively repugnant. Even if it was primally induced and culturally condoned, it was hard for me to not judge men harshly if they were drawn to model looks, blond hair and blue eyes, big breasts or whatever their particular turn-on was. This seemed so superficial when one was really looking to give and receive love. I knew, theoretically, that once one saw with the eyes of love, especially on the soul level, then the beloved becomes transmogrified with beauty. I just didn't know how to quite get there, especially if sex was going to be in the picture.

This weakness in me came out the most when I was in between more serious relationships—on the rebound or just getting back into action. That's when I more easily succumbed to "boy-toys" or blond Vikings. But it was always an important factor. It was obviously time to work on raising the level of my perspective in all my dealings, because the superficial level of the visual aesthetic had been seeping into affairs of the heart for as long as I can remember—and that's a *long* time, karmically speaking.

I made a commitment to try to see the beauty in short, fat, balding middle-aged men—as well, as my usual preferences—not replacing, just expanding my range. This immediately more than quadrupled my options. If I decided to fully own my bisexuality, I could fall in love with most everyone on the planet, in theory anyway.

In practice, this worked pretty well for me with a balding, pudgy guy whom I met at the Christmas party of a scuba club in 1993. I was sitting on his lap, flirting, convinced that he would be just like a cuddly bear in bed. Unfortunately, the guy was scared shitless by my attentions. At least, now that I was aware of this shortcoming, I was willing to try to not be ruled by it anymore.

Just before I went to Egypt with Rush for three weeks in January 1994, I did a reading for the trip. My guides told me to close my eyes when I was in the inner sanctums of temples or anywhere the psychic energy felt particularly intense. Instead of looking around me, I was directed to place my hands on the altars or on the walls and *just feel.* By being still with my eyes wide shut, my inner psychic vision would become more fully activated.

It was a revelation to me that I would see more by feeling more first. By leading with my heart and psychic receptivity, I would get the most from this trip. My channel warned me that, because of my overly developed visual nature, I would miss the most important things by just looking with the physical senses. Only my inner vision and heart/mind could see and feel what truly mattered.

If Egypt was going to be my initiation into the next level of my psychic power through communion with the Divine, then why couldn't it also be my initiation into the next level of relating with other human beings as vehicles for this Divine communion?

After this reading, I felt lazy and whined to Rush," Why do we have to travel all the way to Egypt when we're always there when we're together?"

"For nostalgia." Rush responded. "You have no idea how time falls away when you're floating down the Nile."

# 43

## *When Time Falls Away*

I knew that one day I would have to go back to Egypt with Rush. It took over twenty years before we actually got around to doing it. Our karmic connections psychically were the most positive and powerful from our time together there as High Priest and Priestess, when we would meet for ritual ceremonies. This connection was activated automatically whenever we were together. The psychic juice running between us was so strong it would just overflow and move us into the same multidimensional space that transcended linear time which we were always in together in Egypt.

Rush had already been to Egypt twice before, so he knew the ropes and had a private guide and itinerary lined up for us. I also knew that Rush was ill and sensed that he might be on his way out from cancer by the age of sixty. Time was of the essence. We needed to go before Rush was too weak to make this arduous journey. He was fifty-seven.

A week before our scheduled three week trip in January 1994, the State Department issued a security warning for U.S. citizens traveling to Egypt. There had been a terrorist attack on a busload of European tourists just before the holidays, and most tour companies, here and abroad, canceled all their tours for January. Rush and I concurred that now was an even better time to go because no one would be crowding us out of the sites when we wanted to do psychic energy work.

With my lousy travel karma, especially overseas, I did have Rush check my astrological transits, and of course, he confirmed my worst fears. "It looks like your going to get shot by terrorists," Rush said definitively. After looking at his chart, which had excellent travel karma, I replied," Well, I guess I'll be standing behind you the whole trip." We had a good laugh, and with that tone, we embarked on our journey together.

The flight over on Egypt Air was uneventful. We settled into a four-star Egyptian-run hotel after Abdul, our guide, helped us through customs. The view from the window of our suite was of the three pyramids, seen clearly at a distance through a haze of smog. Abdul was expert at making our every move smooth, easy and effortless. I immediately nicknamed him "the Vizier."

We were so jetlagged that we went to sleep as soon as possible after an early supper. All night long, I watched as literally thousands of energy entities dive-bombed into Rush's being. They were so excited to have one of their "hosts" back. The air was thick with psychic energy that activated my third eye in a way that made me quite dizzy.

The whole time I was in Egypt, but especially Cairo, I had to hold on to walls as I walked because everything would start spinning uncontrollably. The psychic energy frequencies were so high speed that my inner gyroscope went completely berserk. I felt my inner axis starting to shift immediately. Rush's third eye was shifting more on the inner levels, without as much external somatizing. He said his third eye was cracking and popping so intensely, it was almost painful at times. What a team.

That first morning, I showered and plugged my hair dryer with the appropriate adapter into a still-moist outlet in the bathroom without thinking. It seems that I neglected to plug in the adaptor plug to the transformer first—interesting symbolism. Just thinking about it, even now, blows my circuits.

Not only did I blow out what I had plugged in, I also blew all the fuses in our suite of rooms. Since Abdul couldn't seem to find a replacement adapter in all of Cairo (I didn't understand at the time that I could have used the same plug, just *with* the transformer), all our electrical appliances, from electric toothbrushes to my beloved vibrator, became dead weight in our baggage. The good news was that, with Lil' Oscar out of commission, I had even more energy to transmute psychically.

We planned to do our major psychic work in Cairo on the last five days of the trip. We only visited the Sphinx and pyramids once and spent the rest of our first few days doing the Egyptian Museum, the mosques and the old Jewish quarter. It was damp and overcast the whole time. We did manage to warm up a bit doing some energy work daily on a rooftop sundeck overlooking the pyramids from our hotel.

After a few days in Cairo, where we got over our jet lag, we proceeded to our next stop, Aswan. There we had a full-moon boat ride under a clear sky to the temple of Isis in Aswan and a color-and-light show. We flew south the next morning to Abu-Simbel, which Rush said was a must-see. It was very impressive. It felt huge and monumental and grounding, the root chakra of the upper Nile.

Then, after flying back to Aswan, we boarded a cruise ship for a three-day cruise down the Nile. Our boat was not one of the five-star large ships built just for tourists. This one was a four-star smaller Egyptian boat, and we were the only non-Egyptians aboard. It was filled to the rafters with families on vacation, and no one on board spoke any English. We asked Abdul to stay with us on the cruise, in case we needed a translator. It was a very good thing we did.

Because it was such a short cruise, I wanted to get the most out of it. I got up every day at dawn and did my chi gong on deck before anyone else was up. As we cruised down the Nile with the wind slapping me in the face, time really did fall away. I felt as if I could be cruising down the Nile at any point in human history, or every point, or no point at all.

Not only did time fall away; parts of me started falling away too. I felt as if the Nile breeze stripped clean layer upon layer of ego armor that had accumulated over my essential nature since I had last been in Egypt millennia ago.

I remembered who I really was at the core for the first time in this life. I experienced my essential nature as fundamentally pure sweetness. This came as quite a shock—and probably would to a lot of people who had known me up to that point. I had forgotten who I was at the center of my being for so long. I saw all the layers of ego that were falling away as the necessary protection of that sweetness, until I had activated enough psychic power to let it shine through again, like it had before—in Egypt.

That first day, on the deck at dawn, my ego felt swept clean. It felt like a translucent tool that my soul could use for horizontal functioning—no more armor, no more baggage, nothing to defend. For the first time, I felt free of the encumbering burden and bondage of self. I had been praying for this for years. I wept with joy, though I also felt trepidation for what was to come next.

What came next is that I got a case of severe food poisoning the second day on board. I was doubled over with intestinal spasms and had to spend the morning in bed with crackers and soda that Abdul got for me and peppermint tea and Imodium that I had packed. I had eaten salad the night before, forgetting this was an Egyptian boat, and the water the vegetables were washed in would not be OK for me, while the natives onboard would be acclimated to it. Fortunately, Rush had skipped the salad.

By the time we got to our first tour stop, Kom Ombo, in the late afternoon, I insisted on going ashore, weak as I was. Rush and Abdul literally carried me, one on each arm, as we toured the temple complex. I was so fragile that my knees kept buckling, and at one point, I had to lie down near some samples of ancient surgical and medical instruments next to a carving of Sobek, the crocodile-headed god of the Nile. Resting next to these implements that were used for healing made ironic sense to me, as did viewing carvings of Sobek. I had always seen my beagle, Luna, as an incarnation of one of my favorite "crocs" that I used to feed on the banks of the Nile.

In fact, when Luna was bad, which she often was, I used to threaten her, saying that if she didn't shape up, this might be her first and last time as a mammal for awhile. She would turn her head completely upside down and give me her toothy, mischievous crocodile smile. I remembered all this synchronistically with a half-smile as I lay moaning weakly at Kom Ombo, until Rush and Abdul carried me back to the boat.

By the next stop, Edfu, the following afternoon, I was up and about again, but Rush had succumbed this time. He had eaten fish the night before, which I hadn't (still being weak), and he got a much worse case of food poisoning than me. Either that, or his system was much weaker to begin with.

Lying in bed, he took my hand, looked me in the eye and solemnly said, "My time has come. Bury me at Karnak." He actually almost convinced me that he was dying, until I remembered how dramatic Rush could be at times.

I said, "Don't be ridiculous," and promptly got Abdul (thank God, he was on board), to fetch a doctor as soon as we docked. Rush was prescribed some serious medicine, as he was severely dehydrated after leaking from both ends for twelve hours or so.

Once Rush assured me he was stabilized and wasn't going to leave his body just yet, I got off the boat at Edfu with Abdul to tour the temple complex devoted to Horus. As we walked around, Abdul whispered pertinent historical facts about the sites. I didn't absorb it consciously at the time, but Abdul must have said something about Edfu being identically to its sister temple, Dendera, the temple to Hathor, Horus's spouse.

When I got to the inner sanctum (always the third level in), Abdul bribed the guard not let anyone else into the area while I was working with the energy there. I placed my hands on the altar and closed my eyes. Then, a thundering voice inside my head, roared, *"You must go to Dendera."* This message was repeated several times until the inside of my skull felt like it was going to burst, and I yelled back, *"All right! I hear you."* I got visuals of yearly trips up the Nile from Dendera to Edfu, where, Abdul told me later, the priestesses of Dendera went for seasonal ceremonies. The message was so insistent; it eradicated any other thought in my head. I went outside and told Abdul (almost like I had been programmed), "I must go to Dendera, wherever that is."

Abdul told me it was not on the itinerary and that, besides being a special full-day trip from Luxor (our next stop), it was officially off-limits to tourists because of terrorist activity in the area. Not only was it dangerous, he said, it was costly, and he tried to dissuade me from the idea.

I talked it over with Rush. He said he'd already been there once and felt no inclination to return, but I should honor my inner voice and go, even though he was too weak to accompany me. Besides, Rush already knew that Karnak at Luxor was his spiritual home.

We were scheduled to spend three days in Luxor. Abdul had booked us into a quite luxurious four-star Egyptian-run hotel, with excellent food and a view of the Nile from our balcony. We definitely needed some R&R after our cruise, and we spent the first afternoon resting in the sun near the pool, as the temperature was finally warming up into the low 70s.

Our first full day in Luxor, we toured the Valley of the Kings and Queens on the West Bank in the morning. Many of the sites required arduous climbs down and up steep stairs in a modified duck-walking position to see some of the more elaborate tombs. Rush passed on a lot of the strenuous stuff as he was still weak and preserving his energy for Karnak.

Rush's spiritual home was at Karnak because that's where he had been High Priest. This was his third visit, and as we approached it for the first time, along the Avenue of the Sphinxes (and after touring the Temple of Luxor two miles away that leads to it geometrically), the psychic energy was humming so crisply that we immediately entered into an intense altered-state time-warp together.

It was not that Rush and I had never been in a time-warp together, as our energies synergized at that level spontaneously—it was that Karnak itself, a vast temple complex extending over one square mile, was the original sacred space of that time-warp. We were on hallowed ground together, just like in the good old days, and we were grinning from ear to ear.

For two days, we got up at dawn to be at the temple complex as soon as it opened at 7:30 AM. That way, we could be assured of at least an hour and a half before any of the tour buses arrived. Then, we came back in the late afternoon, after the tourists had thinned out and the heat of the day had waned, to meditate at the large sacred pool at sunset. Karnak was relatively empty most of the day anyway because of the threat of terrorist attacks. That gave us an extremely rare opportunity to do serious, uninterrupted work there.

With the place almost to ourselves, except for the guards, we frolicked about, doing our psychic initiation rituals at all the old familiar power spots. At one point, Rush transferred the power to me for moving from being an initiate to one who can initiate others. During this ceremony, in which I moved from being what would have been called a Priestess to a High Priestess, I actually felt ready to move to this level of responsibility. I felt as if I was donning a mantle of golden light.

Timing is everything. The main reason I was ready for this initiation, besides the twenty-some years of psychic work I had done on myself and others, was because of some work I had done the summer before. At a chi gong retreat in California with my teacher Franz, I reached a point of dealing with a new level of power and responsibility on the last day, when we were practicing at the ocean.

We were supposed to be putting together everything we had learned all week with the energies of the ocean and move all this through our being—all the energies of heaven and earth. At a certain point, the energy movements all came together for me in my body. I started weeping with the immeasurable power and energy at my disposal. I wept because I had been given a priceless gift through these teachings—and I wept because of the enormous responsibility that went with all this power. It was overwhelming. As I asked the Higher Forces what to do with this gift of power and limitless supply of energy, I was told: *"There is nothing to do with it … except pass it on."*

The second afternoon at Karnak, we discovered, to the north of the complex, an open air museum that was closed to tourists, and, fortunately, there were no guards there. We snuck into the museum and had several hours of private time there. Rush found a beautiful alabaster and limestone altar carved with erotic images inside of a space of open-air arches and decided to lie down on it for awhile. He recalled that he had "made whoopee" on this altar with young priestesses as part of their initiation into the mysteries. He laughed as he rocked and rolled picking up all the vibrations and memories emanating from the stone altar.

As I witnessed him accessing these memories, I said, "Things haven't changed that much." Since initiating me sexually many years prior, he had been doing it with female students and clients ever since as part of their healing. While not very ethical by modern standards, it was certainly appropriate as part of ritual ceremonies for a High Priest in ancient Egypt.

Because of Rush's predilection to live out his role of High Priest in this life—it was a karmic high point for him, after all—I had learned to warn any women I sent to him for psychic healing, especially the young ones. I told them that he had unorthodox ways of implementing psychic healing and actualizing their psychic powers. Most of them went for it anyway. He nailed them all, leaving them with few regrets—in the long run, anyway. I remembered that, in ancient Egypt, I had sent young initiates to him as well—like lambs to the slaughter, but in a good way. Because then, as now, some of them came out the other side as lionesses.

Rush's home was definitely Karnak, and it resonated vibrationally for both of us in the solar plexus, the power chakra. While I enjoyed visiting with Rush at his home, by the third day it was time for me to return to my home at Dendera. It was calling to me.

Early that morning, Abdul and I set off in a rented car with a driver for a three-hour ride on deserted roads. At checkpoints along the way, we were instructed to give our papers to Egyptian soldiers with machine guns who looked us over suspiciously, as we were traveling in a restricted area and there were no other tourists about.

When we got to Dendera, I felt as if I was entering onto the sacred ground of my spiritual home. Just inside the outer wall, there was a spacious courtyard with large fallen statues of the dwarf god Bes. My heart soared. I remembered the dream ceremony years before where I was proclaimed queen of the dwarves and given the golden key to their kingdom.

As I entered the main temple of Hathor, the goddess of love, joy and beauty, I saw the zodiac carvings on the ceiling. I tried not to hold my breath in anticipation of what was to come. When we got into the inner sanctum, at the back of the temple near a statue of Hathor, Abdul pointed out where the priestesses healed the supplicants through holes leading to the external walls. I felt as if I had found my old office where I had done work similar to what I do now.

Down in the crypts, underneath my old office in the sanctuary, were decorative carvings that looked like pictorial stories of aliens landing on the earth in large space ships. I was amazed that these drawings looked extremely similar to the type of art I do in this lifetime. The drawings in the crypt felt so surreally familiar, I felt as if I had done the original sketches for them as well.

Up on the roof was a chapel of the sun disc with reliefs of the god Osirus, which were used for annual rituals during the seasons of inundation. On the staircase up to the roof, there was a small open court with a drawing of the sky goddess Nut on the ceiling. She is stretched over the ceiling of the sky to protect all beings, earthly and celestial, under her care. This image of Nut protecting the sky was so powerful that I had to get a copy of it in Cairo to keep over my desk at home, so I can feel Nut's protection as I'm writing this now. I tried to find copies of the carvings in the crypt of the alien landings, but, unfortunately, there don't appear to be any. This was one of my few travels when I regretted not having a camera.

On leaving the main temple, I walked down a staircase into the center of the sacred lake, where waterborne ceremonies were held. It was drained and over-grown with plants—mostly large ferns and some small trees. When I looked up at the sun from the center of the lake, I remembered floating on my back there often, in moonlight as well as sunlight, to center and replenish myself for my life of service.

I realized at Dendera, more concretely than ever before, how much continuity there is in my work as a psychic and spiritual teacher. Dendera had been my high point of selfless heart-centered service, when I was a consort to the Divine, com-pletely cloaked in the mysteries. I'm afraid it's been somewhat downhill since then. In those days, sexual union was reserved only for seasonal rituals enacted as part of these mysteries, and I took my responsibilities in this area much more seri-ously than Rush.

While I left Dendera physically that day, I knew I would never again leave it psychically. I would always be there. The memory of my time there is an ongoing inspiration in my work with clients, enacting with them the same mysteries for healing and evolution that I did at Dendera. I am aware that I am working with many of the same souls as clients who have come back to me for the next level of activation or, simply, a refresher course.

From Luxor, Rush and I flew to a resort on the Red Sea for a few days of rest and sun. We snorkeled amidst the most incredibly intense iridescent colors I had ever seen, caused by the concentration of salt in the water. It was mesmerizing to watch thousand of giant clams opening and closing with the rhythm of the waves, flashing neon pink, turquoise and purple speckled mouths at us. I went snorkel-ing everyday on a rented boat, but Rush only went with me once, as he was rest-ing up for the work to come in Cairo. He was starting to get pretty worn out from the intensity of the energy as well as his failing health.

Upon our return to Cairo, my inner gyroscope went completely berserk again. Being on a boat for three days probably exacerbated my destabilization, but I was glad I hadn't gone diving, due to zero visibility beneath the surface. If I had, the psychic "bends" I had would probably have been even worst, although I can't imagine how.

I was being bombarded with high-speed psychic frequencies of energy that were hitting my third eye. I was so dizzy that I had no balance or depth percep-tion whatsoever and had to hold on to something or I couldn't walk straight. In the shower, or any small enclosed space, everything started to spin so fast that I had to sit down and close my eyes. Just thinking about this energy effect now makes me start feeling the spinning again. Rush was faring better outwardly on the physical levels from the effects of this energy, but on the inner levels his third eye was going berserk as well. He told me it was much more intense than on any other visit.

After a dawn horseback ride on the approach to the pyramids, that I took without Rush, we arrived at the Great Pyramid as soon as it opened so we could get a good forty-five minutes alone in the King's Chamber before any tour groups arrived. Once in the King's Chamber, we took turns lying in the sarcophagus and doing energy work with each other from that position.

We knew this was one of the places where the final tests for initiates were done. We wanted a little taste and review for remembrance sake. The final test involved being sealed in the sarcophagus for a week. If one survived, by slowing down all body systems and moving into an altered state, then one became a formal initiate into the mysteries. Many died in the attempt, because they could not master their fear. Those who didn't survive are some of the souls Rush and I seem to magnetize to work with, though we also work with some of the ones who did.

On the flight home, I jokingly said to Rush, about a half-hour outside of JFK, that it looked as if his good travel karma had outweighed my not-so-good karma in that area. Just as I said that, the pilot announced that we were being rerouted to Toronto, as all airports on the eastern seaboard were closed due to blizzard conditions. Rush looked at me, with a look that said, *"You had to go and open your mouth, didn't you?"*

A fiasco ensued in Toronto that was completely typical of my travel karma. Because we were just about the only Americans on board an Egypt Air flight, we were not allowed to leave the terminal at first because none of the other passengers had visas for Canada. When the Canadian authorities finally let all of us get on a bus for a hotel, the front desk wouldn't give us rooms because Egypt Air had no official office in Toronto to represent us. Alitalia was supposed to give us vouchers for hotel rooms, but my experience with lost luggage on Alitalia didn't give me much hope. Chaos ensued.

Finally, with our Egyptian pilot attempting to vouch for us and with over a hundred Egyptians in turbans yelling, I resorted to my usual desperate act in such circumstances. I grabbed a hotel clerk and informed him that if I didn't get a room immediately, I was going to pass out, and he would be liable for the consequences. With room keys in hand, I found Rush, calmly having a beer in the bar and gave him his key. He had no idea of what traveling with me could be like until this.

After a good night's sleep, a hot bath and a meal, we were back on the runway the next day in a plane so decrepit we were afraid it wouldn't be able to take off.

It didn't help our concerns that the flight attendants had us all sit in the front half of the plane to help it take-off. Rush again expressed amazement at the abysmal nature of my travel karma, as he had never seen anything like it. All along the way in Egypt there had been almost daily trivial inconveniences that were par for the course for me, but which he had never experienced before.

I thanked him for acknowledging the courage it took for me to travel at all, considering the nature of my astrological circumstances, and he jokingly said he would never travel overseas with me again. We parted at the airport, back to our separate abodes, more deeply bonded than ever, on more levels than I knew were possible. We were ready to embark on the next leg of our soul's journey.

# 44

## *What Was I Thinking?*

One would think, after Egypt, that my propensity to be led by my visual aesthetic would have come into balance more. The only way I can explain what happened a little over a month after my return is that I was in a reaction mode I have come to call the spiritual cha-cha: two steps forward, one step back. In this case, it was more like a running leap backwards.

I had been celibate since my breakup with Jake back in late August, and spring was in the air. Or at least the sap was starting to rise in my own mind. I always feel as if I'm coming out of hibernation in my cave by the ides of March—and this mama bear was looking for honey.

I was at one of my recovery meetings in Soho, the kind where everyone splits up into circles of eight people to share on a topic after the speaker has qualified and set the tone. Across from me in the circle was a giant of a man. He looked like an oversized, slightly caricatured version of the Dutch actor, Rutger Hauer, one of my visual crushes at the time. I was so mesmerized by this man's size, his rugged good looks and long blond hair, I failed to pay attention to the fact that what came out of his mouth while he was sharing was so slow and plodding—it was the opposite of whatever a mental giant is.

After my initial sighting, I arranged for a mutual acquaintance to set up an intro for me which flowed into a coffee date at the same meeting the following week. This acquaintance, Siggy, warned me on the phone that as much as he liked the giant, whose name was Tom, he was sure I would be so bored that I would fall asleep over dinner with my face in the soup bowl, never even making it to the main course. I assured him that wouldn't happen, as I wasn't particularly interested in talking much anyway.

It turned out that Tom looked so much like Rutger Hauer he had actually worked as his stand-in in movies, as part of working as an extra. No lines required. (Now there's a clue.) He also made a living selling his art on the street, his particular niche being quite beautiful, intricate etchings and woodcuts.

Because Tom was quite talented creatively and could actually make a meager living from his art, I was impressed enough to be blind to the sad fact that he was not as well developed in any other area, except his anatomy.

Tom was hung like a stallion and, it turned out, hadn't been involved with a woman or had sex in the five years since he had gotten sober. While it took a time or two in bed for him to get over some initial atrophy, Tom turned out to be an eager, athletic lover with exceptional stamina. He was a marathoner, not a sprinter. Hallelujah and praise the lord!

The spiritual and psychic high points I had activated in Egypt were culminating in the publication of my first psychic book. At the same time I was doing the final proofreading of my book, I was having the affair with Tom. The reaction mode I was in was so severe that the split in me—between my desire and spiritual natures—felt deeper than ever before. Obviously, what I thought I had worked on healing was rising up with a vengeance to be healed at the next level.

One day in bed in our second month together, I looked up at Tom as he was laboring above me, holding his weight up by his strong arms, as he was pumping me into oblivion for indefinite periods. It was as if I was really seeing him for the first time.

I saw that, with his shoulder-length, straight blond hair flapping on either side of his long, giant-sized, ruggedly strong-boned face, he looked exactly like an Irish setter, even down to the doglike look of unconditional love and devotion in his eyes.

I realized, right then and there, that I was in very deep karmic poo-poo. I was using this poor, sweet giant of a guy as if he were my personal sex pet—one of the darker aspects of my karmic rut. Worse yet, he was in love with me, as only someone with a hermit karmic pattern with minimal social or emotional skills could be. His heart and sexual energies had been activated by me in a one-two knockout karmic punch. This made me responsible for letting him down easily without harming or causing him any suffering except growing pains. If I failed, I was setting myself up for some serious karma repercussions.

The good news was that Tom was coming out of his hermit shell and feeling emotionally alive for the first time in a very long time. The bad news was I lied and told him I was in love with him, and then tried to convince myself I wasn't just saying it so as not to rock the boat. I tried to believe it, but inside I knew I had crossed the line this time—I had never been this emotionally dishonest before in an intimate relationship.

I deluded myself enough so that we had an idyllic spring of romantic hand-holding and late night strolls down foggy West Village streets, sipping cappuccinos at picturesque, little outdoor cafes near where he lived. He made me breakfast in bed and enjoyed feeding me as his beloved mistress, while I enjoyed looking at his body while he fed me—or fed on me. Since we had little to talk about when we weren't in bed, I encouraged going on outings to the Cloisters or biking on paths near the Hudson. Tom was so devoted to taking care of me that if I fell off my bike, which happened a few times as my balance sucked, he loved to clean and bandage my scraped and bleeding knees and shins.

Tom insisted we have a barbeque party in my garden so that all our friends could meet and acknowledge us as a couple. I complied, but nobody showed up from his social circle except one woman, because he didn't really have any friends, only acquaintances. A dozen or so of my friends showed up, mostly in couples. Tom did all the cooking, while I mingled with our guests. It all felt like a sham to me; Tom and I were the least likely couple there. I could see this was true in my friends' eyes as well, although they were all too polite to ever say anything, and I was too perceptive to ever ask.

By the beginning of summer, Tom was beginning to lose his erection in the middle of fucking, and I knew (even if he didn't) that it was because he was feeling used. He wasn't very conscious of why—because he wasn't very conscious. In his emotional insecurity, he wanted promises of commitment from me that were not forthcoming. As his emotional needs were not being met, he became more and more impotent. We spiraled downward.

By the time we went on a biking and camping trip to Cape Cod in August, Tom's sexual dysfunction was so flipping him out that his mood swings became a turn-off. I knew I was not willing to have the kind of patience for the long-term emotional investment Tom needed for a turnaround sexually. It would involve therapy for him, couples counseling for us, sexual sensitivity exercises and all of that.

So I ended it, as I always do, with a clean, clear, unequivocal break. It was a surprisingly hard and painful action for me to take. Maybe I had gotten more swept away in the endorphin rush of pretending I was in love than I had planned. Unexpectedly, in the midst of the pain of the break-up, I felt more incredibly alive than I had ever felt before.

I felt as if I was letting go of the next level of karmic attachment to using men as sexual objects—at least in terms of their physical beauty. It created too much heartache, not to mention karma. I liked Tom, and I loved and cared for him in the sense of my heart being open toward him, but I was not romantically in love with him. There weren't enough components at play for him to represent "the other" for me, and he was much too jammed up emotionally to just be my play-mate with no strings attached.

Tom's pain, because of the imbalance in our feelings for each other, became too much for me to bear. He even asked me to marry him as a last, absurd, des-perate attempt to keep me. He really didn't have a clue. Maybe I could have borne Tom's unhappiness longer if he hadn't somatized it into a limp dick.

This was definitely the weakest link in my karmic rut chain of development. I have no excuses, only sincere regret. My hope is that, in cracking open Tom's heart again, it inspired him to do the inner work to keep it open and not go back into his hermit karmic pattern.

# 45

## *The Concubine Chronicles*

The fall season of 1994 passed uneventfully on the personal front, after my breakup with Tom, and I put all my energies into getting my book ready for publication in the spring.

I was reasonably well toasted on the idea of "pretty boys" being a turn-on anymore. That means I was ready for the next level of my karmic rut to come up to be cleared. I didn't know it yet, but I was moving from a primary attachment to my visual aesthetic of beauty in men—which was just the tip of the karmic iceberg in this department—to a primary attachment to sensual pleasures as the be-all and end-all.

I first met Vic at a winter solstice party at the school where I studied chi gong and tai chi. We had some repartee over the cheese tray about aliens and mucous-producing foods, as he was just getting over a cold and wolfing down large quantities of the stuff. I developed an immediate and extremely strong energetic and visual revulsion to him. My visceral aversion to Vic was equal to his visceral attraction to me. He started following me around the party like a hungry lapdog.

Vic told me he was living with someone and "sort of" engaged; he was a scuba diver and an entrepreneur with a hand in various businesses such as real estate, music and restaurants. When I was thirsty, he waited on me, serving me seltzer on his knees, as if he were making me an offering. This piqued my interest enough, in some vaguely queasy way, to dance with him. Even though it was a fast dance, and I kept my distance, I again felt repulsed by his sheer physicality on the dance floor.

When I left the party, he gave me his card, which I tore up with a shiver as soon as I walked out the door. However, I had given him my number, in an impulse of misguided friendliness and codependence, as he was an acquaintance of Robin, who ran the school. A few days after the party, I told her I would never go out with Vic if he dared to call me. Something not quite right about him for me, and I took that as a warning not to get involved.

Nonetheless, the following Saturday was a slow day; I had no plans until the evening, except to get my hair cut in the afternoon. I decided impulsively that whoever called me first, I would say "yes" to. Of course, two minutes later, the phone rang and it was Vic. He met me at my hair salon, and then we went to a neighborhood French bistro for a lazy afternoon lunch that extended into the evening hours.

Over lunch, Vic told me he couldn't get me out of his mind and was completely mesmerized by me. I took a good hard look at him and realized there was something too obsequious about him for me to feel he was a peer. However, I certainly enjoyed how he was feeding my ego. He looked at me so adoringly and he wasn't bad looking. He was forty-five, dark, with a strong, stocky, bull-like body (a typical Taurian physique), and he seemed quite well off financially.

When he drove me to my recovery meeting that night, I surprised myself by not wanting to get out of the car. I had been enjoying his company and didn't want to part yet. He drove me uptown to his office/bachelor pad and we hung out some more. We had many thing in common in terms of likes, at least on the mundane level—traveling, diving, good food, music, theater, New York City and nature.

Vic asked me to give him a hug before we left his place, which I did. He went into a swoon after feeling our bodies connect for a long moment, and I went back into revulsion mode. I told him that I really liked him as a friend, but not to get any ideas.

Over the next couple of months, Vic wooed me assiduously with expensive dinners, theater and foot rubs. Since I was not dating anyone else at the time, I was using him as a filler, but I was also getting quite used to his attentiveness. Still, whenever he kissed me, I felt immediate revulsion. He was such a wet kisser, and his mouth and tongue were so much bigger and juicier than mine that I felt as if I was being invaded, devoured and drowned all at the same time—not a pleasant sensation. However, he did seem to be growing on me as a person.

We went on separate vacations that February. I went to Belize alone, as Rush was too ill by then to accompany me; Vic went with his fiancé to Anguilla. After returning, we wound up a lunch date by lying down on my bed and hugging, fully clothed. In frustration, because I wouldn't respond to his kisses and kept pushing him away, Vic pulled his erect penis out of his pants to "give it some air."

He placed it in my hand and groaned. I gasped—it was humungous. I had no idea. Even though his hands, feet and even nose were all goodly sized, he was hung beyond any rational proportions. I was so impressed I said to him, "You should have done this months ago and we could have saved some time." At least, during those months, we had laid a foundation for a good friendship. After this, we proceeded to be what I called "fuck buddies."

The problem was that Vic was in love with me, and my feelings for him were not romantic at all. I loved him as a friend. Vic was ready to leave his four-year committed, supposedly monogamous relationship with Vera as, over the years, he had become increasingly negative and critical of her. He wanted to move out of their shared apartment and be with me full time. All he was waiting for was my signal. I warned him, "Don't jump ship on my account. There are sharks in the water."

In fact, I encouraged him to stay with Vera because Vic didn't like living on his own, and I definitely was never going to live with him. I encouraged him to compartmentalize his affair with me and try to be nicer to Vera when he was with her.

We entered into what Rush called "duplicitous duck soup." I inspired Vic to use the joy he found with me to spread a little "sunshine"—love and appreciation—Vera's way, thus ameliorating some of the karmic consequences. I figured if Vic got more from me, he could give more to Vera, and everyone would come out a winner.

This worked quite well for a number of years and suited my purposes perfectly. We had our regular bi-or tri-weekly marathon sexual sessions together, and then Vic would go home to Vera. Afterward, I could enjoy my busy social and professional life quite separate from him.

I had no doubt that I was getting the absolute best of Vic in bed. Outside of the bedroom, I found him a bit too plodding mentally, a typical Taurian trait. However, in bed he was extremely stimulating and in small doses—occasional dining out, a weekend in the country here and there, a few exotic adventure-oriented trips—just about perfect. We found a happy medium.

## Karmic Interlude—The Foot Binding Unwinding

The summer before I met Vic, I had started a series of bodywork sessions with my internal arts teacher, Robin, with a specific focus and purpose. After practicing standing chi gong all spring, I realized I had major physical and energetic blockages in my feet. The area that was the most jammed was in the ball of the foot, called the "bubbling-well point," which is one of the major energy gates in the body for chi to flow through.

Because I ran so much psychic juice from my crown down (I call the energy gate in the crown my "blow-hole" like a whale), standing chi gong became excruciatingly painful to do for any length of time. The energy running through me got backed from my feet into my lower legs, since it could find no release.

I knew that, until I could open my feet, I would never be able to be rooted enough to the earth to stabilize my being for the next level of psychic expansion without frying myself. Even though my feet looked very beautiful and delicate aesthetically, with a very high arch, they appeared at size 6 a little too small for my body size, which is more voluptuous than delicate. This could also have been a depth perception problem—like guys with their dicks.

My feet matched my hands in size and delicacy and were the two parts I was routinely complimented on, by men as well as women, besides my porcelain-like skin. Nonetheless, I was willing to develop peasant feet (be careful what you wish for) if they would help me be stronger in my body so I could more easily do my work. Comfort has always won over vanity for me.

In my first massage session with Robin, while she was working on my feet, I realized, in a spontaneous karmic flashback, that she was the one who had bound them in a past life in China! She was my "amah," or nursemaid in that life and when I was around five or six, the binding began. This memory was first activated in my body at the age of six when I wore toe shoes in ballet class. I started screaming bloody murder at the pain.

I didn't blame Robin for binding my feet; I knew she had saved my life by doing it. After a few years of binding—tighter and tighter—my feet looked like tiny tulips in their little red silk shoes. Then I became highly eligible as a number one concubine for some wealthy master.

At that time in China, I might have died of starvation without the foot binding, as I was too frail constitutionally to be a peasant's wife. Jade Flower was my given name in that life. I don't remember any parents, only my amah.

Not only was I ready to free myself from the karmic bondage of being a sex slave, a slave to sex, or enslaving others—I had also met the perfect souls to help me unwind this karma. First, there was Robin—she had assisted me in winding up the karma in the first place. Second, there was Vic—he was my primary master in the life after Peter sold me to him. No wonder I had irrational aversions to them both! Quite legitimate when seen from a past life perspective, which is often the case.

Not surprisingly, Vic was really turned on by my feet. He loved fondling and sucking them when we were making love, especially when he saw how turned on I got when he squeezed them as he was ramming himself into me. It exponentially increased my orgasmic intensity and multiplicity. One of the reasons the Chinese were into foot binding, besides the aesthetics and the practicality of no escape, was that closing down the bubbling well point turned all the sexual juice running through the energy circuitry back into the genital area. This makes it an exceptionally combustible area to light a fire in.

In addition to the karmic concubine activation, Vic was also more than ready to be *my* slave this time to balance the score. This juxtaposition is what gave our sexual chemistry so much heat at the core. On the one hand, I was his possession. He loved to possess, devour and consume me completely, until there was nothing left. On the other hand—or foot I should say—he loved it when I turned the tables on him and made him my sex slave. We took turns.

The majority of the time, our lovemaking turned out to be a spicy mix of both dynamics—sometimes almost simultaneously.

## *Sensual Perfection*

Why was my relationship with Vic different than any other long-term relationship I'd been in before? I was not romantically in love with Vic, and the visual aesthetic didn't work for me either. Not only that, there was no deep spiritual, psychic or mental affinity with Vic as a compensating factor. To top it off, paradoxically, the sex I had with Vic was consistently, over a period of three years of weekly meetings, the best sex I ever had.

Not being in love with Vic meant I had absolutely no twinge of jealousy about him being with Vera when he wasn't with me. I just allowed myself to be fully open when I was with him, and the rest of the time my focus and energy were on whatever or whoever was in front of me. There was never any wasted mental or emotional energy when Vic wasn't around. This was a very liberating dynamic.

I asked myself: How could I enjoy sex with Vic even more than I had enjoyed sex with Paul, with whom I had been passionately in love? One reason (besides my tendency to rewrite history, always focusing on the present moment as the best ever) was that Vic had no inhibitions or idiosyncrasies in bed. He was a completely sensual being. "Anything goes" was his motto and became mine as well. While his development in the sensual area was part of his karmic rut, similar to mine, it did allow my sensual being to flower in my forties in a way that was unprecedented. Timing is everything.

With Paul, or just about anyone else for that matter, I felt the need to stay attuned to their level of inhibition, sexual hang-up or weak area. My tendency was to compensate for them, as I was very adaptable and had a seemingly wide range. The down side was, by being so sensitive to a lover's needs, I couldn't fully let go and *just be* during lovemaking—except when I was coming, of course. I was busy monitoring the dials to create harmony and wholeness. I naturally shifted to my yang or active mode if I was with a man who as more yin or passive. Conversely, if a man was very yang or aggressive and active, I allowed myself to be more fully receptive or yin.

With Vic, I could just be—however *I was* that day. He took care of *everything*. He intuitively knew my needs, desires and rhythms, which was no easy task as they changed from day to day. I never needed to say anything; it was sensual perfection.

This is not to say that Vic did not have hang-ups or neuroses outside the bedroom. We found easy ways to work around them. For example, the area of Vic's hang-ups mostly had to do with cleanliness, especially in the kitchen. As oral as he was in the bedroom—that's as anal as he was in other areas.

One of my favorite times with Vic was when we spent long, lazy weekends at his isolated country house up in the mountains. On my first visit there, I realized I would never cleanup the kitchen or vacuum well enough to meet his specifications. I just told him that, rather than nagging me, he should just accept this as a sign we could never live peaceably together. He got it.

After that, Vic did most of the shopping, cooking and cleaning. We actually created a game that was very playful and worked for both of us. I would make him wear a butt plug, dog collar and thong while he was cleaning the house. He would get occasional paddles, spankings or whippings if I noticed dust somewhere or if he wasn't cleaning fast enough, or—just for the hell of it.

At a certain point in this game, he started licking me, from my toes upwards, and if he was really good (or bad), he would get a good butt-fucking with one of the large dildos he had brought me to use on him. One was a huge black rubber dick with a sword-like handle. The other one was a strap-on, which was novel and fun for me as an occasional variation. I only wish I had known then that they made double-dildo strap-ons, which would have doubled our fun. Vic had an amazing capacity for pleasure/pain, and usually my arm got tired before he begged me to stop. Then I made him shower, as he sweated a lot, and fuck me silly. A good time was always had by all.

We usually did the whole dominatrix scene when we spent a weekend in the country and then only for an occasional afternoon or evening. Vic just needed to be dominated sometimes to round out his repertoire. While I didn't need to dominate, and mostly did it for him, I will admit that I did enjoy seeing the look in his eyes when his legs were up over his head and I was ramming a big rubber cock up his ass farther than I could have imagined possible—shades of gay lives past, no doubt.

In the mornings at the country house, Vic woke me up by nibbling my toes and slowly making his way upward, while I was still sleeping. I awoke wearing a sleepmask as he ate me out with much slurping, moaning and sniffing. I had never been with anyone *so* into all of my tastes, textures and smells before. He didn't even like me to bathe or use deodorant before sex. Then he entered me and slowly and sensuously made love until I continuously came for at least half an hour. The sensation of being devoured and invaded by some large beast I couldn't see was a delectable turn-on—every time, without fail.

Afterward, I would sit out on the terrace on top of a very private hill, reading the paper nude and sipping juice and coffee. Vic prepared gourmet brunches, with fresh fruit and pancakes, eggs and bacon or smoked trout from a nearby farmer's market. We spent the afternoons swimming in lakes, kayaking in estuaries of the Hudson or hiking near waterfalls. In the evenings, Vic barbequed prime meats and grill vegetables he had brought up from the city, while I practiced tai chi and meditated near a bubbling brook, as the sun set over the mountains.

Vic was truly a master of the mundane; it became one of my nicknames for him. He really knew how to live through enjoyment of all the physical senses. He had it down to an art; after all, it was his karmic rut. The other nickname I had for him was "the wilderness shopper" because, whenever we were out of the city, whether in the country or traveling abroad, he always had on hand every possible gadget from L.L. Bean or other sporting goods catalogs. We were never at a loss and I could just leave it all to him.

The first summer we were together, we went touring for ten days in Nova Scotia and Prince Edwards Island, with the high point of ocean kayaking around seal colonies. We ate such incredibly rich foods as oysters, lobster and pie a la mode at almost every meal, making love at quaint or ritzy bed and breakfast inns all along the way.

We traveled so well together; it blew my mind. We never argued, and we were always in sync about what to do or where to go next, as we planned each day spontaneously. It was a shame, in a way, that I had reached a point in my development where just eating and fucking—even at such a high level—were not enough for me, without the romantic, in-love portion of the program.

Even though I knew the "falling-in-love" part usually falls away, eventually anyway (although it never really did with Paul), I had worked too hard for too long to accept that the world of the physical senses, which I enjoyed so thoroughly with Vic, was all there was to life. I tried once on this trip to share with

Vic on the psychic level. But he couldn't maintain the energy level or handle the communication for very long. He just looked stunned, as if he'd been jolted between the eyes with a psychic cattle prod.

In my twenties with Donnie, I had questioned, "Is this all there is?"—on the subject of eating and fucking. In my thirties with Paul, I had resigned myself, for many years, to the idea that perhaps eating and fucking was all that was realistically possible in a romantic relationship—at least for me. I was ultimately disappointed only because I had set my sights too high, beyond the scope of companionship being the sharing of sights, sounds and tastes of life and each other.

Of course, I loved the world of the senses—it was the sine qua non of my karmic desire rut. I also knew that the physical senses, as well as the personal human emotional range, were some of the primary perks of being in an incarnation. Obviously, one doesn't get to enjoy physical senses (no matter how hard one tries) in any other dimension except the physical. However, I seemed to do my most important psychic and spiritual development on a separate path. Maybe I just needed to accept that that was the way it was for me—until it wasn't. After all, that which we resist—persists.

I realized Vic was the perfect partner to bottom out on the sensual levels with. I even knew it while I was in the midst of doing it. It was like eating slightly *too* rich food at every meal. I recognized that if I did it too regularly for too long it would lower my vibration, slow my soul growth down and ultimately make me ill—and not just spiritually.

At the beginning of our second year together, we went on a ten-day vacation to Belize. Vic had a herpes outbreak just after we arrived in the mountains for three days of touring caves, Mayan ruins and such, before we flew out to one of the atolls for a week of scuba diving. This meant we couldn't have sex for the first five days of our trip.

It was interesting in that Vic and I had never really spent much time together when we weren't moving toward doing it, doing it, or in the afterglow of doing it. Not surprisingly, we still got along well as traveling companions as there was lots to see and do. However, without the glue of our sexual dynamic, I was aware of how limited our interchange would become over time, especially if we weren't busy with stimulating new sights and sounds.

The diving was world class, and Vic was as fabulous a scuba buddy as he was a fuck buddy. I could leave everything to him. We did some quite dangerous drift dives, and without Vic to hold on to me, I might still be drifting out to sea. He was my ballast, in more ways than one; with him, I could just enjoy the underwater ride. However, when we were dining with other couples at the dive resort, I was embarrassed to be seen as a couple with him—not a good sign. He acted too obsequious in that situation, like he was my limo driver.

Nonetheless, I was determined to play out the sensual pleasures Vic and I shared for as long as I could get away with it. It didn't stop me from being open to new amorous adventures, as well. After all, Vic was engaged to be married and living with his fiancée, and just because I saw him exclusively the first year, that didn't mean there wasn't more room on my dance card.

# 46

## Buddha's Delight

If Vic were a meal, he'd be spareribs and cream puffs. If Paul had been a meal, he would have been prime aged meat and chocolate custard-filled éclairs. My next lover, who I met in the spring of 1996, was like neither of these. In fact, he was almost diametrically opposed. If my new friend, William, were a meal, he would be an exotic, stir-fried mix of oriental vegetables, called Buddha's Delight in most Chinese restaurants. At least I was expanding my range.

There was no "meat" in my connection to Will, in the energetic yang sense of density. Once we started hanging out together, there was only the activated karmic memory of two androgynous Taoist wizards in flight. I was introduced to him at a dinner party by my energy arts teacher, Franz. Will was an old friend of his and quite a well-known martial arts teacher in his own right, as well as an award-winning cinematographer.

When I met Will, he was already in his sixties, but he had an ageless quality. With his twinkly blue eyes filled with humor and intelligence and a visual aesthetic sensibility as refined as anyone I had ever met, we had an immediate rapport on many levels. He was of medium height, very slender and wiry, with the energy of a monkey—definitely not my usual taste.

We started going out on a couple of dinner dates and got along great. His insights and perspectives on life were as brilliant to me as mine were to him. He confided in me that he had been going through a sexual dry spell for about a year, and it was starting to get to him. I had seen pictures of him in his thirties, when he had been quite gorgeous in his own way, very much a ladies' man, and growing older in the romantic arena is challenging for the best of us. I tried to tell him that he wasn't my type, but he was persistent and he grew on me. His take on life was emotionally upbeat most of the time, and his love of life and appreciation for being alive were similar to my own.

After our third dinner together, I invited him over to my place. We started doing some push-hands together, which is a form of tai chi sparring. This exercise starts by feeling out the other person energetically. When I felt Will's energy and his grounding to the earth, I was very impressed, as this is the area where I was weakest.

I realized once again, perhaps for the hundredth time, that I couldn't really read someone's physical or rooting energy as much as I thought through my psychic vision *without touching them.* The same lesson I had begun to learn in Egypt! Just because I could read someone psychically and see their soul development didn't mean I could feel the present state of their embodied energy without a hands-on experience. It's the same with reading soul potentials with my psychic vision. I still need to get to know someone personally to experience exactly how much of their potentials have been realized. When I go into a full trance and do soul readings for clients, this is not an issue, because both the potentials and the present stage of development are spelled out.

However, I choose not to do a full trance soul reading as part of my personal dating life. I have too much of an edge as it is; it feels fairer to operate with some blinkers on my psychic vision. Besides, knowing absolutely everything up front could be construed as cheating or a misuse of the psychic gift for personal gain. In addition, I can see in hindsight, how knowing the complete karmic story from the beginning would inhibit me from choosing to play out karma that needs to be healed.

Will and I became lovers that night. It felt like two butterflies mating in mid-air. Will's emotional energy was very wide, but not very deep in terms of emotional intimacy. I was aware of the limitations immediately. My preference is for deep, intense and passionate all the time, which can be a bit wearing on more yin energy types.

Outside of bed, we had a lot of good times together. Sitting at cafes, watching the world go by was continuously entertaining, as we shared our ongoing observations and commentaries on the world at large. One hot summer night in the East Village, we were doubled over with laughter as we watched the scene. Not only did the crowds passing by look like the bar scene in *Star Wars*—there were a lot of aliens running around. They also seemed to have shed any semblance of disguise as humans. They were even walking their alien pets on leases—one looked like a cross between a dachshund and an armadillo. I could never have enjoyed sharing these insights as much with Vic.

However, if I really desired some meaty sex, and not just a steak dinner with Will, I still had my weekly or bi-weekly dates with Vic. While the sex with Will was a fun and pleasurable experience, it was not quite right for either of us. Although it did bond us deeper and faster than just hanging out as friends ever could. This was really the point. Will liked women who were yang or dominant most of the time, and, while I was that way mentally in my style of communication, physically my preference was to be more yin.

We had so many good times hanging out together that our Taoist wizard energies became activated synergistically. I remembered how we used to live in caves in the mountains of China and practice internal alchemy, among other arts. The funny thing is Will and I both live in modified caves in this life, too. His was high above the ground as before, and mine was slightly below street level, in honor of my dwarf heritage.

It was so comforting to have found Will again, my old soul friend. After a couple of months, I realized that the sexual portion of our relationship wouldn't last past the summer. The pheromones were becoming a problem for me—always a warning sign that something is not quite right. It didn't bother me because I knew that being lovers with Will for a season or two had sealed our heart energies open for a life-long bond of friendship—and so it is.

# PART VII

## *WEARING MY LOVE LIKE HEAVEN*

# 47

## *Soul Meeting—California Style*

My third summer on spiritual retreat in the Sonoma Mountains of Northern California was a doozie. It was late July 1996 and I was riding high on life. It was my second summer with Vic and my first summer with Will. Professionally, my book had been out for a year and doing well. It fed my private practice, which was stable and enjoyable.

Spiritually, I had reached a place in my meditation practice where I could sit in my garden for eight hours, with all externals being stable, and experience the full range of emotions rise and fall away with no outer stimulus. From extreme sadness with copious weeping, to monumental joy, bliss and states of ecstasy—all were experienced. I was in a state of just witnessing life and occasionally dissolving into the mindstream of the causal plane. When I came out of my sitting practice, it felt as if a moment had passed, not a whole day.

During the first week on retreat, I was more than ready to move to the next level of my practice. All my externals and internals had never felt more stable and integrated. We were doing advanced chi gong the first week with hour-long meditation sessions every other morning before breakfast.

At the second of these meditation sessions, Franz suggested we focus on some specific block—physical, energetic or emotional—that we wanted to work on dissolving with the intent of our mind. This was the beginning of the inner dissolving practice of Taoist water-method meditation. I couldn't think of anything specific I wanted to dissolve, so I decided to focus on dissolving anything that was keeping me from opening my heart more, even if I didn't know what it was. The unknown is always where the juiciest stuff is anyway. I didn't analyze why I picked opening my heart more; it just felt like the next right thing. In hindsight, I forgot to be careful about what I wished for, as opening the heart more is always a package deal—more love, more joy, but always and also more pain.

I did the dissolving practice for an hour and didn't think much about it for the rest of that day or the next. The following night, while I was chatting with

Rob, a camp acquaintance from Santa Fe, we were interrupted in the most interesting way. Just as we were watching the sunset cast its glow over the mountains from the front lawn of the main house, some guy who knew Rob came up and wanted to chat with me. I was annoyed at the interruption and told him I was busy and would catch up with him the following week if he was still there.

His name was Josiah and he had an ingratiating smile and friendly manner. However, I hadn't noticed him all week in our group of about 60 students until he made his presence known to me. Over the weekend, while I hung out with my friend Niles in Santa Rosa, I started thinking about Josiah and looking forward to seeing him again. I felt sorry I had not been very friendly toward him. In fact, I had been rather off-putting, which is the downside of my reserved Capricorn ascendant persona.

There was a joke (on me) going around camp that summer: "What do you call a dwarf psychic who escapes from prison? A small medium at large." Niles had gotten me a hot-pink tank-top with "small medium at LARGE" stenciled on the back. I wore it back to camp to show that I could laugh at myself. Besides, with my book out and my picture on the back cover, I figured my days of psychic anonymity at camp were numbered. Franz had already started telling people I was a psychic, even though I had asked him not to. I was on vacation from my work and the more people that knew what I did, the more intrusive questions I experienced. Nonetheless, I wore the joke on my back for a day. My ba gua teacher from New York, Alan, who was also at camp, said wearing that shirt was the most yang action he had ever seen me take.

During afternoon break on Monday, our first full day back, I went for a float in the nearby creek. I brought a comical float to camp every year so I could doze on it rather than try to take a siesta in the dorm rooms, which were crowded, very hot and usually noisy.

I preferred being on the water with visually stunning views of green mountains, deep blue skies and an occasional grazing cow. As I drifted on the water, I could drift in and out of a doze, and when I got overheated (I always wore a sun-hat after I got sun poisoning the year before), I could just dive into the refreshing creek. In the record-breaking 100-plus-degree weather, floating in the shady parts of the creek and taking frequent dips was the order of the day.

As I was dozing on my red and gold Egyptian mummy float, wearing a turquoise oversized sun hat, I heard someone swimming up to me. I could feel myself being towed around even though I still had my eyes closed. I opened my eyes and there was Josiah. He was just visible from the chin up, with a twinkle in his eyes, a crocodile grin and the string of the float in his teeth. I was charmed. I let him tow me around on my "barge" as we chatted about lighthearted things in a flirtatious manner. It was magical.

After we got out of the water, we went into the shade near the bank of the creek to stay cool. I was lying on my side on a straw mat, and Josiah and another camp acquaintance, Jan, were sitting in chairs facing me. We joked and had some light banter, as I passed refreshments around.

Surreptitiously, I couldn't resist peaking at Josiah's body, as I was at an interesting angle. He had one leg hanging over the arm of his chair, and his crotch seemed to be pointing right at me, covered in skimpy, wet, navy-blue Speedos. With his lanky 6′3″ frame, shoulder-length auburn hair, long limbs, long fingers, long feet and an elegant, graceful air about him, things began to seem promising. I was beginning to warm up to him, and he seemed enticingly interested in me—in that way.

Not that I was looking for anything. My dance card in New York was already full. I was at camp purely to focus on my internal arts practices—but I think the heat wave was making us all a bit giddy. No wonder India is so overpopulated. What else is there to do in the heat?

Josiah went up to take a nap in his tent on a hill overlooking the creek. I could tell he almost invited me to join him—except it was a little too soon and he was a little too shy. I dozed on my mat, thinking of him lying in his tent. I realized his tent must feel like an oven in the afternoon heat. Otherwise, I might have visited him.

That night after dinner, Franz arranged a special meditation session to coincide with some meteor showers. He wanted to teach us how to use the energies of heaven in our practice. After an initial talk and some indoor instructions, Josiah and I found each other and sat together on my straw mat meditating under the stars. We were deliberately on the other side of the house—away from Franz and everyone else. Just the two of us and the brilliant twinkling night sky, with Franz's voice at a distance.

I told Josiah I had been thinking of him lying all alone up in his tent in the afternoon. He said he had been thinking of me alone on my mat. We started kissing and hugging, with shooting stars all around. As he fumblingly started to fondle my breasts, I asked him, "How old are you right now?"

"Sixteen," he said.

"Me too," I said.

With the electricity between us at an unbelievable level of intensity, and the meteor shower at full blast in a crystal clear sky, Josiah looked me in the eyes and said, "I will always love you."

I am ashamed to say that my first reaction was not romantic—it was cynical. I thought to myself: *Man, these California guys are really smooth, considering I just met him.* Yet, he seemed so touchingly sincere and from the heart. My next reaction was if this was how he was putting the moves on me, it was extremely disconcerting. I did a romantic-pragmatism reality check and noted that it was an inappropriate statement based on linear space and time—and yet and yet—it was completely jamming my left brain ability to function analytically.

At that point, we catapulted into a realm transcending the space/time continuum. In that eternal moment, I saw and knew on the soul level that what he had said was true. On that level, I responded, "I will never leave you." (Which is true, on the soul level, if you want to get technical.) I sensed with my psychic antennae that he had abandonment issues which turned out later to be accurate. Therefore, both of our statements on the soul level were eternally true, even though they had nothing whatsoever to do with our present personalities. Thus setting up, in the first twenty-four hours (as is always the case), the primary themes of our karmic dynamic—and the blessings and curses of same.

With that soul tone set, we wanted to move to the hot tub around 1:00 AM after everyone went to sleep. However, we had to wait quite a while for Franz to leave us alone. He sat near us, in the dark on the lawn, sensing energetically that something was up. He didn't want to miss anything. Either that or he was acting as our chaperone; it was an absurd situation, but endearing at the same time.

Finally, Franz went to bed around 2:00 AM, and Josiah and I slid into the hot tub, the sky blanketing us in its luminous shelter. We were naked and embracing, kissing passionately. Then, as I sat on the rim of the tub, Josiah went down on me. This is always the best of signs, sexually speaking—it's the mark of a true gentleman.

Unfortunately, the tub was not only heavily chlorinated but boiling hot from the heat of the day. While I was barely submerged, my legs spread open to receive his tongue, poor Josiah was getting decidedly overheated and waterlogged. I pulled him out of the tub before he got poached or drowned. I didn't want to lose him yet.

He suggested we retire to his tent for privacy; it was two miles down a steep gravel road near the creek. I had a moment of searing panic in his car as we made a sharp turn and my heart leapt into my throat. I was going to be alone with this guy I had only just met, in the middle of the night in the middle of nowhere.

I reasoned with myself: *This was Northern California, not New York City—they don't even lock their cars here, for God's sake. And it wasn't like I met him in a bar—this was a spiritual retreat, after all. Surely different standards must apply.* I surrendered to the unknown. It is one of my favorite things to do—and this was one of my favorite ways to do it.

## *Karmic/Sexual Interlude—In the Tent*

As soon as we got into Josiah's medium-sized tent, he lit a candle and unzipped some of the vents to let the night breeze in, as it was still hot after the steamy day. A chorus of frogs was singing from the creek below. I looked around and saw a perfectly pristine environment—just some pillows, blankets and a large bottle of Listerine. I was impressed. It looked and felt like a monk's cell.

Quickly, we both got naked and continued kissing on our knees. As Josiah had a very hard erection pointing up toward my mouth, calling for my attention, I went down on him. I was a little disappointed at the size of his penis. Little did I know that it was atrophied from lack of use and that, in time, it would become commiserate with his hands and feet.

As Josiah lifted me up from my kneeling position and lay me down on my back, in that exquisite moment before first entry, he said, "There's something I need to tell you." My first thought was that he was going to tell me he had her- pes. This was definitely no big deal for me, as my ex-husband and several of my lovers had it; all of them had been afraid to tell me, in case I wouldn't sleep with them if I knew. The majority of them had told me *after* we became lovers. Not too scrupulously honest, but I was used to the scenario.

It was worse. "I'm married," he said. My initial inner response was, *"A little late in the game, don't you think?"* However, since it was the middle of the night, in the middle of nowhere, and we were hot and ready to go, I decided to squelch that remark and be a trooper. I responded, "Don't worry about it. I have two lov- ers in New York anyway."

In my mind, this sealed our fate of having just a brief camp romance. His being married probably wouldn't have stopped me. I just wish he had let me know before three seconds of final entry. If he had told me ahead of time there were extenuating circumstances (which there always are, from the cheater's point of view), I would not have considered it a sign of weak character.

On to the main event. It was lovely—just the way I most like it, with lots of soulful eye contact and deep kissing. Josiah growled at me like a lion (he was a Leo after all), as he effortlessly spun me around into different positions. I found out later that he was a teacher of several esoteric martial arts—thus the ease of movement—not to mention his stamina.

By candlelight, as I looked up at Josiah moving above me, with his dark-brown should-length hair swinging on either side of his extremely aquiline, noble face, I had a karmic flashback to when we had been lovers before. He had been an Egyptian Pharaoh and I a High Priestess. (I know it's an archetypal cliché, but that *was* the karmic dynamic.) We engaged in bi-annual ritual sex as part of our seasonal offerings to the gods. He still had the haughty and elegant demeanor of a sun god—even while we were rutting. How piquant.

The next afternoon, we took a siesta in his tent, but we didn't get much sleep. It was too hot for me to even move; it must have been at least 120 degrees in the tent. Nonetheless, Josiah was voracious; I was impressed by his perseverance. I lay almost motionless beneath him as he made love to me; I couldn't believe he had the energy to move, much less get it up in the heat. I found out later that he was a man on a mission. He was storing up sex like a camel at an oasis, before he went home to his sexless marriage. Afterwards, we had a nap, both of us drenched in sweat. Then we had an invigorating skinny-dip in the cool creek before our afternoon meditation session.

When I scanned his energy body while he was resting, I noticed that his power chakra in the solar plexus area was quite undeveloped and had much lower energy than his other levels of development. I mentioned this to him, just for the record.

During our first night and day together, we had skipped the personality level and jumped right to the soul level. Then we had moved steadily to activation of our karmic bond. Finally, without missing a beat, the weak areas of his character and development let their presence be known. Not to mention that I would never again experience Josiah as being as unequivocally yang, assertive or romantic as he was at first, when he was in wooing mode. Isn't that always the way? The symbolic pattern of the relationship was already set.

## *Psychic Interlude—New Moon Ceremony*

That night, Franz had arranged an all night new moon ceremony starting at 9:00 PM. Even though it had been over 100 degrees all day, he had warned us it would get very chilly on top of the mountain in the middle of the night. I brought a thermos of hot ginger-green tea and wore several layers of clothes, but it was not enough. If Josiah hadn't been there to keep bundling me up with blankets and layers of his own clothes, I would have been shivering so much that I might not have made it through the whole ceremony, which lasted five hours. I was impressed with his generosity and am eternally grateful he was there for me, because, psychically, it was one of the most monumental nights of my experience to date.

I had done a reading before camp to focus me on my priorities and themes while meditating. I was informed in the reading that it was time for me to get rewired psychically and it was going to happen during the retreat. A higher frequency of galactic energies was moving into the earth plane, and I wasn't wired strongly enough to handle this new octave of energy.

I hadn't been rewired since the early eighties when I was fitted for, what my channels called, my funnel cap, which allowed me to live on the borderline between inner and outer realities. It allowed me to receive and transmit energy and information without the need to travel outside my body anymore, as I had been for the previous ten years or so. Now, a dozen years later, my psychic circuitry, which is the energy body equivalent to the physical nervous system, was ready for an overhaul. I just didn't know exactly how or when this would occur during the retreat.

The first time I was rewired, I felt as if psychic surgery was being done on my skull and third eye, the pressure was so immense in my head. It had gone on for several days. After it was over, I felt an intense sense of mourning; A layer of attachment to all my past incarnations for identity had fallen away as part of the upgrade. This time, it happened all in one night. Josiah helped stabilize my energy during the hours of chanting as Franz led us in a communion with the heavens through seven different planes of consciousness.

We moved through the physical, energetic, emotional, mental, psychic and causal levels of our being. The rewiring started when we got to the seventh level or body of consciousness, which Franz, in the Taoist water method tradition, calls the body of individuality. It was almost 2:00 AM. I began feeling as if "giant yellow snakes" were invading my energy channels.

As we chanted and moved deeper into the seventh plane, which I call the galactic plane, these yellow snakes were moving through me in a way that felt much too expansive for the channels they were stretching open. I was intensely flipping out, as I had forgotten I was scheduled to be rewired. The snakes moving in through my crown and down through my body felt like alien invaders that were too big for me to handle without rupturing something. I felt like I was going to explode.

Once these snakes moved all the way through me and came out through my hands, feet and perineum, energy started pumping through them at a very high frequency. That's when the light bulb went off, and I stopped being paranoid. I realized that I had just been rewired! The snakes which I had anthropomorphized were actually the new insulation for my wiring. It was much stronger and thicker than before; thus the feeling it was initially too big for me to handle. I was much more familiar with this sensation when it came at me horizontally. Now I could handle more juice without frying my nervous system. Hurrah!

A corollary commitment came with this rewiring, which was communicated to me as the new circuitry was activated. I needed to agree that my primary relationship henceforth would be directly with the galactic forces, a subsidiary of the Divine, if you will. I tried to bargain with the galactic forces, who had just implemented the rewiring. I was assured that I would always be given temporal lovers as well; it wasn't an either/or proposition—always my worst fear, as I am such an extremist.

Not only did I need to surrender to the idea that I had just gotten fucked energetically by the Divine through my crown, but that this was going to be my primary love dynamic from now on. Henceforth, earthly lovers were going to be no more than horizontal vehicles for this direct communion. I was now officially a consort of the galactic forces.

I was a new woman, rewired more powerfully than ever before. Josiah had been facing me and witnessed the whole thing. Not only that, his being there had stabilized and anchored me psychically, a role that Rush had always played me in the past. Also, our energies triangulated on the heart levels with Franz, who was sitting in a direct line behind me, all night long.

That rewiring was one of the most powerful experiences I have ever had. It was more powerful than any sexual experience I could remember—except perhaps with Josiah. Now there's a hook.

After the new moon ceremony, Josiah and I had only two and a half more days together. There was much soulful fucking in the tent and many soulful glances exchanged during breaks in the meditation sessions. It seemed the perfect summer romance—short, *very* sweet and soulful beyond the beyond—even though the sex, on a primal level, left something to be desired. Josiah, on balance, was a bit too yin for me, although his penis was starting to de-atrophy. On the other hand, his enthusiastic comments about how incredible our tantric union was righted the balance. One does like to be appreciated.

Josiah enjoyed swishing around camp in a long Balinese batik shawl that he borrowed from me which he tied as a sarong skirt over his workout pants. With his long hair and graceful elongated movements, it was a bit disconcerting to continually rediscover that he actually had a male sex organ and knew how to use it. I chose to find this yin\yang novelty fascinating rather than go the uh-oh route I had been on with Peter, who had a similar build and facial structure to Josiah, as well as the exact same birthday.

I was aware early on that I was wearing the pants, so to speak, in our male/female balance. Especially since people kept asking if perhaps Peter was gay, before they knew we were dating. I didn't want to go that déjà-vu with Josiah. It's a good thing I can compartmentalize when needed and enjoy the moment without too much baggage.

By the time I had to shove Josiah into his car to go home to his wife and five-year-old daughter (whom I found out about *after* the first night) in Oregon, he was sobbing uncontrollably and babbling about coming to New York City real soon. After he left, I began thinking this might be more than a brief summer fling, after all.

However, I decided it was unequivocally his move, since he was married. I would not initiate contacting him first, just in case when he got home, it all became a dream for him. He called me at camp, as soon as he arrived home and wanted to meet one more time before I left California. My plan had been to go up to the redwoods in Humboldt for a few days with my friend Niles. When Josiah and I met, it was short and sweet, but it definitely made clear that what we had was more than a summer camp phenomenon.

On the way to the airport, I listened to Joni Mitchell's song, "A Case of You," and it perfectly expressed my feelings:

> *Oh You're in my blood like holy wine*
> *You taste so bitter and so sweet*
> *Oh I could drink a case of you, darling*
> *Still I would be on my feet.*

# 48

## *Soul Meltdown—New York Style*

Josiah came to visit me for a few days at the end of September, just in time for my birthday. It had been seven weeks since our parting. During that time, I had been experiencing intensely powerful states of bliss almost daily. I didn't feel as if it was because of him. It was as if he had metamorphosized into "the beloved" as a channel of Divine communion for me. Energetically, on the heart and soul levels, we felt clear, open and strong.

At each moment of awareness during this intensely painful separation, I was simultaneously aware of the eminence, at any moment, of blissful reunion. It was this simultaneous awareness that cracked my heart open to a degree of aliveness I had never felt before. This was what I had asked for during my meditations.

I knew it wasn't really him. Josiah was the catalyst and vehicle for this ecstatic communion. Just like Shams was for the Sufi poet Rumi—whom I didn't discover until a year or so after this period. When I discovered Rumi, he quickly became my favorite poet, not to mention that we shared the same birthday. His philosophy of the spiritual potential of relationship was exactly like mine.

This feeling of the exquisitely painful ecstasy of separation simultaneously with eminent reunion inspired a whole slew of love poems, which I faxed Josiah during our time apart. He even managed to send me a love poem of his own, which duly impressed me, considering he was a composer/musician professionally and not primarily a lyricist. I had already discovered at camp he wasn't much of a talker, but I was verbal enough for both of us—at least in the beginning.

I was still seeing Vic once or twice a week—a girl does have to eat after all. This helped me maintain emotional equilibrium. I've found that creating my own triangle for balance is highly recommended, given that I'm not into unnecessary suffering.

By the time Josiah finally arrived, we had already been through a flurry of poetic faxes, love notes and extended late-night phone conversations. Being a confirmed night-owl worked well with the three-hour time difference. We fell on each other with a deep hunger, further fueled by the bicoastal clandestine romantic nature of our bond.

I had arranged some exciting things to do during Josiah's visit, as it was his first time in the big city. He was a country boy at heart, growing up in Iowa and living in a small town now. I'm afraid it was all a bit of a shock for him.

Our first night together, he felt claustrophobic trying to sleep with me. He felt as if he were being suffocated in a closed sarcophagus. I intuited this was not just a symbolic fear but a karmic memory of a failed initiation ceremony in Egypt. I rearranged our sleeping positions so he could get more fresh air and space.

The day after he arrived was my birthday. We went to the Metropolitan Museum to spend some time in the roof garden and then in the Egyptian wing. After that, we went to Vong, one of my favorite restaurants in midtown, for an elegant dinner. In the middle of the meal, Josiah started having a complete meltdown. Energetically and psychically, it looked as if he were having a really bad hallucinogenic trip, only without a drug trigger—just New York and me. He could only look at me helplessly; he was frozen speechless in his seat. I had to pay the bill and get him home as soon as possible as he was starting to freak out in the restaurant.

Josiah stabilized a bit when we got home to what I call my "cave." My apartment is warm, colorful, and womblike—with stucco arches between rooms and a subterranean feel. I could see his personality structure or persona, on some habitual level of identity, was breaking up or disintegrating before my very eyes. The psychic speed of New York City and our connection catalyzed a complete meltdown of Josiah as he knew himself to be. It was fascinating to watch—as we did "faces" in my large tub by candlelight—but also a bit disconcerting because he was so frightened.

The next day, Sunday, I had arranged a small birthday gathering in the afternoon at my place for six of my closest friends to meet my new love. I even invited Will, as he is quite mellow and not the jealous type. Besides, over the last month, we had smoothly shifted without even a bump to being just good friends.

In the middle of my little party, Josiah started having another meltdown. Sensing his discomfort, everyone left with smiling excuses as soon as they could. In photos from this gathering, Josiah looks like he is moments away from his own execution.

After everyone left, Josiah curled up in a ball on the couch and started sobbing. I tried to hold him, but he turned away from me toward the wall. After he quieted down a bit, he seemed to want to be alone. I said I would go for a walk to give him some space. But he said, "Please don't go. I don't want to be alone." So I held him until his psychic meltdown subsided again.

On our third full day together, I took him to a great brunch place, an outdoor cafe on Union Square, where we could watch one of the best shows in town. It was prime people-watching territory and one of my favorite things to do in any city. Of course, just as our brunch was served, Josiah started getting this sickly look on his face. He looked down at his eggs, looked up at me and said, "I think I have to go home right away." Three days—three meltdowns.

Make no mistake: we had increasingly incredible tantric sex between meltdowns. Josiah was capable of keeping his eyes and heart open, while we were hand to hand and mouth to mouth, even as he was pumping deep inside me for extended periods. Not only did he have excellent control, as he was skilled at separating his orgasms from ejaculation, but our energies automatically formed a complete circuit in all the diverse and enjoyable positions we came up with.

When Josiah would make love to me from behind, if he came as I came, the energy from our combined orgasm would pour out the top of my crown chakra and hands like a golden gift of sensual bliss for the galactic forces. It was an offering to the gods, just like in the good old days in Egypt. It was as spiritual as any sexual act I have ever experienced. And, just like in Egypt, there wasn't much going on during our lovemaking on the personality levels. It was truly soul to soul.

After we sent our offerings "back home," we rested, with him sucking on my breasts or tongue, or both, to complete the circuit and refresh his energies after what he had put out. I have never felt as complete after orgasmic lovemaking if there isn't this sharing in the afterglow. Then, there is the feeling of being perfectly balanced, with no depletion on my partner's part and no overfullness on mine.

Our soul connection was so strong. We spent hours doing "faces," which is one of the best ways to commune on the psychic plane. It was so intense, I felt as if we had already made love—before we had even touched.

When Josiah left after five days, we were bonded more deeply on the psychic levels than ever before. We promised each other to maintain this bond on the soul level through energy practices and meditation until we could meet again.

# 49

## *The First Cut Is the Deepest*

At the time I met Josiah, I was starting a two-year astrological transit of Neptune over my ascendant. I knew very well what this meant, as I had warned many clients about similar transits in their own charts over the years. It meant I would be subject to Neptunian romantic delusions and idealistic projections until this transit past, at which point I would be able to see what was really going on—illusion, fantasy or fact.

I *knew* all of this, yet for the next two years I tried very hard to forget what I knew. I deluded myself that, just perhaps, I might be exempt from Neptunian-romantic-delusion-mode. Ha!

The first year with Josiah was so deep, so sweet and so intense, with so little time actually spent together, that all that depth, sweetness and intensity just naturally spilled over into my relationship with life itself.

The first reading I did with Josiah in September spelled it out. We had met to activate different levels in each other and not necessarily to spend that much time together. The reading called us soul twins—two souls at similar levels of development as peers, at least in the overall balance. Josiah was activating a tonal sweetness of heart energy which I had in me (I had felt it in Egypt), but still didn't allow out much of the time. Josiah had this tone in spades.

After each time with Josiah, this sweetness poured more and more spontaneously from me. It was as if I were continuously falling in love with all of life in its infinite variations and seasons and with all living beings in their myriad forms. I went to cafes and just blissed out sending this heart energy—sweet, compassionate and loving—to all the suffering souls I saw on the street. It was simply overflowing from me most of the time, and nothing less than all of life felt big enough to handle the overflow.

My readings kept reminding me that this sweetness was mine, it was *"cosmic sugar,"* and there was plenty to go around. While Josiah may have been the activator of this sweetness, it was now mine to channel.

193

For Josiah, my function was to be the activator of his power potentials. They were in him, but latent at this point in his incarnation, due to the karmic cul-de-sac through which he was healing personally as well as professionally.

The problem was that as I activated Josiah, he was splitting in two. When he was with me, he tasted the flowering of his true multidimensional nature and co-creative power. Then, when he went back home, he had to shut down this higher frequency of operations. If he didn't, he wouldn't have been able to tolerate the karmic prison of his marriage.

Josiah was choosing not to rock the boat at home at the expense of his own speed of soul evolution, as his wife was prone to periodic anxiety attacks which she refused to get help for. (That's a karmic story I won't go into here.) We agreed there were obvious karmic debts to pay before he would feel free to move on without the baggage of unfinished business, especially with a little daughter whom he adored in the picture.

With each visit, the split in Josiah was getting wider and deeper. That's why his meltdowns were initially much more intense than my own. The readings explained we were dissolving parts of our personality structure or habitual karmic emotional or mental patterns that kept us from communing on the soul levels.

By the time Josiah made his second visit after Thanksgiving, his split was manifesting as major passive/aggressive behavior towards me. This activated an almost continuous three-day meltdown in me. My attachment to wanting Josiah to be fully present emotionally with me fell away with a vengeance. In person, his emotional stance toward me kept getting progressively cooler—in contrast to his communication on the phone getting increasingly hotter. It was very disconcerting.

I was having meltdowns all over the place. The first one started on the stairs leading to the Metropolitan Museum. I had to sit down or I would have fainted. I felt as if the whole structure of my being was completely disintegrating. Josiah took one look at me and said, "Now you know what I was going through in September." Did I ever.

Through our mutual meltdowns, our bond grew exponentially deeper as we watched each other disintegrate to our essence and supported each other in the process. In the next reading we did together, our individual responsibilities in the relationship were outlined.

The reading said it was my job to seal, maintain and patrol the perimeter of a sacred psychic space. This space was one that ultimately transcended the individual soul level and even the causal and galactic planes. It was the place where we fully merged as we flowed into the void and our individual essences dissolved.

Every night, whether we spoke on the phone or not, each of us was to take a few minutes to commune with each other in this sacred space.

Given that Josiah was supposedly working on manifesting more power outward into the physical plane, his job description was initiating all contacts, especially visits to New York and trips together. It was suggested that he maintain a quality of communication that was completely clear and honest with nothing withheld. If his family or financial obligations were not allowing him space or time to be with me, then he needed to explain this to me, so I wouldn't take it as a personal rejection. The readings reminded us that I was very emotionally strong, stoic and capable of handling long separations—as long as Josiah kept the lines of communication wide open.

This worked quite well for the first year. Josiah came for his third three-day visit in late January, while assisting his teacher in a martial arts workshop near New York City. We didn't get much sleep or have much alone time together, but it didn't matter because the tone between us felt so good. It helped that we had already made plans to spend ten days in Jamaica together at the end of February.

## *Jamaica—The Luxury Villa*

Josiah had been offered a few days of studio work with some reggae musicians in Montego Bay. After that, I had booked a week in our own little thatched cottage on the cliffs overlooking the sea in Negril. Josiah was so naive he assumed he didn't even need a passport to get into a foreign country. I was having visions of him being turned away at immigration when we arrived. At the last minute, I convince him to get one.

When we arrived, the "luxury villa" his Rasta friends had arranged turned out to be a four-star dump, (which I had expected), as well as a psychic nightmare for Josiah. The accommodations and energy there were so bad; we decided to split the next morning, two days early, for Negril. It was late, and we were exhausted from traveling all day. Plus Josiah had strained a muscle in his back the week before and was in some pain. If there was any studio work for Josiah, he could commute from Negril—but that turned out to be a sham as well.

I was getting in touch with Josiah's naiveté on many levels. However, we still had to get through that one night at the so-called villa, and while it was a memorable night for me—for Josiah, it was one he will certainly never forget.

Our rundown accommodation was near Rose Hall, where many slaves had been massacred in a revolt in the previous century. So there were many "unhappy entities" milling around on the astral plane in our bedroom that night. I knew how to seal and protect myself psychically and advised Josiah to do the same, as the air was thick with disturbed energy. But he was cocky and arrogant, typical Leo traits. Yet, at the same time, with his soft Piscean moon, he was energetically vulnerable, so there was trouble in the air.

We made love for a while and came together from behind. Just as I sent our mutual ritual orgasmic offering of golden energy to the galactic forces through my crown and hands, I felt Josiah sweep the offering directly from above my head, and circulate it through his body. I asked him what he had just done. He told me that, on impulse, because he was so tired, he wanted all the energy for himself. I admonished him, "It's not good to fuck with the gods' offering." He promised never to do it again.

In energetically opening himself to receive that energy, Josiah had also opened himself to all the "hungry ghosts" in the room, and they fed on him all night long. He didn't get much sleep. This was similar to what happened to Rush our first night in Cairo. Except there, the discarnate entities were dive-bombing into Rush and feeding on him from his overflow, as he was a long-lost but familiar host. In Josiah's case, these unhappy entities were depleting him without his permission because he had left himself open.

The next morning, he couldn't wait to get out of there. Once we settled into our beautiful little oasis in Negril, we had a honeymoon of a time. Our meltdowns only happened on my home turf. We slept, swam and sunned together, making love every afternoon and evening. Sunset was the big event of the day, as it was always visually stunning. At that time, we would have either romantic meals overlooking the turquoise lagoon or drinks floating in the infinity pool near our private terrace.

Josiah's favorite thing was to eat simple peanut butter sandwiches; he didn't like fancy food or spending too much money. In bed, under our mosquito net, he loved patrolling the perimeters of the space and keeping it secure and bug-free. Our canopied bed was as pristine as his tent at camp.

I enjoyed going out people-watching and browsing for local foods and crafts. The locals didn't faze me at all; I just ignored them. Unfortunately, when the locals hit Josiah up for money or to buy ganja, he freaked out. He looked like an easy mark because he would smile and say hello to everyone on the street.

I had already warned him in New York that he needed to learn to keep his guard up. But he was so indiscriminately friendly when we strolled away from our enclosed resort complex that he got inundated with negative attention. Then, he would feel so assaulted he'd have to go lie down. This didn't bode well for my

fantasies of long journeys to exotic third world countries with Josiah as my traveling companion. Especially India.

## *Psychic/Sexual Interlude—Under the Net*

Our last night together in Negril was one of my most memorable times with
Josiah. It stands out as the best of the best. It was a combination of the exotic
locale and the opportunity to have a nine-day romantic holiday that gave us the
time to bond more deeply. It also epitomized what had already become our primary sexual dynamic.

From Josiah's first visit to New York, I started doing channeled readings for
us. Josiah was the conductor, which had been one of Rush's primary functions
with me since about 1987, except for the two years I was with Peter. After each
reading, Josiah would *not* count me back from the trance state, which is my normal procedure after a reading. Instead, he would attempt to ground me back into
my physical body by impaling me deeply with his penis.

Making love this way, directly following a trance session with no count-back,
is the most intense energy dynamic possible. It's like the ultimate free-fall amusement park ride. I could tell that Josiah was getting hooked on it. That's why our
last night in Negril was so special. To top it off, instead of grounding me by making love, the energy from the reading was so intense it took him right into the
galactic dimensions with me—and parts of us never came back.

When we did it in Jamaica that last night, after a beautifully sweet reading,
and with Sting's "Fields of Gold" wafting over from a club across the lagoon, I
wasn't doing it because I needed grounding anymore. In fact, through the Taoist
energy practices I had learned from Franz, I could ground myself in my body
energetically more and more on my own. I made love with Josiah with the trance
energies to seal our union at the highest levels possible. Besides, Josiah's primal
energies were not his strong suit anyway—it was his sweetness.

The hook for Josiah was the intense high frequency energies he could merge
with through me. It was like taking a ride on the galactic autobahn (as I liked to
call it since my rewiring), which ran right through my central channel. What was
the hook for me? That Josiah could *handle* this level of intensity, psychically and
sexually, without getting blown-out—*and* that he kept coming back for more.

Josiah's energy was so sweet; it inspired me to write more love poetry upon my
return to New York. Like how he was the *"sweetest fuck in the galaxy"* and how no
matter where we were, *"whether in the tent, in the cave, or under the net—we were
always on the royal barge floating down the Nile as the sun set."* Of course, once this

hook was deeply set in me—of being turned on by Josiah's appreciation of me—it was time for the cosmic trickster (working through Josiah) to start twisting the hook out.

The first signs were already there in Jamaica. For example, one night in bed, Josiah told me, quite emphatically, he really didn't like parts of my personality. I was shocked by his cruelty. My mental speed and verbal nature were obviously starting to get to him. On another night, while he was lying next to me in the afterglow, he asked me, pointing to my brain, "Doesn't it ever stop?"

I avoided reacting by taking inventory of him. Instead, I suggested we focus on our soul connection, as everything on the personality levels falls away sooner or later anyway, and of course, one can never expect to like absolutely everything about another person. Josiah apologized later for his remarks and said I was right. Obviously, the hook had already started to twist.

We had one more lovely three-day visit in New York in May. At that time, we made plans for an extended tryst together in California that summer. We planned to go to the redwoods for three days and then to Camp Franz for a week. It wasn't until I arrived in California that Josiah definitively let me know he had changed his mind about coming to camp with me, although he had intimated the possibility by fax the week before I arrived.

He said it didn't feel right energetically for him as his energies were needed more at home. I felt he was being deliberately evasive, which I consider a form of dishonesty. I let him know if he really wanted to be with me, then I knew he could arrange it. Therefore, his priorities were shifting and he was getting shifty about them.

Consequently, our brief spell in the redwoods was strained. By the time he dropped me off at the camp pickup point and asked me if he could call me at camp, I told him, to paraphrase Rhett Butler, "I don't fucking care—so don't bother."

It actually turned out better that Josiah wasn't at camp. His decision turned out to be the right one for my needs, if not my wants. Without his demands on my time and energy, I was able to devote my full attention to practicing tai chi. I noted for future reference that mixing my spiritual and internal energy practices with my love life for the sake of expediency was messing up my priorities. Not only that—I wouldn't have met Brian, an artist and tai chi teacher from Santa Fe and Mark, a young potter from rural Oregon. Both became deep friendships over the next few years.

In San Francisco, after the week at camp, I released any residual anger I felt towards Josiah. I realized, for the zillionth time, everything always happens perfectly for soul growth. If I was willing to let go of my ego desires a little sooner, I would suffer a lot less. Of course, Josiah felt left out the whole week I was at camp, and he was home with the wife and kid. He promised me that next summer he would come to camp for two weeks. What a joke—I had a great time without him, so my value just went up. The passive/aggressive cycle of the "terrible twos" in our second year was just heating up.

# 50

## *Sedona*

My ten-day trip to Sedona, Arizona, in late September 1998 was divided into two parts. I spent the first three days with Josiah and the last seven days with my old friend, psychic partner and soulmate Rush. This was the last time I had with Rush, as he passed over from cancer on his birthday a month after the trip. He would have been sixty-one.

I

After my return from California, Josiah and I had made up, more or less, over the phone. I realized he was not capable of being more available, or emotionally present, than he was when he was physically available—and what *was* seemed to be progressively diminishing. In accepting this reality, I decided not to make more of the relationship than what was there now. I also decided not to give added weight because of our soul potentials or Josiah's occasional flowery words on the phone. What was left, truthfully, when we were together wasn't much. Except for infrequent flashes of our former greatness together—usually sexually after I channeled and no more than one time per visit.

I was still seeing Vic and enjoying my times with him, especially in the country, where we could play at our indoor sports as well as our outdoor ones—hiking, swimming and kayaking. I was also aware the karmic clock was ticking. Unwinding was in the wind for me—my readings had started to intimate this more strongly. I was becoming increasingly aware that Vic that I had gone as far as it was humanly possible to go—all the way to the depths of sensual indulgence—and I was slowly bottoming out again. There is a saying that all bottoms have infinite trapdoors—and I was aware of this and in denial simultaneously.

I knew that the level of sensual pleasure I experienced with Vic was my karmic rut par excellence. We had reached a point where it felt as if we were wallowing in mud every time we fucked. Just to prove this point, Vic started to spontaneously snort like a wild boar whenever he got overexcited—which I chose to find amusing.

By the time I had arranged to meet Josiah in Sedona, I had much more realistic expectations of what he was capable of offering me. While it wasn't much, as a romantic pragmatist, I was willing to enjoy sharing sweet heart energy with him, while getting my main food supply elsewhere—from either direct communion with the Divine, other lovers, or both.

Just before I left for camp that summer, I had made a new friend through Will, on whom I had a bit of a crush. Even though this new friendship hadn't been consummated yet, I had high hopes this infatuation would come to fruition upon my return from Sedona. I was actively working it.

This was my fifth trip to Sedona. Josiah and I had a reasonably good time as I had many special energy-vortex power places to share with him. We hiked, swam in the creek at the yin energy vortex, my favorite spot, and did prodigious energy practices amongst the beautiful red rocks and sunsets. It was easier for me not to notice that Josiah's personal interest in me was waning even more, but I did anyway. This scenario of lagging interest only happened when he was actually with me; at a distance, I was always of interest to him. Over the phone, I had become an entertaining distraction from his rather mundane home life. But in person I was becoming more than he was choosing or, more likely, capable of handling.

I was used to periodically having to hear about his rocky relationship with his wife, especially when she lost it with him. I gave him advice about seeking counseling, but he said they had tried that. That it was entirely his wife's emotional hang-ups; she refused to stay in therapy, as there were childhood sexual abuse issues, and it didn't have anything to do with him. Nonetheless, I knew his payoff in having an emotionally imbalanced mate was that he got to be the calm, balanced, "all-right" one and stay closed up in his own little world. I wouldn't let him do that with me. I was emotionally present and noticed when he wasn't, which was most of the time. With me, there was no pay-off for him—just a mirror of his own inadequacies. And he knew it.

I had no problem being in a triangle with Josiah per se, as I had had a lot of practice with Vic over the last few years. Still, I couldn't resist zinging Josiah over dinner our last night together—especially since our lovemaking was less than stellar. I let him know I had met someone I was developing feelings for, who might not be so accepting of me seeing Josiah on the side. Of course, this was a projection of wishful thinking, based on my infatuation in New York.

This information certainly woke him up. He immediately sat up straighter and started showing me some real interest. He asked me how long I thought this new relationship would take to play itself out. I predicted about two years. He said he would weather it out and wait for me. Josiah was truly a good and noble ascetic at heart; it was a variation of the self-denial karmic rut. He'd had too many lives as a monk, wandering in the desert or locked away in self-imposed isolation as an alchemist. As soon as my interest in him flagged and there was the hint of unavailability, he perked up. Self-denial really seemed to turn him on.

When Josiah left after three days to go back to his wife and daughter, I was actually relieved to see him go. I was getting bored with him, except for the sex. I was doing all the talking, initiating and entertaining—a pattern I knew too well to want to continuously repeat.

## II

Rush had been sick for many years, but he hid the extent of his illness pretty well from everyone, including himself. This is one way to play it out. As an energetic hands-on healer for over twenty years, among other careers, he had incredible regenerative powers that he used to help those who came to him with cancer and other illnesses of body, mind or spirit. But his strong genetic predisposition, as well as some karma he needed to play out through his relationship with his body along the lines of human vulnerability, had finally caught up with him.

Rush had just been through a year and a half of the usual Western medicine battle with cancer: radiation, surgery and several rounds of mega-chemotherapy. His colorectal cancer had metastasized to his liver. By the time he came to Sedona, he was jaundiced from chemo, and he had maxed out on all Western medical protocols; he'd begun using alternative healing modalities in a last attempt to stabilize his body. But the tide had already turned.

I had been there when they wheeled him out of ICU after his surgery. The surgeon had promised there would be no need for a colostomy, but when they opened him up, the cancer had already spread too far. They had to cut out more than they had promised him.

Rush was so upset when he found out what they'd done to him, that his business partner and friend, Dion, put him on suicide watch. He had said to her before surgery that he didn't want to live if they did that to him. When he woke up, the first thing he said when he opened his eyes was, "They butchered me."

I held his hand, lifted up the blanket and said, with amazement, "My God, they left your dick! And they left both your hands and feet. I seem to recall you've gotten along with much less when you were a warrior in past lives." That seemed to put things in perspective enough to calm him down somewhat, and he was taken off suicide watch. I already knew that Rush was dramatic regarding his own death, as he had been at the Albert Hotel, in prison and at Karnak. Dion had played right into it. I could see he only needed a little reminder of the broader perspective.

A few hours after they moved him from the ICU, they made Rush sit up in a chair to get his circulation going. Even with the morphine drip, he was in such pain due to all the stitches stretching (from where his rectum used to be all the way up to his ribs), that I thought he might keel over.

Still, he sat up in the chair, holding one of those little sponge sticks in his hand like a scepter. I saw a noble king facing his last and greatest battle. Rush had that magnanimous wizard/king archetype down, even in his most challenging moments—especially in those. I told him of this vision of one aspect of his highest human potential that transcended linear time and space. I mirrored this for him energetically so he could see and feel it resonating back to him.

Rush radiated that noble grace for the next year and a half as he endured all the indignities Western medicine puts cancer patients through in the late 20th century. The deterioration of his body continued relentlessly as the cancer spread. As his karma with his body was getting literally burned through, he acquired a much deeper humility for his vulnerable, wounded humanness. It was a blessing to be in his presence. By the time he came to Sedona, we both knew he was near the end. It was a very precious time for us to be together.

I had introduced Rush to Sedona the year before, between his radiation and surgery, so that he could have some R & R there. He fell in love with it. So much so that he made a trip there over Thanksgiving with Dion and his informally adopted son, David.

Almost every day, we hiked to our special secret place where the yin energy vortex met the bubbling brook and spent many wonderful hours sunbathing, swimming and doing energy practices. Rush said he loved this place so much he wanted to revise his plan to have all his ashes scattered at Karnak. Now he wanted some of them scattered at this sacred spot as well. There, we were truly in heaven. There was no feeling of time passing. We were together in an eternally spacious present moment.

After all we had been through together over twenty-six years and all the roles we had played out together, it felt so good and so complete to just *be* with each other. We reminisced, had some laughs and were quiet a lot as well.

On our last day there, as we were sitting on our terrace overlooking a fountain with the red rocks in the distance, I looked deeply into his eyes and said to him, "Sweets [that was always our special name for each other], it sure would be nice if you could stick around awhile longer."

Rush looked deeply into my eyes and smiled gently. He didn't say a thing. He didn't have too. I knew what he was telling me. I couldn't help tearing up a little—as I do whenever I recall this bittersweet moment.

After that moment of unspoken recognition that he was leaving his body soon, I asked him if he had any regrets about staying in his body over the last fifteen months since his surgery, as there had been so much physical suffering. Without missing a beat, he replied, "Not for a minute."

When we shared a cab back from the airport in New York, at his suggestion I dropped him off first at his place on the Upper East Side. As we parted at curbside, he hugged me and said, "You go home the rest of the way on your own now."

## Rush's Memorial

For Rush's memorial, I asked Horace, my old soul friend and former therapist, to lead the service. I had introduced them years before, and they had become very good friends, helping and supporting each other through difficult times. Rush had a hard time receiving help in general, but because he had already helped Horace out, he was open to allowing Horace to be there for him during his last year.

Horace led the tribute by saying that Rush was less afraid of physical death than any person he had ever met. Rush knew that death was the biggest illusion of all. This allowed him to lead a relatively fearless existence and be a role model for every one who crossed his path.

A few years after his passing, I scattered a portion of Rush's ashes at our sacred spot in Sedona. I keep the remainder in a tiger's eye crystal urn, protected by a statue of Horus, until I make it back to Karnak.

# 51

## *The One Who Got Away—and the One Who Didn't*

I

When I got back from Sedona in early October 1998, I was almost obsessed with seducing the guy I had met during the summer. His name was Kumo, his heritage was Maori, he was darkly gorgeous and not a little bit crazy—and eleven years younger than me, so he was thirty-three to my forty-four. Rush had been thirty-three when I met him and so had Paul and Peter, so I guess that thirty-three was the age of men who did something for me.

Kumo was a world class martial arts champion by the time he was in his early twenties. He could move chi (life force energy) through his body like nobody I had ever seen—at least not in such an adorable a package. It was not just that his rooting power was impressive—his agility, buoyancy and creativity with his juice really got me going. Being a connoisseur of energy and able to psychically read it so well, I found watching Kumo while he practiced the internal arts, not just a turn-on—I was witnessing true, priceless genius in action.

The only problem was that Kumo was not nearly so well developed in any other area as he was in energy cultivation. He had seriously weak flaws in his character bordering on sociopathic behavior. These flaws manifested through his owing large sums of money around town. These were business and personal loans for deals gone sour, as Kumo was much better at promising than delivering. He called it a run of bad luck that had been going on for years. I called it delusions of grandeur and wishful thinking. He thought he should be entitled to special privileges and compensations from others because he was so gifted in the energy arts. Furthermore, he could really sell it, at least in the beginning phases of any new relationship.

If Kumo could get something from you, usually monetary—whether by a hard sell, a soft sell or a combination mixed with loads of charm—then he considered it "his"—with no obligation to repay. So he was a dangerous character. I saw this early on and was warned by many in the martial arts community who knew of his money-borrowing schemes from various soft touches he had already hit on successfully.

I started calling Kumo an "energy idiot savant," which hit the nail on the head. Still, his chi, when he was up (his down-side was a moody Pisces), was irresistible in its exuberant juiciness and love of life. I knew I didn't want to become enmeshed with him on any level. I just wanted a little taste. It was a tricky proposition, because his life really was a mess—and not just because of his irresponsibility with money.

On his best days, Kumo appeared to have the emotional maturity of a budding adolescent. He had an overbearing, autocratic father he still lived with and a deep fear of ever letting anyone else have power over him. He preferred very young girls, jail-bait if possible, and the more "bimbo-like," as he called them, the better. He did not want to risk being challenged in terms of emotional maturity or mental capabilities, given his insecurity about not being formally educated. To top it off, his real preference for absolute control was simply to use hookers when he had the resources at hand. This wasn't often, since money ran through his hands at an almost faster rate than his chi—if you can imagine that.

Knowing all this, how could I even want to be lovers with him? His good looks and especially his energy were, as the song says, simply irresistible. I was still seeing Vic and Josiah and felt confident that I would be capable of compartmentalizing, maintaining healthy boundaries, taking what I could use and leaving the rest. Besides, I was already skilled at dealing with dark characters, such as my father, Paul and Peter, to name a few.

I called my friend, Colleen, who lived in Berkeley with an old friend of Kumo's, to get some advice about him. Colleen was one of those old friends from ages past whose advice had panned out for me before. I respected her opinion, as she did mine. But what she said about Kumo really pissed me off. She said, "In my experience, Leela, sometimes you learn more from the ones who get away." Well, nobody *I* had ever desired had gotten away before; this just made me want Kumo even more irrationally.

By mid-October it became clear, however, that while Kumo really liked hanging out with me, he definitely was not interested in becoming lovers. He was very tactful on the subject because he valued our friendship. I appreciated his discretion.

I decided to let it go. I back-burnered it, because I knew too much pressure always backfires. I didn't want to ruin an interesting new friendship and a truly

lovely energy exchange. He was giving me some chi gong lessons, and I was starting to show him how to use psychic energy by activating his third eye and showing him auras and "faces."

Of course, whenever one really lets go, something magical usually happens.
This time, the cosmic tricksters were definitely at work.

## II

Within days of letting go, on Halloween to be exact, which happened to fall
on a Friday that year, I got a call from my camp friend, Rob, who was visiting
from Santa Fe. He invited me out for dinner, and we met at the Spring Street
Natural restaurant in Soho for a drink. As we chatted at the bar, he asked me if I
would mind going uptown for dinner to an Italian place owned by a friend from
the martial arts scene. Since I was in the mood for pasta, it felt like synchronicity.
So off we went.

Carmine's, was a cozy bustling trattoria, which there was barely room for us to
squeeze into a little table in the center of the room. Periodically, during the meal,
Carmine, Rob's friend and the owner, interrupted our conversation and asked
how everything was going. The food was OK, large portions and above average, if
not excellent cuisine, but the interruptions were beginning to annoy me. Carmine seemed to be getting louder and more intrusive with each one.

Finally, by the end of the main course and after three or four interruptions, I
paused long enough from my focus on Rob and the food to have a good look at
our host. Carmine was extremely social and affable, quite a jovial showman, this
little Sicilian with a booming voice and hearty laugh. He affectionately hugged or
kissed just about everyone coming or going from his establishment. It was definitely his place, and he seemed to be enjoying the show.

After dinner, Carmine pulled up a chair at our table, between Rob and me,
but decidedly closer to me. In fact, I realized, with a shock, his knee was rubbing
against mine. This Sicilian was really brazen. I pulled my knee away, but not too
far. It wasn't that Carmine was bad looking or anything, he was a little too loud
for my taste, personality and clotheswise. He was around thirty-five, about 5' 7",
with a stocky, fighter's fire-plug build and bristling dark hair and eyes. The
expression on his Sicilian peasant face was really starting to get to me. He looked
just like a hungry warthog, with slitted eyes and a wide nose—and he was scoping
me out for his next meal. I was a bit shocked by his primal openness.

After the crowd thinned out a bit, Carmine moved us to a larger table for
after-dinner drinks, dessert and coffee. I was so stuffed; I just had coffee. Rob had
a cognac as we chatted, while Carmine ate his late supper. He showed such cos-

mopolitan European delicacy in his table manners (unfortunately, only a public trait, as I found out later). I was intrigued and impressed by his range. What I liked most about him was he was extremely present and attentive.

He asked me a lot of questions about my psychic business, as well as about the spiritual philosophy underlying my work. He got me to open up quite skillfully, more than I normally would on a first meeting. He was a very good listener, with equally good follow-up questions, and had me totally engaged in a very short time.

While I was in the bathroom, Carmine asked Rob whether we were romantically involved. When Rob informed Carmine we were just friends, Carmine's energy toward me shifted into high gear. He became increasingly territorial, with no guise of civility. Energetically, he literally blew Rob out of the room before he knew what hit him. I felt like I had just been bought and sold—and all I did was go for a pee. I choose to find this amusing.

Carmine asked me, his twinkling little warthog eyes eating me up, if I would like to go to a Halloween party with him. Surprising myself, I was delighted by the invitation. I was in a party mood. Rob said his goodnights and left, while I waited for Carmine to give orders to close up the place without him. We left the restaurant around 1:00 AM.

About a block from the restaurant, standing curbside, Carmine grabbed me. As he aggressively stuck his pointy tongue in my mouth, (I wouldn't exactly call it a kiss—more like a frontal oral breach), he kept hypnotically whispering to me, "Come to my place on 33rd Street, baby," as if he were luring me to the Kasbah. I thought this was a bit too rushed, even for me. I reminded him we had a party to go to. After he caught my drift, he stopped pressuring me and ushered me into a cab to go to the Village. His vibe was one of herding and humoring his next meal.

On the way, we continued to kiss and fondle at breakneck speed, as we zoomed downtown. It took a while to locate the party which was in a loft jammed to the rafters with almost insanely riotous costumed party-goers—drinking, drugging and dancing.

I sat on Carmine's lap as we watched the scene. A fight broke out and Carmine whisked me out of the way, just before some guy would have fallen on me. Carmine didn't just have lightening-fast reflexes when he was being protective; he also had them when he was being aggressive. Carmine was standing snugly behind me as we swayed to the music. Before I could even grasp what he was doing, he had his hand down my pants and was fondling my clit in public. He actually did this twice in rapid succession; I could see we were attracting attention. Carmine had already nicknamed me. "Strega," which is Sicilian for witch—but he was the one casting some kind of spell on me—quite a reversal, especially on Halloween.

At 4:00 AM, we left the party. Carmine walked me home and kept mumbling something about dinner and a movie the next night. He said he didn't want to put any pressure on me; there was no rush. Yeah, right. First he pushed all night, and now he was acting like a wolf in a lamb's disguise. By the time we arrived at my door, I really didn't *want* him to go; I found him too intriguing. I invited him in, of course.

I suggested we take a bath together. As I was undressing and running the water, Carmine stripped down to his white jockey shorts with his undershirt neatly tucked in. He was lying on my bed, totally relaxed, with his legs crossed and his arms behind his head. He looked supremely confident that the food he had so diligently stalked and hunted was about to be served—and he was right.

We made love four times that first night—and what can I say? Well, for one thing, Sicilian tantric sex appears to be an oxymoron. Carmine was so hot-blooded that he had little control, or if he had, then he didn't bother to exercise it with me. But he was adorable in a pugnacious, very male sort of way, with the cutest hairy ass, perfect rock-hard legs, diminutive hands and short but wide feet.

I decided, what the hell. If I wanted finesse, tantric or just an extended erotic session, there was still Vic or Josiah. With Carmine, it was pure primal power. I had finally met my energetic polar opposite.

## Karmic Sexual Interlude-The Philosophy of Attraction

I ended up being with Carmine for a little over two years. I can best describe it as a very entertaining mix of the animal channel, the cartoon channel and occasional reruns of the old "Honeymooners" TV show. I don't know who was more surprised, even in hindsight, that we made it work so well for so long—Carmine, our friends or me.

If someone had described Carmine to me with just the external factors, I probably would have passed on the possibility of a relationship as too improbable. This was before I got an experiential taste of the inner energetic and emotional components of our dynamic. Once again proving to myself that, even as a psychic, I had a definite blind spot in the romance area of my life.

Everyone has blind spots and part of what I do for a living is help others see theirs. But my relationship with Carmine confirmed to me that we are all Divine idiots in some area—and thank God for that. Never a dull moment.

Carmine surprised himself by getting into the habit of calling me for late night chats around 1:00 AM, after he closed the restaurant and finished his nightly viewing of the Discovery channel animal show. These weren't normal late night chats really; they were more like philosophical debates that could go on for hours. When we got together, usually at my place on the weekends, he was as sweet as could be. But on the phone, he was a different animal.

Carmine didn't just like to debate; he was too aggressive and competitive for that. He really enjoyed picking a fight with me and getting me all riled up. I found this incredibly annoying, as I am exactly the opposite of the argumentative type. I prefer peace and harmony. After a few increasingly trying weeks of this, the karmic bleed-through made itself known with a warning label that said *"Uh-oh."*

I started remembering a life with Carmine in ancient Greece. Then, he would have loved to debate philosophy with me and been willing to pay top dollar from his meager soldier's wages for the privilege. However, I rejected him as too plebian. No wonder Carmine chose to find it amusing when I spontaneously nicknamed him "my little plebeian" as an endearment on our second date.

I had been a hetaera in that life: an Athenian courtesan in the golden age of Greek philosophy (4th-5th century BC). As such, my specialty—instead of music, dance or art—was in the arts of philosophical debate and erotic lovemaking. I knew many of the main players in the areas of debate and philosophy, and I kept informed of all the latest schools of thought and scandals.

Carmine was just a soldier in that life; he was from peasant stock and totally self-educated. He was too far beneath my station to debate philosophy with. Accordingly, while I would on occasion deem to fuck him for most of his yearly wages, I did it quickly and with disdain. I never gave him what he really wanted—philosophical debate. This would have shown too much respect for his mental capabilities—and *that* I withheld.

I realized by treating Carmine so shabbily in Greece, I owed him a karmic debt. I needed to treat him with the utmost respect—not just as a man, which was relatively easy, but also and especially mentally. That was not so easy. For while I was willing to pay the debt, it became more challenging as time went on. It was not so much that he was a street kid from rural Sicily via Bensonhurst who was mostly self-educated; it was that the nature of his mind was not flexible. It was very linear, rigid and, yes, just plain argumentative.

The pain for me was that, not only did I need to pretend to enjoy debating with him—but that *he* enjoyed it so much. After all, it was what he had always wanted from me—and now he didn't even have to pay. I was. Over time, I learned that reading to him from Plato, especially about Socrates, was a soothing and romantic type of foreplay for him. I myself preferred the Stoics.

After our first meeting, I found out that Carmine was a four-time national martial arts champion, much like Kumo. Much of the power, dignity and force of will that served him so well in competing in tournaments and in life turned into detriments when it came to the suppleness needed for using his mind at a higher level of operations, for debate or anything else.

It was easy for me to respect what Carmine had made of himself. From a poor, immigrant background, he had worked progressively up the ladder as a busboy, waiter, bartender and restaurant manager for over twenty years, culminating in owning his own restaurant, with backers and a partner. But it was definitively *his* place, imbued with his energy and charm.

I knew I could clone much of his primal, earthy, grounded rootedness from our interchange. But, when he asked if I could teach him how to use his mind as deftly as I maneuvered mine, I was sorry to tell him I didn't think it was possible. As I said this to him, I was thinking to myself: *He's just too pigheaded to be receptive.* Yet, it was this same quality that made his swarthy warthog looks progressively more adorable and endearing to me as a human being, and made him such a champion as a modern-day warrior.

If this philosophical karmic thing wasn't enough of a debt to pay, after about two months of seeing each other, Carmine let the other karmic shoe drop, so to speak—but not before he had skillfully set me up for it. He was a wily character, and his timing, especially when he was in a waiting, yin-receptive mode, was impeccable.

First, he waited until I broke up with Vic. That had been coming for a while anyway, but one of the final straws was when Vic broke up with his fiancé, moved into his own apartment and decided to focus all his emotional needs on me. Not a good idea. The weight of his attention and devotion tipped the scales for me; I developed a real sexual aversion to him. This culminated in my somatizing a minor but annoying vaginal infection. My readings had been warning me for almost a year it was time to stop indulging in my desire rut with Vic. Subsequently, we more or less comfortably shifted to plan B and became just good friends.

The other angle was that Carmine's energy was so strong and territorial, it literally blew my desire for Vic out of the water. Carmine liked to stand over me in the shower after we made love and pee in a circle around my body, especially from the waist down. It was his way of marking his territory—and it seemed to work. I didn't find this demeaning at all. In fact, coming from Carmine's world view, it showed he really cared about me.

Here I am moving from Vic—a guy who enjoyed having me pee squatting directly over his mouth—to Carmine who treated me like a Sicilian peasant woman. He called me "his little girl," even though I was as close to his mother's age as I was to his. I enjoyed cooking for him and derived an irrational amount of pleasure from his contentment in our traditional roles. I finally understood how it felt to have my Venus or yin energies sitting exactly on a man's moon or emotional energies. I had always called this aspect "the love lock" when I did readings for couples—now I experienced why.

Carmine acted out the primitive male role in a way that was so endearing and playful to me, I couldn't help but enjoy playing along. It was just how our emotional dynamic naturally fit together. We took so much delight in each other's company; we were spontaneously smiling and laughing all the time.

After Vic was history, Carmine announced in January that he was officially in training for his summer tournaments. That meant he was limiting his ejaculations to once a month. Carmine believed in the Taoist philosophy of retaining his chi by conserving semen and transmuting it alchemically into power. In this philosophy, once a month was the suggested rate of squirting for a man of thirty-five; he even showed me books to hammer his viewpoint home. Unfortunately, because Carmine appeared to be constitutionally incapable of learning how to separate his orgasms from his ejaculation, it was not a realistic option for me to encourage him to develop that skill.

I wanted to support Carmine in his training program to win these tournaments because I knew his dream was to retire from the restaurant business and teach the martial arts he loved so much. But to do that, he needed to make a reputation by winning more big tournaments. I knew that if Carmine firmly believed retaining his semen was the only way to train, then if he didn't abide by his beliefs, he wouldn't be able to psych himself up to win. All this information put me into a complete ironic karmic tizzy. I knew I needed to balance my karma with him by supporting and respecting his decision to move up from being a foot-soldier to a teacher, even if this meant no nookie for me.

Carmine's fucking style was usually as fast as a jackrabbit, with increasingly minimal foreplay. The honeymoon period wore off quite rapidly for him. The romance usually does wear off, sooner or later; I'd seen it so many times before. In fact, I was so used to it that I called it the old bait-and-switch routine. Therefore, I was realistically prepared for the possibility of the romance and foreplay dying down over time. With Carmine, it happened just as soon as he knew he had sufficiently captured my interest. He started treating me as if we had been married fifty years. He enjoyed feeling no need for pretense or wooing and loved the comfort of having a mate of long-standing. I felt like I was being taken for granted a bit too soon.

Notwithstanding Carmine's kamikaze fucking style, he packed such an energetic punch when he was thrusting and his heart was so sweet, open and vulnerable like a little boy—that I had grown, much to my surprise, very attached in a very short time to having regular sex with him—short and sweet as it and he were.

I adapted to stimulating myself and coming faster with him. Because his chi and heart energy were so juicy and strong, these were enough compensating factors for wanting to stay lovers with him. I definitely felt that the Universe had granted me a fair and equitable substitution, energetically and aesthetically—and *more* than fair integrity-wise—for Kumo. The Lords of Karma in the guise of cosmic tricksters were undeniably at work.

If you combine the fact that I had lost my sexual desire for Rush years before, at a rough time for him, with how shabbily I had treated Carmine in Greece, my karma-uppance had arrived. Carmine sold his restaurant and apartment, stored his stuff with his mother in Bensonhurst, and started living with me almost full time by May. He was committed to being in serious training with his teacher for as long as his money held out; he knew he needed to compete while he was still in his prime, and his teacher was available to train him privately.

Carmine asked me to support his dreams of winning and becoming a teacher. He told me he didn't want to see or be with any other women. He had already played all that out, as he had been quite a womanizer for many years. Plus, the year before, the only girl he ever really loved dumped him, ostensibly, in his mind, because he wasn't rich or well-educated enough for her. He knew I didn't care about external stuff as much, which he especially appreciated given his history.

Carmine told me he genuinely liked me as a person. He believed I was mature and whole enough to understand what he was attempting to do, and I would not stand in his way with any emotional neediness or demands. He saw me as very strong and self-sufficient, and he even encouraged me to try transmuting my sexual chi with him. He also said that he would understand if I needed to use my vibrator, or have other lovers like Josiah in California, as long as I didn't try to mess with his training by sexually teasing him, since he had a low threshold for getting aroused.

Carmine wanted a female companion who could be an energetic ally to exchange energies with on all levels except the genital. I realized that the Universe had finally brought me the final exam in my karmic desire rut in an adorable warthog package.

This was an opportunity for me to get over my strong preference for sexual union as the glue in a relationship with a man. But it was incredibly difficult for me, and I struggled with it for months. Sometime I would slip and lure Carmine into having sex when we were cuddling affectionately; I would cross the line by rubbing against his erect penis until he lost control.

Then something happened. Our first summer together, we moved to a place energetically where his pure yang essence and my pure yin essence started commingling whenever we were alone, in either my apartment or the garden. It was as if our energies were mating in any space we inhabited together—the air was thick and sweet and whole with it. Even though we were still cuddly and affectionate, my desire for physical sex with Carmine actually started falling away—as did my need to use my vibrator to help put me to sleep at night, which was a first.

We had reached a level of alchemical union of our yin/yang essences I had only read about in translations of ancient Taoist texts. I had to pull these books out and reread them, because now this alchemical marriage was actually happening—something I had never conceived of as possible for me.

The first summer Carmine and I spent together, mostly in my garden, was primally blissful. We ate and laughed a lot, practiced our different internal arts and created our own complete little universe. We even had Kumo over a few times for dinner, with lots of storytelling and laughter. Carmine and he became like twin brothers—energetically and visually to me, each other and everyone who saw them together. It was heavenly.

Not only that. Carmine had been training hard, and it was paying off. He was winning national tournaments against guys who were twice his size. I watched some videos of these matches, and he was truly, as he said, "a giant killer." After a tournament, we always celebrated by making love, but it became less and less necessary, even for me. His presence was enough. Not only had I gotten over being a size queen with Carmine, I was actually experiencing sexual fulfillment without physical sexual union. It felt as if we were doing it all the time anyway.

# 52

## *Being in Heaven All the Time*

Carmine kept getting bigger and stronger physically and more full of chi through his training. His body felt as hard and heavy as iron. In fact, while we were watching TV in bed, all I had to do was place my hand on his ming-men (the backend of a major energy storage point along his lower spine), and an overflow of chi from his body would spontaneously back up into my whole being and move me into a state of bliss—and humor.

It was incredible. The Lords of Karma had sent me Carmine as the perfect catalytic gift to help me get over my karmic desire rut. Or, at least, raise the level of it from the tangible to the intangible.

Instead of being into sexual union as a vehicle for communing with the Divine, I was moving to a place where energetic communion was happening most of the time, even when Carmine was away. This communion started occurring spontaneously in my energetic relationship with life itself.

All the years I spent investing in my sobriety, strengthening my spiritual and psychic practices, doing emotional clearing work and, especially, my internal energy practices were starting to come together in the big payoff. Of course, my desire and willingness to choose communion directly with the Divine as a priority, rather than through a mate, was a key factor as well.

I was learning how to mate directly with the pure yang energies of heaven by being a pure yin receptor. The intangible fruits were starting to taste sweeter than I ever could have imagined. Why had I resisted so long? It was like being fucked by the celestial forces in every moment. Who knew? It truly is an acquired taste—but once acquired, not only does it become sweeter and sweeter, it never has to stop, unless *I* close the channel. Now *that's* reliability.

I moved into a space where I was receptive to being entered by heaven as my normal operating mode. The boundaries between my horizontal relationship with life on earth and my vertical relationship with the Divine started to completely dissolve. I was in heaven all the time and simultaneously being fucked by life—but in a good way.

I

Things really started picking up speed as soon as I met Carmine. After our second date, he was staying over at my house when I got the call that Rush had passed over from a heart attack. Carmine held me as I sobbed for hours. I took it as a very good sign that he didn't abandon me in my time of need, even though he did continue to watch his Sunday football game with the sound off as he held me. I was pretty hysterical for a while. After all, my oldest best friend of twenty-six years had just died. Most guys would have suggested I call a female friend to console me. But Carmine could handle it; he didn't split. His solid heart-centered character was unmistakably evident.

In the first few weeks after Rush's passing, and especially in the first few days, Rush made his presence extremely known to me. In fact, sometimes, like when I was taking a bath and trying to relax, I had to ask him to give me a break and chill for a bit. Rush was so excited to be communicating with me so clearly. He felt that I could receive whatever information or messages he was sending for me or anyone else close to him. Many of us joked at his memorial that he was coming through so strongly to so many of us, it was easier to get ahold of him *now* than before he passed, as he was notorious for his lackadaisical attitude about returning messages.

Ever since Rush passed, I have received regular messages from him for myself and for others; his energy essence is always available, although not as close as in the first few months. When the messages are for others, Rush can be relentless with me, sometimes even yelling in my head, until I relay the messages. When the messages are for me, I have to make an effort, not so much to remember them, but to really use them to live by.

One of his first messages was an apology for ridiculing my sobriety for almost twenty years, as he still liked the occasional toke and glass of wine or cognac when he was embodied. Rush said it was only clear to him now, from the other side, how important my sober consciousness was for the stability of my channel system.

Next, he told me that his perspective and appreciation for things human was quite different since he dropped his body. He had always thought my crystal-clear channel to other dimensions for information and energy was my greatest gift. But now, he saw that my enthusiasm for the adventure of life and my ability to infuse others with this was, by far, a more rare and precious gift. Rush encouraged me to cherish and cultivate this emotional tone of enthusiasm and nurture it well, as not many people had even a taste of it or for it. And even if they did, I could teach them how to sustain their enthusiasm by power of example and through direct energetic transmissions.

In addition to getting direct messages from Rush from time to time, I always request special messages from him when I do readings for myself with the galactic forces. For example, Rush pointed out to me when I was slipping with Carmine or anyone else, in terms of karmic obligations. He reminded me that Carmine had made a life for himself in which he carried himself with great dignity—even when, through most of his life, he had suffered great indignities. He had turned all this into forming his character with innate integrity and honor. Rush reminded me to see him this way and treat him with the respect he was due.

Rush said that, from the other side, the name of the game on the earth plane was clearly about expanding one's human emotional range and depth, and any entertainment which moves the emotions, in any form, is a good thing. I started making this a more conscious criterion for those people I chose to have in my life, besides my old standards of karmic connection and vibrational affinity. Now, personalities who are entertaining to be around carry more weight in my preferences I also started to cultivate more facets in my own being that are mischievous, playful and fun to be around. Since then, I have come to realize if I genuinely like and appreciate those around me, my heart naturally opens toward them with more compassion and generosity.

One of my most moving experiences with Rush happened just after he passed over. His consciousness merged with mine so I could see the wonders of the earth through his eyes. I saw the incredible diversity of humankind and, even more than that, the uniqueness of every soul incarnate in human form. All the myriad sights, sounds and colors were magnified in technicolor brilliance a thousand-fold.

Rush told me he had a deep nostalgia for the personal human emotional range with its illusions of separateness, boundaries and individual identity. He said he missed the physical senses as well. I saw that if I didn't experience the full range of emotions in depth, as well as the full enjoyment of the senses (not much fear of that), the karmic longing of unfinished business would pull me back to experience the lesson of humanness once again. Not that I would have minded when I was younger; that's how the wheel of karma turns, after all. But I prefer to do it more by choice next time and less from unfinished assignments or regret. I remembered, once again, through my communion with Rush, how truly rare and precious each human incarnation is as an opportunity for growth and experience which one cannot get in any other dimension except the physical.

I experienced the other side of the equation when Rush gave me a taste of traveling through dimensions of limitless light and co-creative energy with him. He didn't let me travel with him for too long, as he knew I would like it too much (I did), and he didn't want me to lose my focus and enthusiasm for the work and play I have yet to do here.

From all of this, I gained a perspective that I never had so viscerally before. I grasped that heaven and all the dimensions of being that it contains are always available when we leave the earth—but that the experience available through the density of the third dimension is *only* available when one is incarnate in a physical body.

Therefore, *the trick seems to be* to dissolve the space/time continuum and bring heaven into every moment while incarnate, so there really is no where else to go but *here.* In learning to master this trick, I shifted into a new paradigm of being, and a new psychic archetype was born.

Now, I am no longer simply emanating the high priestess archetype for my clients, capable of initiating them into the mysteries of dissolving the space/time continuum. I became a galactic *daikini,* (a Tibetan word for goddess) and started to radiate this energy as well—allowing me to update the old cosmic trickster archetype to a more modern feminine version. With this embodied energy, I can sweeten the shift to a new level of being with play and humor. And not just with my clients anymore either. That was the next boundary that began to dissolve.

II

I knew Rush was in the process of dying for over a year before he fully left his body. Even though I was psychologically prepared for his death, I projected that I would still be devastated. I had asked Josiah if he would be willing to be on call if I needed him when Rush passed, and he agreed.

By the time the actual event occurred, however, I didn't need Josiah to fly out. It wasn't so much because Carmine was there. I just knew it was better for me to be alone and gather around me my inner circle of New York friends, who all knew and loved Rush.

Since Sedona, it was clear that Josiah wasn't capable of being present emotionally for any length of time—except, of course, for that occasional teasing glimmer of our soul connection during psychic and sexual practices together.

This was exponentially confirmed once Carmine was firmly on the scene. Carmine was so *present* and naturally open hearted just being his authentic self. Even when he was sleeping, he felt more present than when Josiah was awake and try-ing to be present. I kept this observation as my private joke, but I did file it away for future reference.

The next time I saw Josiah, six months had passed since our three days in Sedona. Through that half-year, we had maintained our friendship with long weekly late-night phone calls. I was aware that the romance had cooled; the majority of the attempts to keep our conversations lively were coming from my end.

Obviously, I told him about Carmine and decided to tell Carmine about him. Absurdly, Josiah seemed to have a harder time accepting that Carmine was in my life, considering he was the one who was married as well as maintaining other lov-ers on the side. These I heard about periodically, when he was having problems with their demands. Once, he even left a love note for his wife to find, and she put him under house arrest. Then, I got to do therapy on the phone with him—I rationalized that was what friends do for each other anyway.

Josiah arrived in New York City in late March for a two-night stopover on his way back from a music gig in Europe. At this point, I don't think he would have gone too much out of his way to see me, except that New York was a convenient stop on his way home.

He was jetlagged, but sweet to be with, and came bearing a beautiful gift of a tiger's eye pendant. We were both pretty good in the gifts-with-deep-meaning department. This was his second really good jewelry gift, the first being a beauti-ful heirloom hematite and opal pendant. He had also given me a Tibetan bell with an exquisite tone, and I had given him one of my favorite paintings of an Egyptian initiation scene.

Besides, a few days with Josiah was a lovely yin interlude in the midst of Car-mine's full-blown nonstop yang energy. They were complete energetic and tem-peramental opposites, and I enjoyed playing the range. My ba gua teacher Alan, who knew them both, couldn't comprehend how I could be with two men who were so completely different. I explained that was exactly the point!

I had been really pissed off at Josiah in mid-February, when he abruptly can-celed our confirmed plans to spend ten days together in Kauai. He begged off because of business and financial pressures. I really needed a vacation, and every-thing—the condo, the airfare—was already paid for. I really wanted to go, but not alone.

I switched gears and invited Mark, my camp friend from rural Oregon, to join me, and he did. We had such a lovely time together as friends. I really didn't miss all the emotional work of being with Josiah. Mark was so smooth and easy to travel with; we naturally gave each other just the right amount of space and companionship. I resolved to invite Mark to travel with me more often, instead of Josiah, and not just as a backup.

Because things went so splendidly in Kauai, it was easy to let go of any resentment toward Josiah. Naturally, Josiah immediately regretted his decision, just as he had the summer before. The pattern was more than abundantly clear, and I wasn't even trying hard to look: passive/aggressive with a silken sledgehammer.

During Josiah's visit, I invited him to attend a soiree that Will was having. I knew that Carmine, who was a long-time friend of Will's in the small world of the martial arts, wouldn't be able to make it because the party was on a Saturday night when he was needed at the restaurant.

As luck would have it, the day before the party and the day Josiah arrived, Carmine had emergency dental surgery on two impacted wisdom teeth and was very sick from an allergic reaction to antibiotics. Carmine may have been too sick to go to work, but he wasn't too sick to attend the party and check out Josiah. He was still queasy, and his face had blown up to twice its normal size, which is saying a lot. Carmine had an incredibly strong competitive streak, which is one reason why he won all his tournaments. It was curiosity of his adversary that drew him to the party, not any desire to be social. He just couldn't resist.

I told Will I was afraid if Carmine showed up there might be trouble. He had the perfect solution. He gave Carmine a very complex mechanical puzzle to untangle, involving lots of intricate pieces of metal. Carmine sat in a corner, as peaceful as a lamb, and as involved with his toy as a five-year-old boy, which is exactly how he looked, with an expression of amused concentration.

Later in the evening, things got even more amusing. I was sitting in Will's living room with Josiah to one side, overdressed in a custom-made black suit, and very stiff and formal, with his Leo sun and Capricorn ascendant guard up. To my left was Will, in his usual party mode after a few drinks, hugging and kissing everyone and telling them how much he loved them. Next to Josiah was Kumo, in a very giggly, excited mood and, directly across from me, sat Carmine, momentarily without his toy.

There we all were, two of my current lovers, an ex-lover and "the one who got away" trying to one up each other by telling increasingly more outrageous and humorous stories of their exploits. I just sat there watching it all in a long chocolate-brown velvet ensemble and a Mona Lisa smile. Carmine and Kumo were especially entertaining as they were always competing with each other, whether it was martial arts or tall tales. It was hilarious. I was doubled over laughing so hard, I was afraid I was going to pee in my panties. I also found all of the attention quite gratifying to my narcissistic playgirl tendencies. All in all, it was a dream party. No one could have imagined anything this good.

When Josiah and I were leaving the party, I kissed Carmine goodnight as he was making half-hearted attempts to pick up a drunken girl in the kitchen, just to keep his end up. I felt a bit awkward, since Saturday was always one of Carmine's regular nights at my place. Under the circumstances, he was extremely well-mannered and civilized about the situation, with no hard feelings, which I truly appreciated.

The following summer, when I went to Camp Franz for two weeks, Carmine knew I would be seeing Josiah there. By then, we were living together almost eight months, and we had settled into a very comfy routine. The night before I left, as a goodbye gift, Carmine "threw me a good one," to mark his territory, sincerely wished me a good trip and promised to water the garden while I was gone. I was in heaven—and bicoastal.

## III

I should have known, once I arrived at camp and Josiah was running a day late, there was no way our time together could compare to the memories and heat of our intensely passionate first week together. It turned out to be so internally opposite of that first week, with the externals being so similar, the contrast made it especially painful and disillusioning.

At my suggestion, Josiah pitched his tent on a hill overlooking the main house, rather than several miles away, down a gravel road at the creek like the first time. That way, I wouldn't be dependent on him to drive me back and forth to meals and classes, as he tended to dawdle. I had also reserved a bed in one of the dorm rooms in the main house for convenience and to keep my options open.

From our first night together, Josiah was as weird with me as I had ever seen him. He didn't want to talk or make love. He didn't even want me to touch him, which was especially difficult because the air mattress he brought was defective. Consequently, I kept rolling into him as the air leaked out. He'd turn away from me when this happened as if I were a leper or something. It seemed that coming to camp to be with me for two weeks was such an assertive act that it completely overloaded his emotional circuits. He was so immobilized, he seemed almost comatose.

After three days of this ridiculous behavior, I gave up on him energetically and focused all my attention on the classes with Franz. I started socializing with my many camp friends whom I had been neglecting, while trying to coax Josiah out of his zombie-like state. I tried not to take any of it personally. Of course, just as soon as I switched gears, Josiah perked up and promised to make an effort to be more present with me the following week, after a weekend break with his family.

When Josiah returned on Monday, I was in a good mood after spending time on the coast with some friends. He seemed to be in better spirits, and he really did try to be with me, but I felt as if it were mostly for public show. When we sat together in classes or at meals, he held my hand and even cracked a smile occasionally. It seemed important to him to appear to still be a couple.

In private, Josiah was still almost completely shutdown. Sexually, we only made love one time that had any real heat to it, or eye contact, for that matter. That happened our last full day at camp, when I reserved my dorm room for an hour for some privacy during siesta time. It was a desperate act to try to make some connection with Josiah before we parted. The intense heat of the day and the defective air mattress had conspired to make the tent a "no-fucking zone" for Josiah. Yet the conditions were almost identical to our first week of intense love-making, reminding me that nothing seems impossible in the first heat of passion.

After camp, I went to the redwoods in Humboldt with Mark and Morgan, another camp friend from England. This turned out to be the best part of the trip. We had a glorious time practicing our ba gua meditation under the giant trees and then hiking to the Lost Coast to picnic and practice on the beach, surrounded by herds of elk and fields of wildflowers.

Naturally, since I was having a really good time without him, Josiah kept calling me in Humboldt. He insisted on seeing me one more time before I left for the East Coast. I only managed to squeeze in an hour-and-a-half visit with him, after much travel hassles and, even as I did it, I had a feeling the joke would be on me—one more time.

After giving me a tour of his family home, while his wife was at work, and showing me how my painting was prominently displayed in the living room, we went to a nearby Denny's to talk. Josiah wanted me to understand how conflicted he was, how much he had to lose if he got divorced, and how miserable he was for not taking the risk. He was truly in a karmic prison of his own making. I was glad I was not his warden, although he seemed to be attached to needing someone in that role. I was getting very tired of being his confessor—especially since his offerings lately had become increasingly paltry.

I flew home, reflecting on how I had evolved from being a spiritual pragmatist to a romantic one as well. With Josiah, as in most generic affairs with married men, there were lots of promises and talk of love, hot sex and the future. The reality is that nothing happened with Josiah unless I made it happen—and that gets old fast. In my heart, I knew it was just as well he stayed married and on the

West Coast, because if he lived near me and was more available, I would probably get bored with him within six months. The good news is that long-distance affairs get to be played out over years, instead of months, and the bad news is—exactly the same.

Josiah was very good at setting me up with expectations that never panned out in person, except for those enticing glimmers that are always the hook. I was seeing his dishonesty to himself, and his wife, spreading like a cancer that I wanted no part of.

Naturally, by mid-flight, my thoughts turned to Carmine, who was waiting at my place. Carmine had never said the love word and yet I could feel it emanating from him all the time. He would only go so far in expressing how much he really liked me, and this he did often and with affection. He also emphasized that what he liked about me was who I was as a being—not anything to do with my special gifts as a psychic, or anything I could do for him in that regard. It was refreshing to know I was coming home to someone so honest.

It would have been easy to stay angry at Josiah for continually setting me up with false hopes, and to stay angry at myself for letting him. I resolved not to let Josiah's bullshit get to me anymore. It wasn't worth the aggravation. Still, it took another year and a half for me to completely unwind from him. I had to see him three more times, all in California, before the price became too high to pay. The pleasure/pain continuum took a bit longer than usual to shift with Josiah, perhaps because the stakes started out higher to begin with.

IV

Upon my arrival on the redeye, Carmine greeted me in the same way we had parted, but he didn't just "throw me a good one." We actually made love in a leisurely fashion, at least based on his usual speed. Maybe it was because he was still half asleep, but, just as in our brief courtship days, there was eye contact and mutual visual appreciation, along with the always exceptional energetic commingling.

I was really glad to be home and pleasantly surprised that Carmine was there to greet me in such a friendly fashion. I had learned a lot at camp, but not as much as I could have, without the distraction of Josiah's demanding moodiness. But the high point in my memories wasn't camp or Josiah at all. It was my three days in the redwoods with Mark and Morgan, two gorgeous beings in their late twenties, who turned out to be the perfect traveling companions on all levels. I don't know which scenery I enjoyed more: the world class redwoods and Lost

Coast or the energy triangulation with my companions. Probably the combination of both is what made it so memorable.

Carmine and I had a lovely August in the garden. Kumo visited us on Sundays around dinnertime. He was the perfect addition to our little heaven out on the shady deck with cool breezes, even on the hottest days, and always much conviviality and laughter.

In September, Carmine started seriously training again for a big international competition in Taiwan scheduled for late November. That meant the no-nookie rule was enforced again, with occasional slip-ups that stemmed from my instigation, I confess.

## Karmic/Psychic Interlude—The Spiritual Courtesan

In the meantime, Kumo and my relationship had been evolving in a most interesting way since we met the summer before. Once I had surrendered to the fact that I wasn't Kumo's type for a romantic relationship (hooking up with Carmine certainly speeded up that process), Kumo and I were able to move into a dynamic which created a direct energetic bleed-through to a karmic bond we had in India.

It was one of my all-time favorite lives, the one where I had been a very successful Brahmin courtesan. When I met Kumo, I was at a stage in that life in my forties, where I was training young girls, as well as some select young men, in the arts of love, and maintaining several ongoing relationships with long-time lovers. Most of those were Brahmin caste, but Kumo was not. He was from a mixed merchant/warrior class, but he had aspirations. I took him on as a student because he had promise. Just as in this life when, after many late night conversations to help him embrace his karma and not run from it, he started seeing me as his "spiritual mother."

Trying not to be incestuous (most of the time), I looked for some way to harness Kumo's exceptional energetic gifts. My first idea was that he could give me some private lessons in the internal components of chi gong. Unfortunately, after a few lessons, Kumo, being an energy idiot savant, rather seriously injured me by not being sensitive enough to calibrate his energy and step it down enough to my level of capacity.

Out on my deck one evening, Kumo pressed down so hard on my shoulders to check my alignments and root that, when he stopped pressing, I sprang out of my body so far that the cord connecting me to it snapped. There I was, lying passed out on the deck, with Kumo trying desperately to revive me. I was watching this scene from about fifteen feet up. As I looked down at my body lying there, I was thinking, *Oh shit!* I had no choice but to slowly re-enter my body as an act of will. Since then, I have maintained myself in my body by conscious intent, which, over time, has become more or less on automatic. Before then, I was never that immersed in my body, and since then, one could say I have also become non-attached.

After that, I decided: no more private lessons with Kumo. Instead, I asked him if he would be willing to do bodywork on me, especially to open up my feet, which were still energetically bound. After examining my feet at camp, Franz had told me that if they were *his* feet, he would make it his number one priority to get them open as soon as possible. Then the channel for my psychic energies through my crown and my rooting energies through my feet would come more into balance.

Receiving bodywork from Kumo was heavenly—*because* he is an energy idiot savant. Since my sexuality was no longer primarily centered through my genitals, it felt exactly as if we were making love whenever he worked on me. In my darkened living room, with exotic music playing in the background, I lay on the floor, only partially covered by a towel. Usually stripped down to his underwear, Kumo slathered me with oil and did his energy thing, sweating all over me.

He worked very deeply, which was at times, very painful. Sometimes the pain was intense as my karmically bound feet released their trauma. I spontaneously started kicking Kumo in the back as hard as I could, with my free foot, to help relieve some of the pressure. He was a sweetheart and let me kick him, which helped speed up the whole process immeasurably. When he wasn't working on my feet, I just received his energy as a totally receptive vessel.

Afterwards, we sat and talked, sipped tea and nibbled on snacks until late into the evening. I advised him on how to cope with the "karmic salt mines" he was still laboring in, as he tried to pay off his debts and help his family. In our talks, I was operating from the yang side of my mental and psychic nature, and he became the receptive one. It was a perfect balance—my favorite thing.

I tried to explain to Kumo and Carmine why any two-person martial arts practice, whether rou shou (from ba gua) or push hands (from tai chi), was just like having sex energetically to me. The purpose of this type of sparring is to tune into the other person's chi and try to destabilize them by being sensitive to their movements, alignments and root. Since I no longer felt that genital merging was the only way to experience sexual union, it felt almost the same as the physical act to me.

Neither of them had any idea or understanding of what I was talking about. This was probably good because, if they ever did comprehend what I was saying, their heads would be so screwed up they wouldn't be able to compete with other guys; with girls, their dicks would just get hard. Although I did notice that after that Carmine stopped practicing push-hands with one guy he knew was definitely gay.

With my level of sensitivity, I wouldn't consider sparring with anyone, male or female, unless their energy was palatable enough for me to want to be with them intimately, at least in theory. This may be a corollary effect of what happens when the boundaries between vertical and horizontal union with the Divine dissolve.

In any case, my relationship with Kumo continued to evolve both ways. When we did interchange energies it was sweet, just like in India. It was a slice of karma-coated heavenly candy—with no calories, no after effects and no emotional fall-out.

After a year of regular sessions, Kumo announced that my feet were finally open. While they still need maintenance to keep them open (no tight shoes, as I have gone from a size 6 to a size 8 wide in this process), the ramifications, now that my psychic channel is balancing out with my connections to the earth, are still being revealed.

V

When Carmine left in mid-November for the Far East, he planned to be gone for about nine months and to continue his training in Tokyo after his competition. Within days of his departure and, after Josiah canceled a tentative visit to New York once again, I decided it was an opportune time to swear off men for a while and give myself a breather.

About a day after this decision, while I was sitting outside a coffee shop in the East Village having hot chocolate one evening and musing about my vow of celibacy, an old acquaintance named Phil, formerly from the neighborhood, stopped to say hello. Phil had an unrequited crush on me from about fifteen years before, and he immediately started coming on to me. The irony of the timing was hardly lost on me.

Phil wasn't bad looking for an aging hippie. He was about my age and tall, with blond hair and blue eyes, a lanky physique and a sort of rabbity look, so his beard helped. He was a self-proclaimed philosopher/mad poet, with a few small books to his credit. Within five minutes of meeting, he was reciting love poems to me, and they were quite good. The poems hooked me, as I'm sure they had countless times before at poetry readings he did regularly around town.

What I liked the most about Phil was that he seemed *so* into me, and his infatuation had been unrequited for so long. I decided to requite it, after the requisite three dates of the nineties. It turned into a brief affair of about a half-dozen overnight dates, as he lived out of town. Each one got progressively more irritating, which made for an interesting but educational disaster.

Phil got comfortable at my place much too quickly for my taste, especially since he proved to be an eager but mediocre lover. It wasn't so much that he didn't know the moves, his energy and his prick were just so lame compared to Carmine's. I had definitely been spoiled in the energy department by being with someone of world class caliber. The joke was really on me. I had moved from being a size queen to an energy empress—and nothing less than what I had become accustomed to seemed to do.

I decided to follow the advice I always gave to clients: "It's lonely at the top. But it's also lonely in the middle and lonely on the bottom, so you might as well get on with where you're going." I banished Phil from my kingdom. If I had any doubts, they vanished when I realized Phil had been pilfering pain meds (left over from dental surgery) from my medicine cabinet for his "bad back." That, combined with regular beer drinking and cigarette smoking, were too much to tolerate for long anyway.

Interestingly, Phil had been writing a sexual memoir, which I read and tried to promote for him through a writer friend of mine who had good contacts and gives good advice. The only response I got from Jerry, who has known me for almost twenty years, was, "You could do much better than this yourself. And I bet it would be a lot more interesting. That's something that I would want to read for sure." Jerry and his wife, who were also good clients of long standing, had been trying to get me involved in a threesome for many years, until we had all mellowed out with age.

But Jerry's words started percolating. A memoir of my erotic life was something I thought I would get around to when I was eighty and things slowed down a bit. Yet, I wasn't able to sleep at night as the words of this memoir started bubbling up inside me. I realized that the emotional juice and enthusiasm were there now. In a few years, I might be in such a different place that my interest in writing this would be gone. And by the time I was eighty, I had a feeling all these memories would be so far from who I had become—they would seem like earlier incarnations.

I developed a compulsion to get my memories down on paper now. Thus, from a lame affair the seeds of *Cosmic Sugar* were born. I had to put several more serious works-in-progress on the shelf, as writing this became simply irresistible. The good news happened just as soon as I stopped seeing Phil.

Carmine returned after only two months, with more medals, more fame and more attitude than ever. Unfortunately, along with the training Carmine picked up in Japan, he also picked up a little too much of the samurai mentality for my taste. It was rough the first few weeks he was back because his heart was so shielded there was a definite chill in the air. I felt as if I were lying in bed next to a killer, which is the mode he needed to operate in while he was training and competing.

After a few weeks, Carmine slowly thawed, his heart reopened, and things were very good between us again. He even enjoyed hearing me read parts of my first draft of this memoir, although I did read him selective sections. He could handle the sexual parts much more easily than the karmic or psychic stuff, which always weirded him out.

Carmine was especially concerned about his chapter in the book. He suggested I call it "Carmine the Giant Killer." He even suggested I leave the karmic and psychic parts out, as if I could separate myself like that—even though I did manage to with him. I just fed my psychic self elsewhere—at least on the verbal level. Energetically, we communed all the time. He seemed more and more to me like a rotund, smiling, primal Buddha.

In the spring of 1999, Carmine's martial arts teacher passed away suddenly from a stroke. He had been Carmine's mentor and spiritual father for over ten years. Their heart bond had been the deepest Carmine had ever had with anyone. He was disconsolate. Yet, after a period of mourning, he stepped up and took over his teacher's lineage and school. I was so proud of him. I felt as if my karmic work with him, both debts and lessons, was nearing its conclusion.

Knowing this, we had one more loving, bittersweet summer hanging out in the garden, where we were in heaven all the time. It was a combination of alchemically commingling our energies at the highest levels, the humor of animals playing on the Discovery Channel and the comfortability of being married fifty years—all rolled into one.

During this last spring and summer, I saw Josiah twice briefly on my way going or coming from classes or camp with Franz in Northern California. These visits were loving and friendly, but I could feel our reasons for coming together unwinding as well. I was becoming more peaceful with the inevitability that everything falls away at the perfect time.

I had predicted, after a couple of years of sobriety, it would take me at least ten years to learn how to accept life on life's terms, and another ten years to learn how to do it gracefully. Near the end of my second decade of sobriety, I was just beginning to get the hang of what grace felt like in the dance of life.

That fall was busy and productive with my private practice and writing. No matter how much was going on, I always felt my internal core was stable and more substantial than ever before. Any external turbulence felt like a ripple on the periphery of my being.

Reluctantly, Carmine started thinking about having to gear up to go back to work in the restaurant business. His money was running out after two years, and his teaching, which he loved, didn't pay all his bills. He went into a depression, as only a sensitive Piscean can. He took to our bed and slept for days at a time. He seemed to lose interest in interchanging energies with me on any level, and we started squabbling over silly things.

When it was too cold to hang out on the deck anymore, our living area got smaller. I started feeling as if Carmine were an immovable object taking up space in our bed. I couldn't get him interested in talking, cuddling or engaging with me at all. He would just lie there, grunt and switch channels on the remote. As a New Year's millennium gift for us both, I pushed him out of our cozy nest so that we could fly. I wanted to do this while things were still relatively good between us, with no acrimony or recriminations. And it worked. We parted as loving friends in early January 2000.

I wish I could say my parting with Josiah was as loving and on as high a road, karmically speaking. Sadly, on a trip to California for a week in March, Josiah's behavior was so cumulatively lame and dishonest and his inability to be emotional present so absent that I hit my tolerance levels for insidious psychological abuse. He got a Dear Josiah letter while performing music one night at a club. I just dropped it at his feet and walked out. No applause. Even though he was the one who was truly ending it slowly with a whimper, my style has always been more of a decisive bang, once I get fed up enough.

When I got back to my hotel room, I felt an overwhelming sense of release and relief that I had cut the cord. This is always a good sign that one has made the right decision. So much weight had been lifted; I spontaneously danced a little laughing jig. I had just liberated myself from a three-year Neptunian delusion that had less and less reality in present time and space. Even a psychic can fool herself some of the time, if the illusion is pretty enough and hits the right karmic chords.

Now, in the late spring of 2000, I am in a space full of love, wonder and excitement for all of life—including me. And that ain't a bad place to be. As I meditate and practice the internal arts in a bliss state in my beautiful garden, I feel how abundantly the Universe provides everything needed for soul growth. If energy is the true currency of life, I have come to realize that heart energy is the gold standard. On that measure, I make my stand.

In closing, I want to share a prophetic dream I had on the night before my wedding in 1987. I dreamt I walked into an ante room where a group of white-robed, bearded Indian gurus sat playing poker. I sensed that if I moved out of this room and into the next, there was a staircase that would take me to the wedding chapel. I became paralyzed with fear.

One of the gurus, who looked just like the trickster Rajneesh, turned to me, raised his right hand up, with his palm facing me, and kindly said, "Do not be afraid. There is nothing to fear."

I replied, "How can you say that?"

The guru smiled gently and responded, "You are always in heaven. *You just forgot!*

Now, I have remembered … and may I never forget again.

# *EPILOGUE*

I

I just read the last chapter which I wrote over six years ago. All I can say is, "Ha!"

At that time, the cosmic karmic tricksters had lulled me into a temporary state of contentment with my aloneness as I sat meditating in my garden. After about ninety days, I headed out for my last summer of a seven-year cycle at Camp Franz in Northern California.

Josiah and I had not spoken since the split in March. I had no desire or expectation to see him while I was out West. My good friend Will was coming to camp with me, and we planned to spend a few days after camp in the redwoods in Humboldt with my friend Mark, the potter from Oregon.

I was more than at peace with these plans. It has always been easier for me to become celibate in between relationships than to keep my sexual energies open for any sporadic possibilities, thus minimizing emotional and energetic turbulence. I had deliberately and comfortably transmuted these energies into a higher frequency psychic/spiritual level of operation. I was looking forward to building up some momentum on this development at the retreat, which was an advanced one-week chi gong intensive.

And I say it again, "Ha!" What is it they say about the best laid plans? Literally, in my case.

As soon as I arrived at the retreat center, high up in the Sonoma Mountains, I began unpacking in my dorm room when there was a light tapping on the door. I looked up and there was Josiah, unannounced, uninvited, hat in hand, so to speak, and smiling shyly.

I'd been holding unresolved resentment toward him for months, remnants of the rage I felt when I broke things off. Seeing him in his sweetest wooing mode, the same that had caught my attention six years previously, was discombobulating. He asked if he could speak with me. We went out on the balcony overlooking a gorgeous mountain vista of rolling hills.

Josiah apologized profusely for not being there for me emotionally or any other way in March, with the usual excuses of family pressures. I fell for it, of course. Why? He knew how to push all the right karmic buttons that fed my ego in our ongoing reincarnational drama of the Pharaoh supplicating to the High Priestess for absolution. And, boy, did I give it to him.

We stumbled into my bed in the dorm room after hastily locking the door and made mad, passionate make-up love—one of the best kinds. It was eye to eye and mouth to mouth, with deep penetration on all levels of our being, except the personal, as usual.

We emerged from the dorm room, rumpled and grinning, to find a couple of very confused women who had been waiting to get into *their* room. We apologized and wandered out on the grounds looking for a place for Josiah to set up his tent for what, we had agreed, would be a one-week retreat in paradise—in other words, a mutual folly à deux.

While looking for a campsite, we found a small metal trailer that was as yet unoccupied. We knew the accommodations were fully booked, so we found the posted list of attendees and their designated room assignments. We discovered that the two guys who had been given the trailer had opted to camp out instead, as the trailer had only one small bed and was quite stuffy. This was probably a smart move since we were in the middle of a heat wave of 110+ degrees during the day. We would be baking like sardines in a large tin can.

Nonetheless, we decided it was a heaven-sent omen. When we tented on the last retreat, it had been inconvenient and uncomfortable, exacerbating our dynamic at the time. Rather than risk a repeat, we moved Josiah's stuff and some of mine immediately into our new "home" and even found a fan to cool our sweat. I decided to keep my dorm space as well, for storage and extra bathroom privileges.

We anointed the new bed with our conjoined energies and emerged, rumpled and grinning once again, to the bemused eyes of Franz and William, old, old friends, who were soaking in the hot tub next to our new home. We could read in their eyes what we knew to be true. A new chapter in our karmic dance had just begun with a bang.

The next week was a very happy memory, even in the midst of it. I was subtly aware that hindsight nostalgia was operational in present time, especially in peak moments. A cycle was ending—and not just with Camp Franz.

Josiah and I had exquisite afternoon siestas every day. Although I did notice he was much more selfish in bed than he had been in our very first week together in the summer of 1995. I probably shouldn't have been surprised, but I still felt some disappointment. I hoped his initial wooing generosity in regard to oral sex, compliments and stroking might be back after our four month breakup—but it was not to be. I also noted that he wasn't into kissing as much as the week progressed, and he preferred doing it doggy style a bit more than ever before. Our relationship had always been more on the soul or psychic plane than on the personality level, but now it was becoming even more impersonal. It was still open-hearted, but cooler in tone and definitely more about the energetic and pleasure circuitries we were activating than anything else.

Still, Josiah was a consummate swordsman—so he got his, and I certainly got mine. But he was more detached and less affectionate, with less hugging and cuddling than ever before. I had gotten used to much more with Carmine, preferred it that way and noted the difference.

By our last night of lovemaking, Josiah's body language announced he wanted me to service him orally on my knees. Then he entered me from behind with no kissing, no foreplay. And I knew, *I knew* this was the last time—and not just for that week.

One of my favorite tantric practices has always been to imagine that it is the first time, with all the anticipation and danger of a strange cock entering, or that it is the last, with the bittersweet taste of nostalgia. Either way, this technique brings one's awareness fully into the present moment with a sharp focus that dissolves the space/time continuum and brings one into the eternal now.

With Josiah that last night, it was more than just a meditation technique. With every exquisite stroke I embraced the knowing that, "*This is it, this is it,*" with full presence. I felt truly all right with it. I accepted it as *done.* And it ended as it had begun—sweet.

The next day after lunch, Josiah wanted to have a closure talk in the trailer before our public goodbyes. He took my hand, looked me in the eye and said, "Where do we go from here?" I looked him in the eye and said, "I don't know." But I did.

## II

About five months after my last meeting with Josiah, starting in January 2001 and running through November of that year, I am chagrined to admit that, karmically speaking, I didn't just regress, I fell off a cliff.

In the ancient Hindu board game of *Leela* (which means cosmic play in Sanskrit), one's spiritual growth is marked by the throw of a die (symbolizing karma) through seventy-two aspects and eight planes of consciousness. One can move ahead in a slow steady way, one throw at a time. Or if one lands on a square with an arrow signifying good karmic choices, one's growth can accelerate faster and skip to a higher level in just one move. But if one is at a higher level in the game and lands on a square with a snake, one can slide back down to the first plane of consciousness which is ruled by *maya*, or illusion.

In hindsight, that is what happened to me. I had cultivated a taste for the intangible fruits of merging with the Divine through my spiritual practices, but then I fell down the rabbit hole, the slippery slope, landing on the biggest snake in the game. It's called *tamas* in Sanskrit, and among other things it connotes darkness, ignorance, sloth and indulgence on the sense level.

The online dating scene is the worst possible neighborhood for someone with a karmic pleasure rut to hang out in. It was a place I swore I would never get into because I was into people in a live way and meeting men online seemed too removed and mental to me. After camp with Josiah, I "forgot" to consciously shut down my sexual energies and consistently switch back to vertical feeding from Source. Therefore, I was emotional unstable. So when I discovered how much fun playing in the online scene was, and how it fed my second chakra ego identity, I quickly became addicted to it. It was an even more terrifying and rapid descent than when I hit bottom with drugs, alcohol and promiscuity twenty years prior.

Once I got into the groove of how the online dating scene worked, I worked it like a pro. With my personal ad plus photo on multiple dating sites, I ultimately racked up about 1,500 responses. Talk about feeding my ego. No, talk about feeding the black hole in me. And you know what they say about black holes. Especially when you consider that one of the archetypes I most identify with is the Hindu goddess, Kali the Devourer.

Here is the dating technology I honed: If the guy's initial letter passed muster (only about 100 did), I requested a photo and birthdate, so I could set up their astrology chart for compatibility. From this, only about fifty looked reasonable. Then I moved on to the phone call for further screening. If they sounded depressed, overly horny, too kinky, boring or charmingly sociopathic and dark (been there, done that), they were disqualified. This left about forty guys I met for coffee over a ten-month period—more than one a week would have been too draining.

Only one slipped through my discrimination process in the first few months. He convinced me to meet without seeing a photo because of "computer problems." Since it was a slow week, and he promised "I wouldn't be disappointed," I obliged. He looked and acted like the creature from the black lagoon: creepy, passive/aggressively insecure, deeply pock-marked and slimy. When I immediately told him there was no chemistry and I wanted to split without chitchat to save us both time, he became extremely hostile in a scary way and even followed up with a nasty email. Lesson learned.

Of the forty or so coffee dates, I ended up having a number of one-night stands or short affairs with a variety of men to boys. I put it that way because the crop kept getting younger as I loosened my original criterion. The initial standards expressed in my ad were: a man over thirty-five, spiritual and sensual, a playmate and potential mate, with an open heart and emotionally available.

What I got were a lot of sensual playmates or wannabes, all emotionally under-developed, lonely and very horny—and the cutest ones were all under thirty-five. Since this was what the Universe was offering me, I rationalized that I'd accept—at least until some emotionally mature mate material arrived. In the final stages of this almost yearlong run in the shallow end of the karmic dating pool, I ended up with a small harem of exotic foreign pretty boys, mostly East Indian, culturally sex-starved and all under thirty.

My bottom was that while they kept wanting more, I couldn't even keep their names straight (no excuse, but two of them did have the same name). My indifference to the whole scene was beginning to sicken me. I knew I was going to have to shut the entire situation down sooner rather than later, before it deadened my heart and spirit. I was changing sheets so often it felt like I was running a bordello—and while karmically familiar, if the purpose was pleasure, there were rapidly diminishing returns.

After 9/11, I had my last playmate in this karmic cycle of review. I knew it was a test to see if I could bottom out and let go of this phase of boys I had been toying with over the summer. That was in part a reaction to online dating being such a disappointment in terms of finding a potential mate.

His name was Enrique. He was twenty-seven, a Brazilian martial arts champion and teacher, with the looks and energy of a panther. In bed, all he wore was a necklace of large white tiger's teeth set against his café au lait skin. He was sexually voracious and wanted a regular weekly fling, but I kept saying to myself, *"This is the end, my friend, the end."*

Just as I was getting ready to pull my ads and shut down this cycle cold turkey, I got a response that piqued my interest. The energy in the letter was strong, emotionally stable and mature, if a bit straight and earthbound in tone, which could also make it a good polarity to balance my energy.

I requested a photo and birthdate, but after a week with no response, I emailed again. This was something I had never felt motivated to do before. If someone didn't respond the first time, one strike and he was out. But this time he responded, and his astrology chart was strong and compatible, and his photo was even stronger. His name was Max. He was a Pisces with a huge open heart and capacity for pleasure; I could tell this even before I met him.

I gave him my phone number. When he called, I insisted we meet for dinner that night, no chitchat. It was December 7, 2001. The Universe sent me a mate, just as my aversion to superficial playmates was kicking in. Max met my entire criterion and then some.

Looking back on my sex-addiction slip, I could rationalize it was despair over not manifesting a mate immediately that precipitated my descent—not to mention impatience. My response to hopelessness was doing what I did best—pleasure rutting with a vengeance. It was my lowest bottom—because I had so far to fall.

All human beings are addictive by nature. For over twenty years, I had refined my level of addiction from drugs and alcohol to spiritual and energy practices, in and out of bed—and then I lost it. May I never forget and never need to repeat. Amen.

III

On our first date, my initial impression was that Max was sad, depressed and deeply wounded in his sexual self-esteem. Yet at the same time, once he relaxed a little with me, he exuded an incredibly open-hearted sensuality.

Max was in his midforties, from a Sicilian working-class background, divorced just over a year and living in his own home in a pricey section of New Jersey. He was conservatively dressed in a Burberry trench, charcoal pinstripe suit and wingtips that fit the part he played as a senior vice-president in a large corporation. We looked as if we came from different universes, not necessarily a bad thing for chemistry.

As I had intuited from Max's photo, he was a big bear of a guy; his sensual lips and huge paws won me over immediately. He probably weighed over 275 pounds, and at 6', he was well overweight. But it didn't bother me, even though I could tell he was in denial that his college linebacker, weight-lifter physique had headed south. He was still quite strong and muscular, which felt powerful and protective to me, like having my own personal bodyguard.

Max wasn't just wounded from a twenty-year marriage which had slowly become stagnate and sexless. He was equally disheartened from a year on the dating scene. He told me he was almost ready to throw in the towel and become celibate, as I was—obviously for different reasons.

After some decent conversational bonding, by dessert we were holding hands and igniting some exciting chemistry both visually and energetically. I invited Max to walk me back to my place and asked him in when we got outside my door. That is, if he didn't mind waiting a few minutes while I tidied up, as I wasn't expecting company. He refused. That's when I got my first taste of his bull-headed tendencies (Taurus rising). Months later, he admitted he was suspicious it was all a scam, and as soon as he got inside my place he was going to be robbed. Max had such low self-worth; he couldn't believe I actually liked him enough to invite him home.

After I let him into my messy place, we proceeded to make-out fully clothed on the bed for a good long while. Then he slowly moved down and gave me the most incredible head I've ever had. After I came a few times (very unusual for me, as I'm spoiled by my vibrator and most men can't compete), he sat up and very formally asked, "May I remove my pants?" What a gentleman! I found Max's manners in the bedroom quite endearing.

We made love, and while it was obvious it had been a while for him, the X factor was definitely there. Lying in bed in the afterglow, Max placed the back of his hand over his face, plaintively asking aloud, "Why me?"

"Why not you? I responded. "I like you and we have good chemistry. You're a catch!"

"You're a witch!" he responded.

Max was overwhelmed. He couldn't believe his dry spell with women was truly over after he had given up hope. This confirmed what I had read in the restaurant: Max's sexual confidence was deeply wounded from his ex-wife's sexual rejection and his bad luck dating. Since everyone is wounded somewhere, it's better to find out up front the nature of a potential mate's wound—and be OK with it, because it certainly isn't going to be healed overnight, if at all. With my long-standing Mother-Teresa-of-the-bedroom complex, not only was Max's wound easy to accept—as a challenge, it was pure catnip.

On our second date the following weekend, Max took me to his home in New Jersey. On the way we stopped for brunch at a diner. He ordered a burger and fries smothered in gravy. I could see that verbal self-restraint was going to be an ongoing theme in our relationship. In his initial letter to me, Max had said he was "big, but not fat." Far be it from me to burst his denial. I mainly choose to operate as a power of example in personal relationships, unless I am directly asked for my opinion. In my profession, I *am* asked and paid to answer from a psychic perspective of higher truth. But Max wasn't asking. I have long held that the first twenty-four hours together symbolically tell the tale of the entire arc of a relationship—at this point, we're less than eight hours into it.

Max's house was set on a hill surrounded by forest in an affluent area of large homes with lots of acreage. The view from his house was all trees, and for some reason, it had the feeling of a rustic log cabin in the midst of the Bavarian Alps. It felt very fairytale-like, and I was beginning to feel like Goldilocks. Inside, it was very spacious but somewhat sparse as his ex-wife had taken well over half the furnishings. Things got cozier after Max lit a huge fire in the living room and another in the eat-in kitchen.

We made love on quilts in front of the fireplace in the living room. Then Max grilled some juicy pork chops that we ate in front of the fireplace in the kitchen. I felt as if I had died and gone to heaven! I wasn't even shy about asking, with a grin, if I could take a leftover chop home with me. I had found my true sugar daddy—sweet, loving, giving, affectionate and providing meat on the bone. For a girl like me, there was nothing more I could need or want from a man.

This was reinforced right after the weekend when I went with a girlfriend on a trip to the Bahamas over the holidays. One day, while I was over-adventurously snorkeling alone where no one could see me, I got sucked out of a cove by a wicked riptide rapidly pulling me out to sea. I was trying to swim sideways toward the shore and making no headway. The current was getting stronger, and I was becoming exhausted. Then I heard Max's voice in my ear whispering, *"Relax, Baby, I've got you."* Instantly, I felt my body relax in his arms as if he were carrying me. The next thing I knew, I hit a large boulder in the water and was able to grab it and claw my way, hand over hand, from rock to rock until I made it back to shore. That was when I knew for sure that Max was truly sent as my protector.

## *Karmic Interlude*

On our next date, we went to my favorite Greek restaurant in midtown. It was our first dress-up date. Over dinner, Max told me about the only past life he remembered. He spoke as if the memory was viscerally ever-present in his being.

It was a life in pre-Christian times in Britain, where he was the Mage, or leader, of a group of Druids. Because of a decision he made, he felt responsible for the loss of hundreds of his people. Max started weeping as he told me. I could see his karmic guilt kept him stuck in middle management in his career and unhappy in love as self-punishment.

I imparted this in a spontaneous psychic reading and advised that perhaps it was time to parole himself from karmic prison—he had paid long enough. My side of this reincarnational drama appeared in a vision as I was speaking to Max. I was a Druid High Priestess when he was Mage, and while we held each other in mutual respect in our roles, he had an unrequited desire to be lovers.

While we were making love the following weekend, I experienced another reincarnational bleedthrough. Max was a Sultan, very similar in looks and body-size, and I was one of hundreds of harem concubines who coveted the perks that came with his favor. My desire went unrequited in that life; I could feel it being carried into the present moment.

Both of us had karmic desires to be lovers that were simultaneously being fulfilled as we merged in union. It doesn't get much better than that—it felt completely balanced and deeply healing.

In our second month together, the next level of karmic healing arose when Max fervently announced in bed he was in love with me. His impulsive moon in Aries felt as if it were trying to steamroller my cautious moon in Cancer. I had to literally place my hand on his chest and say, "Whoa, you are moving way too fast for me."

Over the next few months, as I was slowly falling in love with Max, my main focus was on getting over my visual aesthetic karmic rut for pretty boys, which, fortunately, I had just bottomed out on *again.* Whenever I looked at Max, especially when he was naked and sitting hunched over at the edge of my bed, I kept saying to myself, *"But he looks like a bowling ball with hair!"* Although it was true he was bald on top and matted with black fur like a bear from the neck down, he just kept growing on me over the course of our first year together.

Max was so good to me on all levels, and he was so good in bringing out the best in me, that he became absolutely beautiful in my eyes. On our first anniversary, as we continued to move deeper into intimacy, I told him I loved him and gave him a key to my place. My karmic pretty boy days were finally over. My new preference in partnership, or should I say, deal-breaker criterion, is mature, giving, huge open-heartedness.

In year two, we fell into a very comfy pattern of sleepovers at my place in the city during the week and alternate extended weekends at Max's place in the country. We ate out, ordered in or I cooked at my place: at Max's, we cooked together. All our time together was generously interspersed with lots of cuddling, making love, dancing, laughing and just fooling around having fun with the unselfconsciousness of children.

I had never met anyone who had more capacity for joy and pleasure than I did, and it stretched my heart wide open. We loved giving each other gifts and doing for each other so much that most of our early disagreements were about wanting to be the giver. We had to negotiate our generosity by agreeing that I would "do" for him more at my house where he would graciously receive as my guest, and we would switch roles at his house. We switched that order in bed, with flexibility the key. I found this was the best way to get Max to learn how to relax and receive from me in bed. I really enjoyed expanding his range in this area. Sometimes just a foot massage or a surprise gift could put him over the top, and he would weep.

Our arrangement was ideal for more than three years. We had enough time together and enough space apart. It was the perfect balance.

The unwinding began just after our third anniversary in December 2004. Max, who had ballooned up to more than 340 pounds, announced he was going to have a new type of obesity surgery, the lapband, which was less drastic than gastric bypass. I was thrilled and relieved. I had become increasingly concerned about his weight impacting his health; he had injured knees that weren't healing and progressively worsening untreated sleep apnea. The only reason I hadn't said anything was because my readings repeatedly advised me to be a power of example through my diet and exercise habits and to allow Max to do something in his own way in his own time. And he had!

I had gained 30 pounds over the same three-year period, codependently keeping up with Max's preferences for red meat dinners and rich desserts. I knew his surgery and the dietary changes it would force on him would give me the opportunity to lose weight more easily. Max always said how much he liked my curvy plumpness and the fact that my bra size had gone up to a 40DD; he always made me feel positively svelte in bed—easy considering his massive size.

Now the jig was up for both of us. I was genuinely happy about it. Even before Max made his surgery announcement, I knew something big was coming because we both had major Uranian transits on the near horizon. That always means extensive changes, at times with unpredictable outcomes.

Max had surgery in February 2005. The weight just fell off him. Within six months, he lost more than 100 pounds. We were both ecstatic with the results. No more injured knees, his sleep apnea and snoring completely disappeared, and just as I had always teased him, for every 30 pounds of weight loss his manhood grew an inch. What's not to like?

By July, Max started getting strange with me. He became critical of my weight and even accused me, after a lengthy make-out session in bed, of not liking to kiss him all that much. He started getting selfish in minor and some not so minor ways. For example, in the past when he smoked a cigar in the car, he put it out if I said it was giving me a headache. No more. He was becoming increasingly belligerent, and at the same time, less available on weekends. And when we were together, I could feel his heart closing off toward me when we were in bed. Who was this man? What happened to the Max I knew and loved? His personality change accelerated as his weight continued to fall away.

On August 15th, after more than a month of this weirdness, Max dropped a bombshell. He had been "seeing" someone for over a month whom he had met at work. He was breaking up with me! One of my first thoughts was, *"Well, I guess I healed his sexual wound!"*

Max said it was the hardest decision of his life, but it wasn't fair to me or to "her" to not come clean. He said he had to do this for himself. I had just been studying his transits, and I agreed. It felt surprisingly crystal clear to me. Max said if it didn't work out he would "never say never" about coming back to me. But because I firmly believe in the sharp growing pain of clean breaks, I asked him to please leave my keys on his way out.

After Max left, I went into shock. I walked through my house chanting, "I'm stable at the core. I'm stable at the core," and called friends for support.

By the next morning, I had a vision of myself as a frog in a large pot filled with tepid water on the stove. The heat was being turned up bit by bit; I wasn't aware I was slowly being stewed to death. Max had tipped over the pot and saved me from stagnation. I had been in denial because being with Max had grown overly comfy on the lower chakra levels, including the more personal levels of the heart.

More importantly, I had always felt it would not be my move to initiate a break-up, since I sincerely did not want Max to be wounded again. But the new Max wasn't the same as the old Max. If his heart wasn't unconditionally open toward me anymore, for whatever reason, then his breaking-up saved me from incurring the karma of hurting him.

The evening after Max left, I went to my weekly mantra chanting class with a new spiritual teacher I had been studying with for just over month. Isn't timing interesting? His ethereal chanting moved me into a state where I went from weeping to laughing hysterically through my tears at the cosmic humor of it all. I thought, *"Wow, this guy is the real thing, and his chanting really delivers the goods!"* The Universe had provided the ideal replacement therapy to get over Max in a healthy way.

I immediately closed down my sexual energies and recommitted myself to deepening my daily meditation practices, even getting up before dawn, after lifetimes as a night owl. I had been searching for a new spiritual path for more than five years, and I had manifested one at the absolutely perfect time. I was ready to accelerate my evolution. It became clear that my relationship with Max might have become an impediment to the next leg of my journey. *C'est la vie.*

Max's company relocated him to California about a year after our break-up. Before he left, we got together for some tea and closure. We looked like different people—he'd lost 150 pounds and I'd lost 40. After a half-hour of light chitchat,

Max said he had to go. As we hugged goodbye, his composure broke. He started weeping and said, "Breaking up with you was the worst mistake of my life." This confirmed my suspicion that the affair with "the other woman" had tanked, since he had been keeping in touch with little gifts, notes and calls. I reassured him it wasn't a mistake as I kept patting his back. I told him I was sure he'd meet someone else, if he just gave it time. We parted as heart-centered friends—for life, I hope.

In hindsight, as happy as I had been with Max, the greatest gift he gave me was tipping over the pot. I felt freer than ever before from the karmic bondage of my second chakra identity. I was finally ready to more fully immerse my energies, without distraction, into communion with the Divine as my primary relationship. It was the perfect fit I had been yearning for.

In fact, the day after Max broke up with me, the final piece of our karmic puzzle fell into place. It was as if a veil had been lifted from my psychic vision. I remembered that, in my Brahmin courtesan life, one of my favorite long-time clients had begged me to teach his obese adolescent son the arts of love so he would be marriageable. Max was my last student before I retired into a spiritual life.

I taught Max in that life to be proud of his skills as a lover—but there was unfinished business. In India, I did it as an obligation; this time I did it with an open heart. The test was to love unconditionally, without remembering the missing piece. I couldn't pass the final karmic exam with Max if I knew the answer ahead of time. That would be cheating, even for a psychic.

I chose to shelve the manuscript of *Cosmic Sugar* while I was with Max because I didn't want to hurt him. Even with a pen name, it would have been hard to keep publishing a book secret.

Now is the perfect time. My sense pleasures continue to give me the taste of sugar melting on my tongue. In addition, through spiritual practices, the higher pleasures of Divine union allow *me* to dissolve like sugar in the cosmic ocean of becoming. The entire world has become my body of bliss. It is not either/or—it is *and* and *both*.

# AFTERWORD:
## Like a Circle
### in a
## Spiral

Erotic love as a spiritual path is not a new concept. Eros and divinity have been closely linked for millennia, from Eastern Taoist and tantric practices to Western esoteric mystical paths. However, the chasm between sex and spirit grows increasingly wider in American mainstream culture. We are bombarded with dogma emphasizing celibacy or monogamy as the high road. Conversely, the media inundate us with sexual content devoid of heart or soul.

The majority view of the psychological community and religion is that traditional family life, which attempts to rein in the passions by restricting sex to a single partner for life, is the best path for emotional maturity. As for spiritual growth, detachment from desire (outside of conventional marriage) is encouraged because it is seen as sinful or the root of all suffering.

A few years ago, I was interviewed for a book on love relationships. Dozens of spiritual teachers and couples therapists were asked to contribute. The editor informed me I was the only one who advocated the position that monogamy might not be optimal for everyone's soul assignment. My view on marriage was that it was appropriate for less than 10 percent of the population as a *primary* spiritual path, based on karmic predisposition. As a dissenting voice, I was not included.

It appears that the mass consciousness is only capable of finding erotic love spiritually acceptable within quite rigid parameters. Because we live in a relative plane, the average perspective on life is one in which the relative truth of duality reigns—dark/light, male/female, bad/good. It is only from a higher, non-dual level of truth that Eros and spirit are potentially one and the same—interdependent, interpenetrable, indivisible.

Even the Dalai Lama, when asked about tantric practices—which embrace sexual union as a vehicle for enlightenment—believes that road is too tricky for most human beings to navigate without getting bogged down in a desire rut. Obviously, based on my own challenges, I have no argument with his assessment in general.

However, it's clear that women need more empowering archetypes to expand their range of choices for identity. In the conventional roles of wife and mother, there is a loss of freedom and autonomy. In the business world, a woman is successful at the expense of sacrificing her yin power. And in spiritual orders, there is the surrender of all things sensual or emotional, except as it relates to union with God.

Through modern human history, with few exceptions, if a woman chose not to relinquish her full sensuality *and* power, her only option was to become an outcast from society. That meant becoming some kind of prostitute, no matter how one euphemizes it as a courtesan, geisha, hetaera, concubine, harem girl, high-priced call girl, or sacred temple prostitute. A stigma was attached, either through benign neglect or outright condemnation.

One could go outside the norm in another way and become a healer, shaman, wizard, or medicine woman—all vocations commanding respect and even fear. Also roles that, while allowing a woman to own her power, had a price attached—being categorized as a witch. This reductive labeling traditionally led to persecution when things weren't going well. The trade-off for being powerful was being viewed as suspect and a potential scapegoat.

In looking forward, the criterion for what constitutes a spiritual path needs to become more all-encompassing. Ideally, any path that offers inner growth and bliss can be acknowledged as a steppingstone to Divine communion. We need to endow what we are passionately drawn to with meaning and value—regardless of what it is. Then the investment of heart and soul unfolds spontaneously as an innate expression of our being.

That means a calling in any sphere can be just as spiritual as being locked away in a nunnery *if we intentionally use it for evolution*. This new paradigm for inner development includes athletics, parenting, helping professions, the military, business, teaching, humanitarian pursuits, political action, any form of creativity and the sensual arts, to name a few. And let us not forget that all jobs—from ditch digger to sanitation worker to housekeeper—if done with integrity and mindfulness, can be vehicles for awakening, as well.

Everyone is on "the path," whether they are consciously aware of it or not, because each person's circumstances are perfect for karmic healing. All roads, no matter how circuitous—even those appearing to lead into darkness—ultimately lead back, in one life or another, to reunion with Source. There are no wrong choices or mistakes—only lessons we need to learn time and again.

Releasing judgment is the master key that liberates us from our limiting beliefs. For example, a famous New Age spiritual teacher and author, considered an authority on meditation, came to me in confidence and admitted he didn't know how to meditate. I taught him with no disapproval, albeit a tad of personal amusement.

Furthermore, have you noticed how many perennially horny spiritual teachers are incapable of living by the standards they teach because of inner karmic demons they haven't yet exorcised? Still, it is possible to accept their imperfect humanness without rejecting their teachings, which come from a higher aspect of their being. When we are free from mental rigidity, the paradoxical nature of personality is full of entertainment value.

At this stage in the evolution of consciousness, the majority of people on the planet, gurus included, are still bottoming out on their karmic ruts. As a race, we are far from reaching that magical point where personal and Divine will come together. The first step in approaching this alignment is in giving up attachment to our habitual karmic identities and surrender to the Tao, the flow of life.

When observing this process en masse, boundless patience, compassion and a *very* long-range perspective are needed, since every bottom has a trapdoor leading to countless more. There are as many levels of heaven and hell as there are souls incarnate—courtesy of our belief ruts.

No one is exempt from the inexorable laws of karma. We are all players in *leela,* cosmic hide-and-seek. Here's how it works: Our souls courageously choose a new incarnation as the perfect vehicle to maximize karmic healing. Then, as we are sliding down the birth canal, there is the *"oh-shit-what-have-I-done!"* moment. That's when we viscerally experience being in a vulnerable little baby's body and realize we're stuck again in the density of the physical plane. This insight is followed by, what I call, the master-erase—we forget what our assignment was to begin with. And then the game begins again in earnest. I have found a good dose of cosmic humor helps in digesting this view—because *leela* is neverending.

One of the goals of this Divine play is in remembering our true Self. Try as we might to get filled by people, places and things, until we cultivate a taste for the sweetness of merging with Source, what we have been searching for remains elusive. We keep looking in the wrong direction—when it's inside us all along. The Divine experiences Itself through the illusion of separateness in the earth plane. I like to see us as God's little hand puppets, secretly whispering to each other, "Hello, is that *You* in there?" The fun really begins when we recall that we are only one Being—with billions of faces. Then we are at a point in the game where we can consciously send a little joy and gratitude back home.

If we want to open to our true nature—pure being, consciousness and bliss—mastering two types of fear is required. Anxiety about physical death is a carryover from our animal brain's survival instinct. The best antidote for this primal fear is through maintaining unconditional faith in one's eternal nature and the knowledge that death is the ultimate illusion.

Fear of annihilation of the "little self" is felt at a less conscious level for most. The Divine creates souls out of the cosmic ocean from an impulse to know Itself. This makes fear of dissolving back into that space quite legitimate. The optimal solution is to stabilize at the stillpoint within through meditation. Once we get in touch with that which is unchanging in us, we experience the beginningless and endless, spontaneous arising and dissolving of all forms—including our own.

When I was stuck in my desire rut, I couldn't have imagined how expansive my new identity is. My old predisposition still whispers from deep inside—but at least it no longer shouts, and the compulsion to act from it is gone. Fear of losing essential parts of being no longer exists as layers of personality continue to fall away—all in their own time. What is left is an awareness of the ephemeral nature of the earth plane and the preciousness of each moment on our paths of awakening.

My hope for the readers of this story is that you are able to release judgment about my journey of becoming whole and embrace your own journeys, karmic warts and all. From this, your vision of others will be transformed. That which we resist not only persists—what we judge "not OK" in ourselves or others keeps us separate from the Divine.

The wheel of karma grinds exceedingly slow and fine. Sooner or later, in this life or another, we will choose spiritual evolution as our primary goal. The karmic storyline of our incarnation remains the same, but as we consciously choose more wisely, the themes become more subtle and the stakes rise in the game.

As we embrace what is necessary to be experienced as grist for the mill, the space/time continuum dissolves and we are in the Eternal Now. Through this unconditional acceptance of what is, every step of the journey is simultaneously felt as being in heaven. This is by no means a static state—it is a continuously evolving spiral of expansion.

As joy in being permeates existence, there becomes nowhere to go but here—and the reality of no escape becomes the ultimate sweetness.

Leela Jones
New York City
March 2008

978-0-595-49228-2
0-595-49228-2

9 780595 492282